SCIENTIST TO PRESIDENT
DR. A.P.J. ABDUL KALAM

SCIENTIST TO PRESIDENT DR. A.P.J. ABDUL KALAM

Prof. Ramesh Chandra
Ph.D. FRSC (London)
Founder Director,
Dr. B.R. Ambedkar Center
for Biomedical Research
University of Delhi,
and
Vice-Chancellor
Bundelkhand University, Jhansi (U.P.)

GYAN

GYAN PUBLISHING HOUSE
NEW DELHI-110002

Scientist to President : Dr. A.P.J. Abdul Kalam

(*Biography*)

Rs. 540

ISBN: 81-212-0807-6

Published in 2002 in India by
Gyan Publishing House
5, Ansari Road, Darya Ganj, New Delhi-110002
Phones : 3282060, 3261060, Fax (011) 3285914
E-mail : gyanbook@vsnl.com
Website : http://www.gyanbooks.com

Laser Typesetting at: Sharma Graphic, New Delhi
Printed at: Mehra Offset Press, New Delhi

Contents

Appendices

Foreword

It is a great honour for me to write a Foreword to the book *Scientist to President: Dr. A.P.J. Abdul Kalam*, the Biographical sketch of Dr. Avul Phakir Jainulabdeen Abdul Kalam, who is popularly known as the Missile Man. The author, Prof. Ramesh Chandra, an eminent Biomedical Scientist and Vice Chancellor of Bundelkhand University, Jhansi (Uttar Pradesh) has elegantly woven the theme in twenty chapters by describing Dr. Kalam's career from early childhood to the Presidency of India, the largest functioning democracy in the world.

Dr. Kalam was born into a middle class Tamil Muslim family in the town of Rameswaram in Tamil Nadu which was known as Madras State in the colonial period. Although his parents did not have much formal education, they led a life of spirituality and scholarly pursuit. To quote from Dr. Kalam's autobiography "Wings of Fire", "events from the *Ramayana* and from the life of the Prophet were bedtime stories my mother and grandmother would tell the children in our family". Clearly, the Kalam family was open minded and brought up their children to follow a similar path. It is not surprising that Dr. Kalam is known to quote from both the *Quran* and the *Bhagavad Gita* with equal ease.

Dr. Kalam is undoubtedly one of the greatest technologist of India. He is credited with the development of India's missile technology which is crucial for its needs for national defence. It is of interest to ask the question as to what factors helped him succeed in his mission and achieve his goals. One of the necessary requirement is the existence of an environment in which technology leaders of the caliber of Dr. Abdul Kalam are given the freedom and opportunity to flourish. Such a catalyst is provided by India's resolve to be a secular democracy in which, thanks to the vision of the framers of its Constitution—notably Baba Saheb Dr. B.R. Ambedkar—every citizen is guaranteed an equal opportunity irrespective of their sex, religion or caste.

Secondly, it was under the visionary leadership of the late Prime Minister Jawaharlal Nehru that India made a resolve to invest in the development of science and technology. Thus, India's Nuclear Energy programme headed by Dr. Homi J. Bhabha was initiated and, a number of National Research Laboratories under CSIR headed by Sir S.S. Bhatnagar were established. Also, about the same time a Defence Science programme led by Dr. D.S. Kothari was started. On a personal note, I began my scientific career at the National Physical Laboratory, New Delhi and the Atomic Energy Establishment, Trombay at the time when these facilities were in their infancy.

It is indeed fortunate that ever since its independence, the leadership of India have been consistently supportive of its science and technology programmes. In spite of considerable opposition from some countries that view India's Science and Technology programmes as an economic and military threat, India has forged ahead by creating many other programmes such as the Space Research Institution headed by Dr. Satish Dhawan and, a missile-based defence system led by Dr. Abdul Kalam.

Dr. Abdul Kalam has proven to be a superb leader and manager of high technology. A partial list of his successful missile launches includes Prithvi, Agni, Akash, Trishul, Nag and Pokhran II. The development of such a sophisticated high technology requires enormous funds which are not easily available in a third world economy. Buying the technology from abroad is not a visible option. Therefore, one is forced to be creative to develop technologies with the limited resources that are indigenously available. It is a well-established fact that there is no dearth of competent and creative scientists and technologists in India. Dr. Kalam used this fact to his advantage and put together a team of highly talented individuals who believed in their mission with a passion. Furthermore, he expanded his team by constantly consulting and bringing in technical support from experts such as the late Dr. Vikram Sarabhai, Dr. Arunachalam, Dr. Satish Dhawan, Dr. Brahm Prakash and many others.

There is a great deal to be learnt from the way he interacted with the members of his team. Speaking from my own experience, no high technology project is free from some temporary bottlenecks or snags. Dr. Kalam was no exception but he was inspiring to his team members even under conditions of extreme disappointment. He was accessible, willing to listen to all inputs and treated everyone with respect. He leads a very simple and humble life. Although, I have not had an opportunity to meet him in person, I have talked to him over the telephone and found him delightful. Young men and women could not ask for a better role model.

In recognition of his services to the nation, Dr. Kalam has been honoured with numerous awards that include the highest civilian award of Bharat Ratna and several honorary degrees. Very shortly he will assume the office of President of his motherland. Although, in the past India has had a scholar, Dr. S. Radhakrishnan as the President, Dr. Abdul Kalam is the first scientist elected to be the head of the State. This new assignment brings in unique challenges that would be different from Technological Challenges. India is a nation of one billion citizens of whom a large fraction lives below the poverty level and suffers from social and economic deprivation. Casteism is deeply rooted in the minds of many. Religion-based hatred and bigotry which Dr. Kalam himself experienced as a boy, still persists. Although his technological experience can help alleviate economic misery, a great deal of creativity would be required to change social behaviours. I wish him well.

Shobha Singh, Ph.D.
Distinguished Member of Technical Staff (Retd.)
AT&T Bell Laboratories,
Murray Hill, New Jersey, USA &
Research Fellow & Director (Retd.)
Polaroid Corporation,
Cambridge, MA, (USA)
44, Pine Street
Weston, MA-02493, USA

Preface

In the long-drawn academic struggle in the field of scientific research, Dr. A.P.J. Abdul Kalam had to face numerous ups and downs. Born in a humble family with limited economic means, there could be no hope that this youngest child of his parents would shine like a meteor on the international horizon. At a time when he had to face acute financial difficulty for higher education, his sister came forward to support him. A serious and disciplined student as he was, he could do well in the MIT, Madras, as well as elsewhere in his later career. His ardent desire to join the IAF could not be fulfilled, but the pious advice and appeal of Swami Sivananda at Rishikesh made him adamant to eke out his future career in scientific research under the Defence Ministry, Government of India.

This afforded him ample opportunity to probe into new arena of scientific research in the company of renowned scientists like Prof. Vikram Sarabhai, Dr. Arunachalam, Dr. Satish Dhawan and others. His well-disciplined scientific talent generated ever lasting impression on his colleagues. Consequently, with the successful launching of Agni, Akash, Trishul, Nag, Prithvi, Pokhran II and others, there was a new feather in his cap. Combined with a sense of disciplined work, simplicity and humility, Dr. Kalam did not look back, but forward with the idea of developed India. The Government of India recognised his immense scientific services and awarded him the highest civilian award of Bharat Ratna. Subsequently, numerous academic institutions invited him to speak on his new inventions. They showered high academic honours on him with much love and respect.

This was not the end of journey. He ardently believed, "I had a long way to go but I was in no hurry. I went in little steps—just one step after another—bent each step towards the top". In fact, day in and day out, he worked consistently along with several colleagues whose goodwill and cooperation he sought at every step. Sometimes sleepless nights were spent in discussion even without meals. This was the sense of sincere dedication which made him a most popular and eminent scientist.

With full faith in the verses of *Quran* and *Gita,* which he recites daily, he has generated self-confidence in him. He is non-political and ardently believes in the goodness of human beings. Thus, his life is action-oriented which made him well-engaged for more than five decades. He is quite impartial in his action and thought and does not believe in seeking or offering 'cheap' favour.

Look at this Missile Man from any angle, he will appeal to you as a most simple person, and unassuming with an open mind. He wears simple clothes with a rubber chappal and long saintly hair, with malice towards none. There may be several social institutions having his financial stamp. But he would never divulge it. In one of the academic gathering in the capital, where he was the main speaker, he was offered a cheque of fifty thousand rupees. He politely handed it over to the Home Minister present there requesting him to donate it for social cause.

With all facts and figures, his life may be called a unique saga of scientific achievement which has been respectfully acknowledged by millions of scientists and others not only in India but all over the globe. Indeed, the road from Rameswaram to Rashtrapati Bhavan in the capital was complex and difficult which took him full five decades to traverse. One may say that he could never think that he would be given such an honour unprecedented in the history of Indian sub-continent. In fact, destiny does play an unexpected and significant role, and an ardent believer in the 'dictum of action' in *Gita* must one day be rewarded as Dr. Abdul Kalam has been.

I have a well-deserved apology for a short span of time in writing the Biography of the Missile Man, the Scientist President. The time between the announcement of his candidature and the final voting may be measured with my anxiety to finish this work by the time of his entry into Rashtrapti Bhavan. So in this short duration, a few prominent academics came forward to help me in this task.

It is a unique honour to seek the advice of the most eminent scholar, President of India, Dr. K.R. Narayanan on numerous occasions. Undoubtedly Dr. Suraj Bhan, at present Governor of Himachal Pradesh and Vishnu Kant Shastri, Governor of Uttar Pradesh had always been very kind and helpful to me and a most respectable source of inspiration. I feel beholden to Dr. S.R. Bakshi, an eminent social scientist and Dr. Sangh Mittra of Indian Council of Historical Research for their academic support during this period. Lastly, I must thank my wife Dr. Sujata Chandra and my son Ankush and daughter Avishi who had always cooperated and supported me in this stupendous task. I am grateful to Dr. Shobha Singh, an eminent United States based Scientist, who had gone through this book and written the foreword of this book at a very short notice. I would fail in my duty if I don't thank and acknowledge the help, encouragement and cooperation of my other family members, my mentors, teachers, students and co-workers.

Besides I have used some of the learned and scholarly writings of Dr. Kalam, news and views from newspapers and comments of eminent persons. I am grateful to all of them. The life story of this eminent scientist should appear to be well-weaved from scattered threads.

Prof. Ramesh Chandra
Founder Director,
Dr. B.R. Ambedkar Center
for Biomedical Research
University of Delhi,
and
Vice-Chancellor
Bundelkhand University, Jhansi (U.P.)

Introduction

It is the biographical sketch of an eminent scientist who played a most significant role in the scientific history of the Indian sub-continent. Born in a humble family with limited financial assets, his father had to eke out his domestic responsibility by plying boats and taking passengers to a particular distance. But with the limited means, the family was well-contented and satisfied and there was no complaint of any kind on its lips. It was indeed a God-fearing family not spreading their domestic commitments to unbearable burden.

As a student Dr. Kalam did not show any kind of 'greatness' in his daily behaviour. One could say that he was one of the hard-working young student with normal behaviour. After high school education, he had to face financial difficulties when he was selected for an engineering course in the MIT, Madras. His sister came forward to help him at any cost. Probably she knew that her brilliant youngest brother in the family will have to lose his academic career if not given financial support.

The educational career in the MIT was a serious one and it made young Kalam more serious when the responsibility of supporting the family hovered around him. He received the degree from MIT, with confidence to face the academic world. As he has mentioned in his Autobiography, young Kalam had much fancy to fly in the air and attain the heights unprecedented in the annals of a common human being. He applied for a flying course as GD Pilot in IAF and was called for the interview at Dehradun. It was a novel experience for an ambitious young man to travel in the North for a career which he cherished very much. He did well in all the tests, but unluckily his name was ninth and the vacancies in the final list were eight. He felt much disgusted at this unexpected setback and felt as if something very precious has been snatched from him.

At this point of time, he visited Rishikesh in order to see the abodes of *Rishis* and *sadhus*. Incidentally, he met Swami Sivananda to whom he narrated the whole story of his recent failure at Dehradun. He consoled him and advised him not to lose heart.

There were, he opined, several avenues to carve out a good career. Probably this advice greatly touched upon the heart and mind of young Kalam.

> *"To live only for some unknown future is superficial. It is the climbing a mountain to reach the peak without experiencing its sides. The sides of the mountain sustain life, not the peak. This is where things grow, experience is gained, and technologies are mastered. The importance of the peak lies only in the fact that it defines the sides. So I went on towards the top, but always experiencing the sides. I had a long way to go but I was in no hurry. I went in little steps—just one step after another—but each step towards the top."*

Now he reached Delhi and received an appointment order for the post of Senior Scientific Assistant with the basic salary of Rs. 250. Young Kalam accepted this position with a sense of reluctance. But he did not know that a grand career awaits him. He had a trip to Rameswaram and vividly mentions some of the interesting episodes of his family and the place in his well-written Autobiography.

> "I normally ate with my mother, sitting on the floor of the kitchen. She would place a banana leaf before me, on which she then ladled rice and aromatic sambhar, a variety of sharp, home-made pickles and a dollop of fresh coconut *chutney.*"

> "The famous Shiva temple, which made Rameshwaram so sacred to pilgrims, was about a ten-minute walk from our house. Our locality was pre-dominantly Muslim, but there were quite a few Hindu families too, living amicably with their Muslim neighbours. There was a very old mosque in our locality where my father would take me for evening prayers. I had not the faintest idea of the meaning of the Arabic prayers chanted, but I was totally convinced that they reached God. When my father came out of the mosque after the prayers, people of different religions would be sitting outside, waiting for him. Many of them offered bowls of water to my father who would dip his fingertips in them and say a prayer. This water was then carried home for individuals. I also remember people visiting our home to offer thanks after being cured. My father

always smiled and asked them to thank Allah, the benevolent and merciful."

"The high priest of Rameshwaram temple, Pakshi Lakshmana Sastry, was a very close friend of my father's. One of the most vivid memories of my early childhood is of the two men, each in this traditional attire, discussing spiritual matters. When I was old enough to ask questions, I asked my father about the relevance of prayer. My father told me there was nothing mysterious about prayer. Rather prayer made possible a communion of the spirit between people. "When you pray," he said, "you transcend your body and become a part of the cosmos, which knows no division of wealth, age, caste, or creed . . . ."

On the whole, the small society of Rameshwaram was highly stratified and very rigid in terms of the segregation of different social groups. However, his science teacher Sivasubramania Iyer, though an orthodox Brahmin with a very conservative wife, was something of a rebel. He did his best to break social barriers so that people from varying backgrounds could mingle easily. He used to spend hours with him and would say, "Kalam, I want you to develop so that you are on par with the highly educated people of the big cities."

"One day, he invited me to his home for a meal. His wife was horrified at the idea of a Muslim boy being invited to dine in her ritually pure kitchen. Sivasubramania Iyer was not perturbed, nor did he get angry with his wife, but instead, served with his own hands and sat down beside me to eat his meal. His wife watched us from behind the kitchen door. I wondered whether she had observed any difference in the way I ate rice, drank water or cleaned the floor after the meal. When I was leaving his house, Sivasubramania Iyer invited me to join him for dinner again the next weekend. Observing my hesitation, he told me not to get upset, saying, "Once you decide to change the system, such problems have to be confronted." When I visited his house next week, Sivasubramania Iyer's wife took me inside her kitchen and served me food with her own hands."

Luckily, Dr. Kalam had to work with the best scientists of India.

He eulogises the highest scientific talent of Prof. Vikram Sarabhai, Dr. Satish Dhawan, Dr. Arunachalam and others. He indeed learnt from them and put all the precious scientific threads in his valuable dictionary. Working at Kanpur, Bangalore, Hyderabad and other places was a novel scientific experience. Prof. Sarabhai had much faith in him and did not hesitate to recommend as much funds as he asked for. Other senior scientists did recognise his talent with love and respect.

His visit to NASA and other international scientific installations paid him very rich dividends and he was instrumental in utilising this new experience in new kinds of missiles and rocketry. Affectionately known as the Missile Man on account of new discoveries in Prithvi, Agni, Akash, Nag, Pokhran II and others, the government of India honoured him with Bharat Ratna, the highest civilian award.

Being the Principal Scientific Adviser to the Defence Minister, Government of India, he supervised the chain of scientific laboratories with appreciable output on the part of numerous young scientists whose cooperation he sought at various levels. He engaged himself so much in this task that on several days he would have nominal rest, not caring for the regular meals.

"Man needs his difficulties because they are necessary to enjoy success. All of us carry some sort of a super-intelligence within us. Let it be stimulated to enable us to examine our deepest thoughts, desires, and beliefs."

"Once you have done this—charged yourself, as it were, with your commitment to your work—you also need good health and boundless energy. Climbing to the top demands strength, whether it is to the top of Mount Everest or to the top of your career. People are born with different energy reserves and the one who tries first and burns out easily will do well to reorganise his or her life at the earliest."

"The pursuit of science is a combination of great elation and great despair. I went over many such episodes in my mind. Johannes Kepler, whose three orbitals laws form the basis of space research, took nearly 17 years after formulating the two laws about planetary motion around the sun, to enunciate this third law which gives the relation between the size of elliptical orbit and the length of time it takes for the planet to go around the sun. How many failures and frustrations must he have gone through? The idea that man could land on the moon, developed by Russian mathematician Konstantin Tsiolkovsky, was realised after nearly four decades—and by the United States, at that. Prof. Chandrasekhar had to wait nearly 50 years before receiving the Nobel Prize for his discovery of the 'Chandrashekhar Limit', a discovery made while he was a graduate student at Cambridge in the 1930s. If his work had been recognised then, it could have led to the discovery of Black Hole decades earlier. How many failures must Von Braun have gone through before his Saturn launch vehicle put man on the moon? These thoughts helped to give me the ability to withstand apparently irreversible setbacks."

In fact he showed much consideration to the views of the younger generation of the scientists. They could meet him and discuss with him several scientific problems. He was keen to give them academic awards and their talent was always well-rewarded. So far so, the DRDO, ISRO and other organisation could show their deep and fruitful roots on the Indian soil.

In his approach to life, Dr. Kalam is secular. He recites verses from *Quran* as well as *Gita*. He is respected by one and all. Look at him, he is indeed very simple in dress and food. So mentally, he does not like pomp and show.

On account of numerous qualities, his name has been recommended for the Presidentship of India. Several political parties including BJP, Congress and others have sponsored his candidature for the highest executive office in our country. A noble person like him who has achieved meteoric laurels would definitely be well-fitted in the historic building of Rashtrapati Bhavan.

1

Early Career

Abdul Kalam was born on October 15, 1931, in a *humble Tamil* family at Dhanushkodi in Rameswaram district of Chennai. It is the capital city of the Southern State of India. His father Jainulabdeen Marakayar was not a well-educated person, nor did he possess wealth in excess. Mother Ashiamma had gained formal education. His father possessed great innate wisdom, true generosity of spirit and was a spiritual person. In a remote belt of a spiritually charged island town, at the southern tip, his father rented boats to fishermen.

Abdul had a materially and emotionally secure childhood. Being the youngest in the family he was pampered a lot. His neighbours remember him as an introvert interested in reading. In the environment that he grew up, books were a scarce commodity. Mr STR Manickam, his neighbour, who encouraged him to read books, says, " I used to have a library and Kalam was always there. He used to read everything he could lay his hands on."

He always used to eat with his mother, sitting on the floor. His decision to become a vegetarian was partly due to his financial constraints—but later on, he cultivated it as a habit. Kalam believes that he has inherited *honesty* and *self-discipline* from his *father*, while faith in goodness and *kindness* were the traits inherited from his *mother*.

Dr Avul Pakir Jainulabdeen Abdul Kalam—'200 percent Indian', as his colleagues call him, had made India proud in myriad ways. "We must think and act like a nation of a billion people and not like that of a million people. Dream, dream, dream! Conduct these dreams into thoughts, and then transform them into action," said the man who dreamt for India, and acted on its behalf to place her in the exclusive Space Club. He moves a first world dream for the third world nation. He is a vegetarian and teetotaller , who recites the *Quran* and the *Bhagwad Gita* with equal faith and devotion and has an unparalleled career as a defence scientist to be crowned with the highest civilian award of India—The Bharat Ratna.

As the Scientific and Technology Advisor to the Prime Minister of India, he propelled India into the select club of Missiles possessing countries. He resigned from the post to take up a more ambitious programme of teaching and creating scientific temper in the minds of young inquisitive and knowledge-thirsty Indians. His potent concoction to 'hurl ' India in the Superpower Countries Club, 'Vision 2020', spells nothing short of a revolution at grassroot levels. His 'mantra' or gospel for India are: 'freedom, development and stand up to the world'. After the Pokhran blast, *Bombay Times* labelled him as The Missile Man. The English translation of his poem Tumult reads:

"Did I explore space to enhance science, or did I provide weapons of destruction".

Dr. APJ Abdul Kalam is the father of India's indigenous missile programme. His three visions for India—Freedom, Development and Self-Reliance, are arrived at on the basis of achievements and progress made by India, and during his own career as a missile scientist. Recipient of several awards including the Padma Bhusan (1981), the Padma Vibhushan (1990), he has been honoured with India's highest civilian award, the Bharat Ratna (1997).

Abdul Kalam has specialized in Aero Engineering from Madras Institute of Technology. Besides being a chairperson to Technology Information, Forecasting and Assessment Council (TIFAC), he has also been appointed Principal Scientific Advisor to the Government of India and accorded the rank of Cabinet Minister. He had contributed to a large extent to the development of the Satellite Launch Vehicle III, which injected the Rohini Satellite into orbit. At 70, he overlooks overall scientific development of the country on issues relating to scientific and technical policies in different sectors. He also advises on matters relating to technological self-reliance and foreign collaboration.

Known as a Missile Man on account of his numerous scientific and humane achievements, his chequered career witnessed numerous challenges. He was happy to face them and thought their solution in one way or the other. This is evident from the following few details of his brilliant career:

October 15, 1931 : Bom at Rameswaram.

1950 : Kalam joined St. Joseph College, Trichi for BSc degree.

1954 : Joined Madras Institute of Technology (MIT).

1958 : Employed at DTD & P (Air) as Senior Scientific Assistant.

1962 : INCOSPAR took the decision to set up the Equatorial Rocket Launching Station at Thumba.

November 21, 1963 : India's 1st rocket Nike-Apache launched.

November 20, 1967 :Rohini-75 rocket was launched from TERLS.

1968 : Formed the Indian Rocket Society.

December 30, 1971 : death of Dr. Sarabhai.

October 8, 1972 : Successful testing of the RATO system Sukhioi16 jet aircraft performed.

1974 : Death of his brother-in-law, Jallaluddin.

1976 : His father Jainulabdeen passed away at the age of 102. Soon afterwards his mother also passed away.

July 18, 1980 : India's first Satellite Launch Vehicle, SLV-3 lifted off from SHAR.

January 25, 1981 : Padma Bhushan award announced.

May 31, 1981 : Next SLV-3-D, took off.

February 1982 : Appointed Director of DRDL.

July 27, 1983 : IGHDP launched.

June 26, 1984 : Devil missile was fired to flight test the first indigenous strap-down Inertia 1 Guidance System.

August 3, 1985 : Foundation stone of the Research Centre. Imarat (RCI) was laid down.

September 1988 : Second flight of Prithvi.

May 22, 1989 : Agni missile launched.

January 26, 1990 : Conferred the Padma Vibhushan.

1990 : Jadavpur University conferred him the honour of Doctor of Science.

1991 : Received an honorary degree of Doctor of Science from IIT, Mumbai.

1997 : APJ Kalam awarded the highest civilian honour of India: the BHARAT RATNA.

Climbing to the top demands strength, whether it is to the top of Mount Everest or to the top of one's career.

To live only for some unknown future is superficial.

I was willing to accept what I couldn't change.

There are forces in life working for you and against you. One must distinguish the beneficial forces from the malevolent ones and choose correctly between them.

As a child of God, I am greater than anything that can happen to me.

We should not give up and we should not allow the problem to defeat us.

Great dreams of great dreamers are always transcended.

Be more dedicated to making solid achievements than in running after swift but synthetic happiness.

Those who cannot work with their hearts achieve but a hollow, half-hearted success that breeds bitterness all around.

To succeed in your mission, you must have single-minded devotion to your goal. Man needs his difficulties because they are necessary to enjoy success. You have to dream before your dreams can come true. Life is a difficult game. You can win it only by retaining your birthright to be a person.

Do we not realize that self respect comes with self reliance?

God, our Creator, has stored within our minds and personalities, great potential strength and ability. Prayer helps us tap and develop these powers.

The Earth is the most powerful and energetic planet.

A Team led by E. Vijayalakshmi Visited Rameswaram

The narrow, slushy lane led through a timber yard, past houses with peeling plaster and crumbling walls. The smell of fish was all-pervading. We soon reached our destination, House No. 2 on Mosque Street in Rameswaram. An old man responded to our tentative knocks. Was he A.P.J. Abdul Kalam's brother? we asked . A barely perceptible nod. Could we talk to him about his famous brother?

A.P.J. Mohd. Muthumeeran Marakayar glared at us. "Why didn't you call and come?" he demanded. Desperately, we spun tales. But the old man wouldn't buy. The premium for talking about his famous brother was a warning over the phone so that he could be 'ready' for us. Muthumeeran Marakayar, or 'chinna' Marakayar as he is known in Rameswaram, is a very dominant personality. Decades ago, one stern look from him could arrest the naughtiness of his siblings. Today, one of them, 'Aavul Pakkiri Jainulabiddin Abdul Kalam, 66, is making history.

"Of course, I am happy about the Bharat Ratna my 'thambi' was awarded. Four of us attended the ceremony in Delhi last March. Kalam took care of us there. We didn't have to spend a paisa, "he said, opening the conversation. Apparently, when Kalam was notified about the Bharat Ratna he first informed his brother."He then asked me to organise a 'biriyani' party for friends and relatives for which he sent us money. We held prayers and had a big party in this house", said Muthumeeran.

"Kalam was the first graduate in the family. The rest of us didn't even finish school", said Muthumeeran. He remembers that Kalam "was always experimenting with something or the other." Kalam began at the 'Samiyar' school in Rameswaram, and moved to the Schwartz school in Ramnathapuram town. Graduation was from St. Joseph's College in Tiruchi.

"We used to hear of his good academic performance at Tiruchi. Even then we used to say that he would go very far, "recalled Venkatasubramania Shastrigal, 71, a good friend of Kalam at Rameswaram. Kalam then went on to do aeronautical engineering at the Madras Institute of Technology.

Kalam's father, Jainulabiddin Marakayar was a panchayat board president. He also owned a few boats which ferried pilgrims between Rameswaram and Dhanushkody. But after a cyclone ravaged Dhanushkody in 1964, the operations were limited to ferrying passengers between Rameswaram and ships anchored off the coast.

Kalam's father had an excellent relationship with the main Ramnathasamy temple in the town. According to Muthumeeran, in return for supply of small boats every year, his father was accorded certain honours by the temple authorities during temple festivals. He is bitter that this tradition is no longer honoured.

Abbul Kalam was perhaps marked out to be different right from the beginning. Since he was the youngest in the family, he got his fair share of pampering from the elders. But neighbours remember him as a reserved boy who was very interested in reading books. "I used to have a library and Kalam was always there, asking for books", said S.T.R. Manickam who has known Kalam since he was a boy. "He used to read everything he could catch hold of. It was amazing."

In a way, this library was the foundation on which Kalam built his career. A fact he acknowledged in a new year card he sent to Manickam last year. In chaste Tamil Kalam had written, "your library was, in my youth, a source of great inspiration to me." Manickam who treasures this card, proudly displayed it to *The Week*.

Kalam is quite attached to home town. The last time he visited the place was three years ago for a relative's wedding. "He came surrounded by security. We just peeked at him from outside," commented a neighbour. Added 'chinna' Marakayar, "All of a sudden there were security guards all over."

But the doors of the house were open to all his friends and acquaintances. "I went to meet him and we sat and spoke about the good old days. He has not forgotten us in spite job becoming such a big man," said Venkatasubramania Shastrigal. "As a young boy he sometimes used to come and deliver the papers at the behest of his brother who was a newspaper agent. Today, he is making news."

There is no question of not approving of the nuclear tests. After all, ask residents, isn't one of its heroes their own brother? And a very forthright one at that. Confirmation of this is the term 'Kalamitous' that his colleagues invented to describe his frustration whenever the tests were delayed. Kalam regularly keeps in touch with his family through phone and he also helps them financially when the need arises. But one thing is taboo: he won't use his influence to get a family member or relative a job.

Said 'chinna' Marakayar with just a tinge of annoyance in his tone, "He will never recommend a relative or friend. Well, we also don't ask him now." The youngsters in the family thought are quite impressed by their famous uncle', said Kalam's grand-nephew Sheikh Dawood, 'He always asks us to study well. We are all inspired by him.".

Kalam, according to his family, is a strict vegetarian. Adept at playing the *'Rudra Veena'*, he is a *fan of the Tamil poet* Subramania Bharathi. He never did marry. He once told a friend, half-jocularly, that if he had married, he would never have achieved even half of what he has managed to. "When he was posted in

Thiruvananthapuram, we almost fixed an alliance for him. But my wife and daughter fell ill and we got distracted by that. After that he left for Hyderabad," recalled Kalam's brother.

The man , ascetic in looks and behaviour, is quite religious. According to his brother, Kalam prays twice a day, in the morning and at night. "He is so busy throughout the day. Where can he get time to make the five prayers every day?"

Rameswaram residents want to hold a felicitation ceremony for Kalam. Manickam has written to Kalam about it, but enhanced security considerations might prevent Kalam from visiting his home town soon. "We are crossing our fingers and hoping he would be able to make it here soon," said Manickam.

So far no tangible benefits have accrued to the town because of Kalam. But the residents have no complaints. As front-page news on Pokharan continue to mention Kalam, Rameswaram residents swell with pride. "Abdul Kalam, "as the visibly proud waiter at the TTDC hotel said, "is a son of the soil. That is enough for us."

In the lovable memory of his respectable parents, Dr. Kalam could find easy time to pen a few lines in their memory. He gave vent to his feelings to befiting the love and affection of his dear parents which contributed much in building up his grand scientific career.

To the memory of my parents

My Mother

Sea waves, golden sand, pilgrims' faith,
Rameswaram Mosque Street, all merge into one,
My Mother!
You come to me like heaven's caring arms.
I remember the war days when life was challenge and toil—
Miles to walk, hours before sunrise,
Walking to take lessons from the saintly teacher near the temple.
Again miles to the Arab teaching school,
Climb sandy hills to Railway Station Road,
Collect, distribute newspapers to temple city citizens,
Few hours after sunrise, going to school.

Evening, business time before study at night.
All this pain of a young boy,
My Mother you transformed into pious strength
With kneeling and bowing five times
For the Grace of the Almighty only, My Mother.
Your strong piety is your Children's strength,
You always shared your best with whoever needed the most,
You always gave, and gave with faith in Him.
I still remember the day when I was ten,
Sleeping on your lap to the envy of my elder brothers and sisters
It was full moon night, my world only you knew
Mother! My Mother!
When at midnight I woke with tears falling on my knee
You knew the pain of your child, My Mother.
Your caring hands, tenderly removing the pain
Your love, your care, your faith gave me strength
To face the world without fear and with His strength.
We will meet again on the great Judgement Day, My Mother!

APJ Abdul Kalam

2

The Parents

Dr. Kalam was born in a humble Tamil family in the Island town of Rameswaram in Madras state. His father, Jainulabdeen, possessed neither much formal education nor much wealth; despite these disadvantages, he possessed great innate wisdom and a true generosity of spirit. He had an ideal helpmate in his mother, Ashiamma. He does not recall the exact number of people she fed everyday, but he is quite certain that the number of people she fed was larger than all the members of her own family put together.

"My parents were widely regarded as an ideal couple. My mother's lineage was regarded as the more distinguished one, one of her forbears having been bestowed with the title of 'Bahadur' by the British.

"I was one of many children—a short boy with rather undistinguished looks, born to tall and handsome parents. We lived in our ancestral house, which was built in the middle of the 19th century. It was a fairly large pucca house, made of limestone and brick, on the Mosque Street of Rameswaram. My austere father used to avoid all inessential comforts and luxuries. However, all that was needed was provided for, in terms of food, medicine or clothes. In fact, I would say mine was a very secure childhood, both materially and emotionally.

"I normally ate with my mother, sitting on the floor of the kitchen. She would set a banana leaf before me, on which she then ladled rice and aromatic sambhar, a variety of sharp, home-made pickles and a dollop of fresh coconut *chutney*".

The famous Shiva temple, which made Rameswaram so sacred to pilgrims, was about a ten-minute walk from his house. The high priest of Rameswaram temple, Pakshi Lakshmana Sastry, was a very close friend of his father's. Indeeds his father could convey complex spiritual concepts in very simple, down-to-earth Tamil. He once told me, "In his own time, in his own place, in what he really is, and in the stage he has reached—good or bad—every human being is a specific element within the whole of the manifest divine Being. So why be afraid of difficulties, suffering and problems? When troubles come, try to understand the relevance of your sufferings. Adversity always presents opportunities for introspection."

"Why don't you tell this to the people who come to you for help and advice?" I asked my father. He put his hands on my shoulders and looked straight in my eyes. For quite some time he said nothing, as if he was judging my capacity to comprehend his words. Then he answered in a low, deep voice. His answer filled me with a strange energy and enthusiasm:

> Whenever human beings find themselves alone, as a natural reaction, they start looking for company. Whenever they are in trouble, they look for someone to help them. Whenever they reach an impasse, they look to someone to show them the way out. Every recurrent anguish, longing, and desire finds its own special helper. For the people who come to me in distress, I am but a go-between in their effort to propitiate demonic forces with prayers and offerings. This is not a correct approach at all and should never be followed. One must understand the difference between a fear-ridden vision of destiny and the vision that enables us to seek the enemy of fulfilment within ourselves.

"I remember my father starting his day at 4 a.m. in the morning by reading the *namaz* before dawn. After the *namaz*, he used to walk down to a small coconut grove we possessed, about 4 miles from our home. He would return, with about a dozen coconuts tied together thrown over his shoulder, and only then would he have his breakfast. This was his routine even when he was in his late sixties." In the humble environs of his boyhood, books were a scarce commodity. However, the personal library of STR Manickam, a former 'revolutionary' or militant nationalist, was sizeable. He encouraged him to read all I could and I often visited his home to borrow books. Another person who greatly influenced my boyhood was my first cousin, Samsuddin. He was the sole distributor for newspapers in Rameswaram.

He recalls his close friends in his childhood in the Rameswaram Elementary School and they were Ramanadha Sastry, Aravindan and Shivaprakashan. They belonged to the orthodox, Hindu Brahmin families. In fact, Ramanadha Sastry was the son of Pakshi Lakshmana Sastry, the high priest in the Rameswaram temple. As children, none of us ever felt any difference amongst ourselves because of our religious differences and upbringing. Later, he took over the priesthood of the Rameswaram temple from his father; Aravindan went into the business of arranging transport for visiting pilgrims; and Sivaprakasan became a catering contractor for the Southern Railways.

"The Second World War was over and the freedom of India was imminent. 'Indians will build their own India,' declared Gandhiji. The whole country was filled with an unprecedented optimism. I asked my father's permission to leave Rameswaram and study at the district headquarters in Ramanathapuram."

3

Route to Higher Education

At the age of fifteen, young Kalam joined the Schwartz High School, Ramanathapuram.

Iyadurai Solomon was a great teacher because he instilled in all the children a sense of their own worth. Solomon raised my self-esteem to a high point and convinced me, the son of parents who had not had the benefits of education, that I too could aspire to become whatever I wished. "With faith, you can change your destiny," he would say.

"And by the time I completed my education at Schwartz, I was a self-confident boy with the determination to be successful. In 1950, I joined the St. Joseph's College, Trichi, to study for the Intermediate examination. He confessed that he was not a bright student in terms of examination grades".

His elder brother Mustafa Kamal, who ran a provision store on the railway station road, would call him in to give him a little help and then vanish for hours together leaving the shop in his charge. He sold oil, onions, rice and everything else. "The fastest moving items, I found, were cigarettes and bidis. I used to wonder what made poor people smoke away their hard-earned money. When spared by Mustafa, I would be put in charge of his kiosk by my younger brother, Kasim Mohammed. There I sold novelties made of seashells."

"At St. Joseph's, I was lucky to find a teacher like the Rev. Father T.N. Sequeira. He taught us English and was also our hostel warden".

His stay on the St. Joseph's campus was for four years. His teachers at St. Joseph were the true followers of Kanchi Paramacharya, who evoked people to "enjoy the action of giving". The vivid memory of our mathematics teachers, Prof. Thothathri Iyengar and Prof. Suryanarayana Sastry, walking together on the campus inspires him throughout his life. He read about Tolstoy, Scoot and Hardy and then moved on to some works on philosophy. It was around this time that he developed a great interest in Physics.

"When I joined the B.Sc. degree course at St. Joseph's, I was unaware of any other option for higher education. Nor did I have any information about career opportunities available to a student of science. Only after obtaining a B.Sc. did I realise that Physics was not my subject. I had to go into engineering to realise my dreams. I could have joined the Engineering course long ago, right after finishing my Intermediate course. Better late than never, I told myself as I made the detour, applying for admission into the Madras Institute of Technology (MIT), regarded as the crown jewel of technical education in South India at that time."

At MIT, three teachers shaped his career. "Their combined contributions formed the foundation on which I later built my professional career". These three teachers they were Prof. Sponder, Prof. KAV Pandalai and Prof. Narasingha Rao. Each one of them had a very distinct personality, and meritorious academic career.

"Prof. KAV Pandalai taught me aero-structure design and analysis. He was a cheerful, friendly and enthusiastic teacher, who brought a fresh approach to every year's teaching course. It was Professor Pandalai who opened up the secrets structural engineering to us. Even today I believe that everyone who has been taught by Prof. Pandalai would agree that he was a man of great intellectual integrity and scholarship—but with no trace of arrogance. His students were free to disagree with him on several points in the classroom".

Prof. Narasingha Rao was a mathematician, who taught him theoretical aerodynamics. He still remember his method of teaching fluid dynamics.

His last year at MIT was to have much impact on his later life. In those days, a new climate of political enlightenment and industrial effort was sweeping across the country. He had to test his belief in God and see if it could fit into the matrix of scientific thinking. The value system in which he was nurtured was profoundly religious. He had been taught that true reality lay beyond the material world in the spiritual realm, and that tremendous knowledge could be obtained only through inner experience. At this point of time, young Kalam made up his mind to appear in an essay competition, organised by the MIT Tamil Sangam. He wrote an article entitled, "Let us make our own Aircraft" in Tamil. It stood the test and Kalam was awarded the first prize by the Editor of the Tamil weekly, *Ananda Vikatan*.

Soon thereafter, Kalam was sent to Hindustan Aeronautics. Limited (HAL) at Bangalore as a trainee. It imparted him a useful practical experience regarding the various components of the aircraft. He gained knowledge of piston and turbine engines, concepts of gas dynamics and diffusion processes.

"Let Us Make Our Own Aircraft" in Tamil. The article evoked much interest and I won the competition, taking the first prize from 'Devan', the editor of the popular Tamil weekly, *Ananda Vikatan.*

"My most touching memory of MIT is related to Prof. Sponder. We were posing for a group photograph as part of a farewell ritual. All graduating students had lined up in three rows with the professors seated in the front. Suddenly, Prof. Sponder got up and looked for me. I was standing in the third row. " Come and sit with me in the front," he said. I was taken aback by Prof. Sponder's invitation. "Your are my best student and hard work will help you bring a great name for your teachers in future." Embarrassed by the praise but honoured by the recognition, I sat with Prof. Sponder for the photograph. "Let God be your hope, your stay, your guide and provide the lantern for your feet in your journey into the future," said the introverted genius, bidding me adieu.

"From MIT, I went to Hindustan Aeronautics Limited (HAL) at Bangalore as a trainee. There I worked on engine overhauling as part of a team. Hands-on work on aircraft engine overhauling was very educative. When a principle learnt in the classroom is borne out by practical experience, it creates a strange sense of excitement —akin to unexpectedly running into an old friend among a crowd of strangers. At HAL, I worked on the overhauling of both piston and turbine engines. The nazy concepts of gas dynamics and difiusion processes in the working principle of *after burning* came into sharper focus in my mind. I was trained in radial engine-cum-drum operations.

I learned how to check a crankshaft for wear and tear, and connecting rod and crankshaft for twist. I did calibrations of a fixed-pitch fan fitted to a super-charged engine. I opened up pressure and acceleration-cum-speed control systems, and air starter supply systems of turbo-engines. Getting to understand feathering un-feathering and reversing of propeller engines was very interesting. The demonstration of the delicate art of *beta* (blade angle control) by HAL technicians still lingers in my memory. They had neither studied in major universities, nor were they merely implementing what their engineer-in-charge was suggesting.

Two alternative opportunities for employment, both close to my long-standing dream of flying, presented themselves before me when I came out of HAL as a graduate aeronautical engineer. One was a carrier in the Air Force and another was a job at the Directorate of Technical Development and Production DTD&P (Air) of the Ministry of Defence. I applied for both. The interview calls arrived from both the places almost simultaneously. I was asked to reach Dehra Dun by the Air Force recruitment authorities and Delhi by DTD & P (Air). The boy from the Coromandel Coast took a train to the North. The destination was more than 2000 km away. It was to be my first encounter with the vastness of my motherland."

4

Search for Service

This involved a long and tedious journey from South to North. But it was indeed very essential for him to carve out a career after getting the coveted degree from the MIT. He halted at Delhi for a few days and felt much excited amidst new environments. At Dehradun, he could not make it before the Selection Board of the Indian Air Force. He was ninth is the batch, whereas there were eight vacancies. He missed the chance but felt much disgusted and disappointed.

After meeting Swami Sivananda at Rishikesh, he got much consolation and mental satisfaction. When the Swami apprised the young engineer almost the truth in the struggle of life, he made up his mind to face the reality with confidence and hard work. Desire, when it stems from the heart and spirit, when it is pure and intense, possesses awesome electromagnetic energy. This energy is released into the other each night, as the mind falls into the sleep state. Each morning it returns to the conscious state reinforced with the cosmic currents. That which has been imaged will surely and certainly be manifested. You can rely, young man, upon this ageless promise as surely as you can rely upon the eterally unbroken promise of sunrise... and of Spring."He was advised, "Forget this failure.... search instead for the purpose of your existence. Become one with yourself, my son ! Surrender yourself to the wish of God".

"I returned to Delhi and enquired at the DTD &P(Air) about the outcome of my interview. In response, I was handed the appointment letter. I joined the next day as Senior Scientific Assistant on a basic salary of Rs 250/- per month. If this was to be my destiny, I thought, let it be so. Finally, I was filled with mental peace. No more did I feel any bitterness or resentment at my failure to enter the Air Force. All this was in 1958."

Kalam was posted at the Technical Centre (Civil Aviation). During his first year in the Directorate , he carried out a design assignment on supersonic target aircraft with the help of the officer- in-charge, R. Varadharajan, and won a word of praise from the Director, Dr Neelakantan. To gain shop- floor exposure to aircraft maintenance, he was sent to the Aircraft and Armament Testing Unit (A and ATU) at Kanpur.

"Three years passed. Then the Aeronautical Development Establishment (ADE) was born in Bangalore and he was posted to the new establishment. Dr. OP Mediratta, Director of the ADE, asked Kalam to lead the team. He was given three years to launch the engineering model into flight. The project was, by any standards, bigger than our collective capabilities. None of us had any experience in building a machine, let alone a flying machine. There were no designs or standard components available to begin with. All we knew was that we had to make a successful heavier-than-air flying machine. We tried to read as much literature as we could find on hovercrafts, but there was not much available. We tried to consult people knowledgeable in this area but could find none. One day, I simply took the decision to proceed with the limited information and resources available." There is always the danger that a person with my kind of background—rural or small-town, middle-class, whose parents had limited education—will retreat into a corner and remain there struggling for bare existence, unless some great turn of circumstance propels him into a more favourable environment. I knew I had to create my own opportunities.

"Part by part, sub-system by sub-system, stage by stage, things started moving. Working on this project, I learned that once your mind gets stretched into a new idea, it never goes back to its original dimension".

V.K. Krishna Menon, the Defence Minister who was keenly interested in the progress of small project, which he envisioned as the beginning of the indigenous development of India's defence equipment. Whenever in Banglore, he always made it a routine to review the progress of this project. "His confidence in our ability ignited our enthusiasm".

"When the project was about a year old, Defence Minister Krishna Menon made one of his routine visits to ADE. Kalam escorted him into the assembly shop. The minister fired one question after another at him, determined to ensure that the prototype would go into test flight within the coming year. He told Dr. Mediratta, "GEM flight is possible with the gadgets Kalam now possesses". He was sure about his competence in flying the machine, he had made, and therefore shook his head in negation. Observing this wordless communication, Krishna Menon dismissed the insulting suggestion cf the Group Captain with a laugh and signalled to me to start the machine. He was very happy. "You have demonstrated that the basic problems of hovercraft development are solved. Go for a more powerful prime mover and call me for a second ride," Krishna Menon told him. The skeptical Group Captain (now Air Marshal) Golay, later became a good friend of Kalam.

"The project was completed ahead of schedule, we had a working hovercraft with us, moving on an air cushion of about 40 mm with a load of 550kg, including the tare weight. Dr. Mediratta was visibly pleased with the achievement. But by this time, I was out of office and the project was mired in controversies and was finally shelved.

"In fact, Kalam was unwilling to face reality. He had put my heart and soul into *Nandi.* That it would not be used was something beyond his comprehension. He was disappointed and disillusioned.

"Ten - minute ride in the hovercraft, a few centimetres above the ground. We were not flying, but were definitely floating in the air. The visitor asked me a few questions about myself, thanked me for the ride and departed. But not before introducing himself—he was Prof. MGK Menon, Director of the Tata Institute of Fundamental Research (TIFR). After a week, I received a call for the Indian Committee for Space Research (INCOSPAR), to attend an interview for the post of Rocket Engineer. All I knew about INCOSPAR at the time was that it was formed out of the TIFR talent poor at Bombay (now Mumbai) to organise space research in India. I went to Bombay to attend the interview. I was unsure about the type of questions I would have to face at the interview . There was hardly any time to read up or talk to any experienced person. Lakshmana Sastry's voice quoting from the *Bhagawad Gita* echoed in my ears:

> *"All beings are born to delusion—overcome by the dualities which arise from wish and hate—But those men of virtuous deeds in whom sin has come to an end, freed form the delusion of dualities, worship Me steadfast in their vows."*

Kalam was interviewed by Dr. Vikram Sarabhai along with Prof. MGK Menon and Mr. Saraf, then the Deputy Secretary of the Atomic Energy Commission, different from that at DTD and P(AIR). There was no need for anyone to justify his position or to be at the receiving end of the others hostility. Some time in the latter half of 1962, INCOSPAR took the decision to set up the Equatorial Rocket Launching Station at Thumba, a sleepy fishing village near Trivandrum (now Thiruvananthapuram) in Kerala. Dr. Chitnis of the Physical Research Laboratory, Ahmedabad had spotted it as a suitable location as it was very close to the earth's magnetic equator. This was the quiet beginning of modern rocket- based research in India. The place selected at Thumba lay between the railway line and the sea coast, covering a distance of about two and a half kms and measuring about 600 acres. Soon after this, Kalam was asked to proceed to America for six-month training programme on sounding rocket launching techniques, at the National Aeronautics and Space Administration (NASA) work centres.

5

Trip to NASA and Aftermath

Kalam started his work at NASA at the Langley Research Centre (LRC) is Hampton, Virginia. From LRC he went to the Goddard Space Flight Centre (GSFC) at Greenbelt, Maryland. This Centre develops and manages most of NASA's earth-orbiting science and applications satellites. It operates NASA's tracking networks for all space missions. Towards the end of my visit, I went to the Wallops Flight Facility at Wallops Island in East Coast, Virginia. This pace was the base for NASA's sounding rocket programme.

What makes life in Indian organizations difficult is the wide-spread prevalence of this very contemptuous pride. It stops us from listening to our juniors, subordinates and people down the line. You cannot expect a person to deliver results if you humiliate him, nor can you expect him to be creative if you abuse him or despise him. The line between firmness and harshness, between strong leadership and bullying, between discipline and vindictiveness is very fine, but it has to be drawn. Unfortunately, the only line prominently drawn in our country today is between the 'heroes' and the 'zeros'. On one side are a few hundred 'heroes' keeping nine hundred and fifty million people down on the other side. This situation has to be changed.

As the process of confronting and solving problems often requires hard work and is painful, we have endless procrastination. When he returned from NASA, India's first rocket launch took place on 21 November 1963. It was a sounding rocket, called Nike-Apache, made at NASA.

In the maiden Nike-Apache launch, he was in charge of rocket integration and safety. Two of his colleagues who played a crucial role in this launch were D Easwardas and R Aravamudan. Easwardas undertook the rocket assembly and arranged the launch.

Aravamudan, whom we called Dan, was in-charge of radar, telemetry and ground support. The launch was smooth and without any problems. We got excellent flight data and returned with a sense of accomplishment.

To implement his future plan Prof. Sarabhai had a detailed discussion with young scientist on science and technology in India. A new generation—scientists and engineers in their 30s and early 40s—was being charged with an unprecedented dynamism. Our biggest qualifications at INCOSPAR were not our degrees, but Prof. Sarabhai's faith in our capabilities. The successful launch of Nike-Apache, he made chose to share with them his dream of Indian Satellite Launch Vehicle. "Prof. Sarabhai's optimism was very contagious. The very news of his coming to Thumba would electrify people and all laboratories, workshops and design offices would hum with unceasing activity. People would work virtually round the clock because of their enthusiasm to show Prof. Sarabhai something new, something that had not been done before in our country—be it a new design or a new method of fabrication or even an out-of-the way administrative procedure. Prof. Sarabhai would often assign multiple tasks to a single person or a group. Though some of those tasks would appear totally unrelated in the beginning they would at a later stage emerge as deeply interconnected. When Prof. Sarabhai was talking to us about the Satellite Launch Vehicle (SLV), he asked me, almost in the same breath, to take up studies on a rocket-assisted take-off-system (RATO) for military aircraft. The two things had no apparent connection except in the mind of this great visionary. I knew that all I had to do was to remain alert and focussed on my purpose, and sooner or later, an opportunity to do a challenging job would enter my laboratory".

"Prof. Sarabhai was ever-willing to try out novel approaches and liked to draw in young people. He had the wisdom and judgement which enabled him to realise not only if something was well done, but also when it was time to stop. In my opinion, he was an ideal experimenter and innovator. When there were alternative courses of action before us, whose outcome was difficult to predict, or to reconcile varying perspectives, Prof. Sarabhai would resort to experimentation to resolve the issue. This was precisely the situation at INCOSPAR in 1963. A bunch of young, inexperienced, but nevertheless energetic and enthusiastic persons was given the task of fleshing out the spirit of self-reliance in the field of science and technology in general, and of space research in particular. It was a great example of leadership by trust".

Soon after this great experiment, Thumba Equatorial Rocket Launch Station (TERLS) came into existence with the collaboration of USA, USSR and France. In fact the Indian leader, Prof. Vikram Sarabhai had taken up the challenge with full confidence. He had deep involvement in the space programme and now made sincere efforts to develop and manufacture rockets indigenously. And to give a quick boost to several programmes experimentation in space were launched at the space science and Technology centre and the Physical Research Laboratory at Ahmedabad.

The next phase quickened the programme in this direction. It was the Rohini Sounding Rocket (RSR) Programme. In fact, the RSR programme was responsible for the development and fabrication of sounding rockets and used for scientific investigation in our sub-continent. So for several hundreds of these rockets have been launched for various scientific studies.

Historically, these rockets had much development in the 18th century during the reign of Tipu Sultan. After his demise, more than 700 rockets were captured by the British. These rockets had been taken to England by William Congreve and were subjected by the British to what we call 'reverse engineering' today. There were, of course, no GATT, IPR Act, or patent regime. With the death of Tipu, Indian rocketry also met its demise—at least for 150 years. Meanwhile, rocket technology made several useful strides abroad. Konstantin Tsiolkovsky in Russia (1903), Robert Goddard in USA (1914) and Hermann Oberth in Germany (1923) gave rocketry new dimensions. In Nazi Germany, Wernher Von Braun's group produced V2 short range ballistic missiles and showered fire on the Allied Forces. After the war, both the USA and the USSR captured their share of German rocket technology and rocket engineers. With this booty, they started to run their deadly arms race with missiles and warheads. Rocketry was reborn in India thanks to the technological vision of Prime Minister Jawaharlal Nehru. Prof. Sarabhai took the challenge of giving physical dimensions to this dream.

6

New Experiments

I

Prof. Sarabhai showed deep interest in the functioning of Thumba. He listened to everyone attentively. He considered the collective understanding of the problem, the main attribute of effective leadership. He once told me, "Look, my job is to make decisions; but it is equally important to see to it that these decisions are accepted by my team members."

In fact, Prof. Sarabhai took a series of decisions that were to become the life-mission of many. We would make our own rockets, our own Satellite Launch Vehicles (SLVS) and our own satellites. And this would not be done one-by-one but concurrently, in a multidimensional fashion.

Prof. Sarabhai assigned Kalam the task of providing interface support to payload scientists. Almost all physical laboratories in India were involved in the sounding rocket programme, each having its own mission, its own objective and its own payload. And Kalam not only had to interact with scientists from TIFR, National Physical Laboratory (NPL), and Physical Research Laboratory (PRL), but also with payload scientists from USA, USSR, France, Germany and Japan.

Kalam was involved with rocket preparation activities, payload assembly, testing and evaluation besides building subsystems like payload housing and jettisonable nose cones. Working with the nose cones led him into the field of composite materials.

Meanwhile, two Indian rockets were born at Thumba. They were christened *Rohini* and *Menaka*, after the two mythological dancers in the court of Indra, the king of the sky. The Indian pay loads no longer needed to be launched by French rockets. Could this have been done but for the atmosphere of trust and commitment which Prof. Sarabhai had created at INCOSPAR? He brought into use each person's knowledge and skills. He made every man feel directly involved in problem solving. By the very fact of the team members' participation, the solutions became genuine and earned the trust of the entire team resulting in total commitment towards implementation.

"Early next year, Prof. Sarabhai wanted to see me urgently in Delhi. By now I was accustomed to Prof. Sarabhai's working method. He was always full of enthusiasm and optimism. In such a state of mind, sudden flashes of inspiration were almost natural. On reaching Delhi, I contacted Prof. Sarabhai's secretary for an appointment and was asked to meet him at 3.30 a.m. at Hotel Ashoka. Delhi being a slightly unfamiliar place, with an unfriendly climate for someone like me, conditioned to the warm and humid climate of South India, I decided to wait in the hotel lounge after finishing my dinner.

"I have always been a religious person in the sense that I maintain a working partnership with God. I was aware that the best work required more ability than I possessed and therefore I needed help that only God could give. I made a true estimate of my own ability, then raised it 50 percent and put myself in God's hands. In this partnership, I have always received all the power I needed, and in fact even felt it flowing into me. Today, I can affirm that the kingdom of God is within you in the form of this power, to achieve your goals and realise your dreams.

"Waiting in the hotel lobby at 1 a.m. for an appointment two hours later was certainly not a reasonable proposition, neither for me nor for Prof. Sarabhai. But then, Prof. Sarabhai had always exhibited a strong component of unorthodoxy in his character. He was running the show of space research in the country—under-staffed, overworked—nevertheless in a successful manner.

"Prof. Sarabhai ordered coffee for Kalam and Group Captain V.S. Narayanan and unfolded his plan of developing a rocket-assisted take-off system (RATO) for military aircraft. This would help our warplanes to take-off from short runways in the Himalayas. Hot coffee was served over small talk about what's happening. It was totally uncharacteristic of Prof. Sarabhai. But as soon as we finished coffee, Prof. Sarabhai got up and asked them to accompany him to Tilpat Range on the outskirts of Delhi.

"It was about an hour's drive to the Range. Prof. Sarabhai showed us a Russian RATO. "If I get you the motors of this system from

Russia, could you do it in eighteen months time?" Prof. Sarabhai asked us. "Yes, we can!" Both Gp Capt VS Narayanan and I spoke almost simultaneously. Prof. Sarabhai's face beamed, reflecting our fascination. I recalled what I had read, " He will bestow on you a light to walk in."

"After dropping us back at the Hotel Ashoka, Prof. Sarabhai went to Prime Minister Nehru's house for a breakfast meeting . By evening, the news of India taking up the indigenous development of a device to help short run take-offs by high performance military aircraft with myself heading the project was made public. I was filled with many emotions—happiness, gratitude, and a sense of fulfilment.

Indeed the RATO motors were mounted on aircraft to provide the additional thrust during the take-off . The Air Force was in dire need of a large number of RATO motors for their S-22 and HF-24 aircraft. The Russian RATO motor shown to us at the Tilpat Range was capable of generation a 3000 kg thrust with a total impulse of 24500 kg-seconds. The development work was to be carried out at the Space Science and Technology Centre with the assistance of Defence Research and Development Organisation (DRDO), HAL, DTD and P (Air) and Air Head Quarters.

The plan mainly centred around the early ideas which had been born at INCOSPAR, it included utilization of satellites for television and developmental education, meteorological observations and remote sensing for management of natural resources.

The other development was the formation of a Missile Panel in the Ministry of Defence. Both Narayanan and Kalam were inducted as members. The idea of making missiles in our own country was exciting, and they were spending hours on end studying the missiles of various advanced countries.

Gp. Capt Narayanan had much enthusiasm for indigenous guided missiles. He was a great admirer of the brute force approach of the Russian Missile Development programme. " When it could be done there, why not here, where space research has already prepared the soil for a bonanza of missile technology?" Narayanan used to provoke Kalam. The two wars in 1962 and 1965 made the Indian Government realize the urgently of effective missiles. A large number of Surface-to -Air Missiles (SAMa) were obtained from the USSR to guard strategic locations. Gp Capt Narayanan passionately advocated the development of these missiles in the country.

While working together on RATO motors and on the Missile Panel,

Narayanan and Kalam played the roles of student and teacher interchangeably wherever required. He was very eager to learn about rocketry and Kalam was very curious about airborne weapon systems. The depth of Narayanan's conviction and his force of application were inspiring. Right from the day of our visit before dawn to the Tilpat Range with Prof. Sarabhai, Narayanan was away busy with his RATO motor. He had arranged everything that was required before being asked. He obtained funding of Rs. 75 lakhs with a further commitment towards any unforeseen costs." You name the thing and I will get it for you, but do not ask for time," he said.

At this point of time, Defence R and D was heavily dependent on imported equipment. Virtually nothing indigenous was available. Together, they made a long shopping list and drew up an import plan. But this made Kalam unhappy—was there no remedy or alternative? Was this nation doomed to live with screwdriver technology? Could a poor country like India afford this kind of development?

II

The Satellite Launch Vehicle (SLV) had also been conceived by this time. Prof. Sarabhai was concentrating with full attention on the east coast in order to let the launch vehicle take full advantage of the earth's west to east rotation. He finally selected the Sriharikota island, 100 km north of Madras (now Chennai), and thus the SHAR Rocket Launch Station was born. Crescent-shaped, the island has a maximum width of 8 km and is along the coastline. Area-wise, the island is as big as Madras city. In 1968, the Indian Rocket Society was formed. Soon after, the INCOSPAR was reconstituted as an advisory body under the Indian National Science Academy (INSA) and the Indian Space Research Organization (ISRO) was created under the Department of Atomic Energy (DAE) to actually conduct space research in the country.

It was felt necessary by Prof. Sarabhai hand-picked team to give form to his dream of an Indian SLV. He gave him the additional responsibility of designing the fourth stage of the SLV. Dr VR Gowariker, MR Kurup and AE Muthunayagam were given the tasks of designing the other three stages.

Kalam laid the foundation for Stage IV on two rocks- sensible approximation and gnawed support. He had always considered the price of perfection prohibitive and allowed mistakes as a part of learning. He had always supported learning on the part of his team members by paying vigilant attention to each of their attempts, be they successful or unsuccessful. Although he provided access to all the information that his co-workers in Stage IV needed, to be full partners, he found he could not spend enough time to be a useful facilitator and a source of support. "I wondered if there was something wrong in the way I managed my time. At this stage, Prof. Sarabhai brought a French visitor to our work centre to point out the problem to me. This gentleman was Prof. Curien, President of CNES (Centre National de Etudes Spaticales), our counterpart in France. They were then developing the Diamont launch vehicles. Prof. Curien was a thorough professional. Together, Prof. Sarabhai and Prof. Curien helped me set a target. While they discussed the means by which I could reach it, they also cautioned me about the possibilities of failure. While I could arrive at a better awareness of Stage IV problems through the supportive counselling of Prof. Curien, Prof. Sarabhai's catalytic intervention motivated Prof. Curien to reinterpret his own progress in the Diamont programme".

Prof. Curien advised Prof. Sarabhai to withdraw Kalam from all the minor jobs which posed little challenge and to give him opportunities for achievement.

Meanwhile they told us that they did not need our Stage IV any more. It was a great shock, making him relive the disappointments, at Dehra Dun, when Kalam failed to get into the Air Force, and at Bangalore, when the *Nandi* project was aborted at ADE.

"Prof. Sarabhai was an exemplar in the art of team-building. On one occasion, he had to identify a person who could be given the responsibility for developing a telecommand system for SLV. Two men were competent to carry out this task—one was the seasoned and sophisticated UR Rao and the other was a relatively unknown experimenter, G Madhavan Nair. Although I was deeply impressed by Madhavan Nair's dedication and abilities, I did not reckon his chances as very good. During one of Prof. Sarabhai's routine visits, Madhavan Nair boldly demonstrated his improvised but highly reliable telecommand system. Prof. Sarabhai did not take much time to back the bound experimenter in preference to an established expert. Madhavan Nair not only lived up to the expectations of his leader but even went beyond them. He was to later become the project director of the Polar Satellite Launch Vehicle (PSLV)".

Having deep interests in new development in 1968, Prof. Sarabhai came to Thumba. He was shown the operation of the nose-cone jettisoning mechanism. They were all anxious to share the results of our work with Prof. Sarabhai. "We requested Prof. Sarabhai to formally activate the pyro system through a timer circuit. Prof. Sarabhai smiled, and pressed the button. To our horror, nothing happened. We were dumbstruck. I looked at Pramod Kale, who had designed and integrated the timer circuit. In a flash each of us mentally went through an analysis of the failure. We requested Prof. Sarabhai to wait for a few minutes, then we detached the timer device, giving direct connection to the pyros. Prof. Sarabhai pressed the beetton again. The pyros were fired and the nose cone jettisoned. Prof. Sarabhai congratulated Kale and Kalam; but his expressions suggested that his thoughts were elsewhere. We could not guess what was on his mind. The suspense did not last for long and I got a call from Prof. Sarabhai's secretary to meet him after dinner for an important discussion".

Prof. Sarabhai was staying at the Kovalam Palace Hotel, his usual home whenever he was in Trivandrum. Kalam was slightly perplexed by the summons. Prof. Sarabhai greeted him with his customary warmth. He talked of the rocket launching station, envisaging facilities like launch pads, block houses, radar, telemetry and so on—things, which were taken for granted in Indian space research. He also asked Kalam to consider if his work was possibly being affected by any problem of which he was hitherto unaware. He finally put his finger on the key issue. Prof. Sarabhai spent the next hour in redefining our tasks, and, in the small hours of the morning, the decision to set up a Rocket Engineering Section was finally taken.

"It has been well-said about the working of mind of Prof. Sarabhai. Mistakes can delay or prevent the proper achievement of the objectives of individuals and organizations, but a visionary like Prof. Sarabhai can use errors as opportunities to promote innovation, and the development of new ideas. He was not especially concerned with the mistake in the timer circuit, least not all with pinning blame for it. Prof. Sarabhai's approach to mistakes rested on the assumption that they were inevitable but generally manageable. It was in the handling of the crises that arose as a consequence that talent could often be revealed. I later realised by experience, that the best way to prevent errors was to anticipate them. But, this time, by a strange twist of fate, the failure of the timer circuit led to the birth of rocket engineering laboratory".

"It was my usual practice duty to brief Prof. Sarabhai after every Missile Panel Meeting. After attending one such meeting in Delhi on 30 December 1971, I was returning to Trivandrum. Prof. Sarabhai was visiting Thumba that day to review the SLV design. I spoke to him on the telephone from the airport lounge about the salient points that had emerged at the panel meeting. He instructed me to wait at Trivandrum Airport after alighting from the Delhi flight and to see him there before his departure for Bombay the same night". "When I disembarked at Trivandrum, there was a pall of gloom in the air. The aircraft ladder operator Kutty told me in a choked voice that Prof. Sarabhai was no more. He had passed away a few hours before, following a cardiac arrest. I was shocked to the core; it had happened within an hour of our conversation. It was a great blow to myself and a huge loss to Indian science. The night passed in preparations for airlifting Prof. Sarabhai's body for the cremation in Ahmedabad. For five years, between 1966 to 1971, about 22 scientists and engineers worked closely with Prof. Sarabhai. All of them were to later take charge of important scientific projects. Not only was Prof. Sarabhai a great scientist, he was also a great leader. I still remember him making his review of the bi-monthly progress of the design projects of SLV-3 in June 1970. Presentations on stages I to IV were arranged".

After an interim arrangement with Prof. MGK Menon at the helm, Prof. Satish Dhawan was given the responsibility of leading ISRO. The whole complex at Thumba, which included TERLS, the Space Science and Technology Centre (SSTC), the RPP, the Rocket Fabrication Facility (RFF), and the Propellant Fuel Complex (PFC) were merged together to form an integrated space centre and christened the Vikram Sarabhai Space Centre (VSSC) as a tribute to the man to whom it owed its existence. The renowned metallurgist, Dr Brahm Prakash, took over as the first Director of VSSC.

The RATO system was successfully tested on 8 October 1972 at Bareilly Air Force Station in Uttar Pradesh, when a high performance Sukhoi-16 jet aircraft became airborne after a short run of 1200 m, as against its usual run of 2 km.

Prof. Sarabhai had established a number of successful industrial enterprises. He was aware that scientific research could not survive in isolation, away from industry. He founded Sarabhai Chemicals, Sarabhai Glass, Sarabhai Geigy Limited, Sarabhai Merck Limited, and the Sarabhai Engineering Group. His Swastik Oil Mills did pioneering work in the extraction of oil from oilseeds, manufacture of synthetic detergents and of cosmetics. He geared Standard Pharmaceuticals Limited to enable large-scale manufacture of penicillin, which was imported from abroad at astronomical costs at that time. At the Vikram Sarabhai Space Centre, work on the SLV went on at full swing. Prof. Dhawan in consultation with Dr. Brahm Prakash, picked him for job. He was appointed the Project Manager—SLV, and reported directly to the Director, VSSC. Dr. Brahm Prakash advised him to take care of the performance. "Everyone will work to create their bit of SLV; your problem is going to be your dependency on others in accomplishing the total SLV. The SLV mission will be accomplished with, and through, a large number of people. You will require a tremendous amount of tolerance and patience," he said. It reminded me of what my father used to read from the *Holy Qur'an* on the distinction between right and wrong: "We have sent no apostle before you who did not eat or walk about the market squares. We test you by means of one another. Will you not have patience?". The primary objectives of the SLV Project were design, development and operation of a standard SLV system, SLV-3, capable of reliably and expeditiously fulfilling the specified mission of launching a 40 kg satellite into a 400 km circular orbit around the earth. Soon Dr. Kalam took up the executive responsibility of implementing the project within the framework of policy decisions taken, the approved management plan, and the project report; and also within the budget and through the powers delegated to him by the Director, VSSC. Dr. Brahm Prakash formed four Project Advisory committees to advise Kalam on specialized areas like rocket motors, materials and fabrication, control and guidance, electronics, and mission and launching . He was assured of the guidance of outstanding scientists like DS Rane, Muthunayagam, TS Prahlad, AR Acharya, SC Gupta, and CL Amba Rao, to name a few.

"I projected a requirement of 275 engineers and scientists for SLV-3 but could get only about 50. If it had not been for synergistic efforts, the whole project would have remained a non-starter. Some young engineers like MSR Dev, G Madhavan Nair, S Srinivasan, US Singh, Sunderrajan, Abdul Majeed, Ved Prakash Sandlas, Namboodary, Sasi Kumar, and Sivathanu Pillai developed their own ground rules designed to help them work efficiently as a project team, and produced outstanding individual and team results. These men were in the habit of celebrating their successes together—in a sort of mutual appreciation club. This generated good morale, and helped them a great deal to accept setbacks and to revitalise themselves after periods of intense work."

Each member of the SLV-3 project team was a specialist in his own field. It was natural therefore that each one of them valued his independence. To manage the performance of such specialists the team leader has to adopt a delicate balance between the hands-on and the hands-off approach. The hands-on approach takes an active interest on a very regular basis in the members' work. The hands-off approach trusts team members and recognises their need for autonomy to carry out their roles, as they see fit. It trades on their self-motivation. When the leader goes too far with the hands-on approach, he is seen. as an anxious and interfering type. If he goes too far hands-off, he is seen as abdicating his responsibility or not being interested. Today, the members of the SLV-3 team have grown up to lead some of the country's most prestigious programmes. MSR Dev heads the Augmented Satellite Launch Vehicle (ASLV) project, Madhavan Nair is the chief of the Polar Satellite Launch Vehicle (PSLV) project and Sandalas and Sivathanu Pillai are Chief Controllers in DRDO Headquarters. Each one of these men rose to his present position through consistent hard work and rock-like will power. It was indeed an exceptionally talented team!

III

Dr. Kalam took up the leadership of executing the SLV-3 project, he faced urgent and conflicting demands on his time—for committee work, material procurement, correspondence, reviews, briefings, and for the need to be informed on a wide range of subjects.

In fact his day would start with a stroll of about 2 km around the lodge he was living in. He used to prepare a general schedule during his morning walk, and emphasize two or three things He would definitely like to accomplish during the day, including at least one thing that would achieve long-term goals.

Prof. Dhawan came up with a clear statement that all the manpower and funds at VSSC and SHAR would have to be directed to us. From our side, we evolved a matrix type of management to achieve productive interfacing with more than 300 industries. The target was that our interaction with them must lead to their technology empowerment. Three things I stressed before my colleagues—importance of design capability, goal setting and realisation and the strength to withstand setbacks. Now, before I dwell on the finer aspects of the management of the SLV-3 project, let me talk about the SLV-3 itself.

"Through mechanical engineering, these materials are transformed into hardware. In fact, of all the engineering disciplines which feed directly into the development of rocketry, mechanical engineering is perhaps the most intrinsic one. Be it a sophisticated system like a liquid engine or a piece of hardware as simple a fastener, its ultimate fabrication calls for expert mechanical engineers and precision machine tools. We decided to develop important technologies like welding techniques for low alloy stainless steel, electro forming techniques, and ultra-precision process tooling. We also decided to make some important machines in-house like the 254 litre vertical mixer and the groove machining facility for our third and fourth stages. Many of our subsystems were so massive and complex that they implied sizeable financial outlays. Without any hesitation, we approached industries in the private sector and developed contract management plans which later became blueprints for many government-run science and technology business organisations.

"By now promoted to Air Commodore, Narayanan took over as Director, DRDL. He mobilized this young laboratory located in the south-eastern suburbs of Hyderabad to take up this enormous task. The landscape dotted with tombs and old buildings started reverberating with new life. Narayanan was a man of tremendous energy—a man always in the boost phase. He gathered around him a strong group of enthusiastic people, drawing many service officers into this predominantly civilian laboratory. Totally preoccupied with the SLV affairs, my participation in the Missile Panel meetings gradually dwindled, and then stopped. However, stories about Narayanan and his *Devil* were beginning to reach Trivandrum. A transformation of an unprecedented scale was taking place there".

"During my association with Narayanan in the RATO project, I had discovered that he was a hard taskmaster—one who went all out for control, mastery and domination. I used to wonder if managers like him, who aim at getting results no matter what the price, would face a rebellion of silence and non-cooperation in the long run".

"New Year's day, 1975, brought with it an opportunity to have a first-person assessment of the work going on under Narayanan's leadership. Prof. MGK Menon, who was working then as Scientific

Advisor to the Defence Minister and was head of the DRDO, appointed a review committee under the chairmanship of Dr. Brahm Prakash to evaluate the work carried out the *Devil* Project. I was taken into the team as a rocket specialist to evaluate the progress made in areas of aerodynamics, structure and propulsion of the missile. On propulsion aspects, I was assisted by BR Somasekhar and by Wg Cdr P Kamaraju. The committee members included Dr. RP Shenoy and Prof. IG Sarma who were to review the work done on the electronic systems".

"As work on the SLV gained momentum , Prof. Dhawan introduced the system of reviewing progress with the entire team involved in the project. Prof. Dhawan was a man with a mission. He would effortlessly pull together all the loose ends to make work move smoothly. At VSSC the review meetings presided over by Prof. Dhawan used to be considered major events. He was a true captain of the ISRO ship—a commander, navigator, housekeeper, all rolled into one. Yet, he never pretended to know more than he did. Instead, when something appeared ambiguous, he would ask questions and discuss his doubts frankly. I remember him as a leader for whom to lead with a firm, but fair hand, was a moral compulsion. His mind used to be very firm once it had been decided on any issue. But before taking a decision, it used to be like clay, open to impressions until the final moulding. Then the decisions would be popped into the potter's oven for glazing, never failing to emerge hard and tough, resistant and enduring.

"I had the privilege of spending a great deal of time with Prof. Dhawan. He could hold the listener enthralled because of the logical , intellectual acumen he could bring to bear on his analysis of any subject. He had an unusual combination of degree—a B.Sc. in Mathematics and Physics, M.A. in English Literature, B.E. in Mechanical Engineering, M.S. in Aeronautical Engineering followed by a Ph.D. in Aeronautics and Mathematics from the California Institute of Technology (Caltech) in USA.

"Intellectual debates with him were very stimulating and could always mentally energise me and my team members. I always found him full of optimism and compassion. Although he often judged himself harshly, with no allowance for excuses, he was generous to a fault when it came to others. Prof. Dhawan used to sternly pronounce his judgements and then pardon the contrite guilty parties".

"In 1975, ISRO became a government body. An ISRO council

was formed consisting of Directors of different work centres and senior officers in the Department of Space (DoS). This provided a symbolic link as well as a forum for participated management between the DoS which had the governmental powers and the centres which would execute the jobs. In the traditional parlance of government departments, ISRO's centres would have been subordinate units or attached offices, but such words were never spoken either at ISRO or DoS. Participative management, which calls for active interacting between those who wield administrative powers and the executing agencies, was a novel feature of ISRO management that would go a long way in Indian R&D organisations.

"The new set-up brought me in contact with TN Seshan, then Joint Secretary in the DoS. Till then, I had a latent reservation about bureaucrats, so I was not very comfortable when I first saw Seshan participating in a SLV-3 Management Board meeting. But soon, it changed to admiration for Seshan, who would meticulously go through the agenda and always come for the meeting prepared. He used to kindle the minds of scientists with his tremendous analytical capability".

"The first three years of the SLV project was the period for the revelation of many fascinating mysteries of science. Being human, ignorance has always been with us, and always will be. What was new was my awareness of it, my awakening to its fathomless dimensions. I used to erroneously suppose that the function of science was to explain everything, and that unexplained phenomena were the province of people like my father and Lakshmana Sastry. However, I always refrained from discussing these matters with any scientist colleagues, fearing that it would threaten the hegemony of their meticulously formed views.

"Gradually, I became aware of the difference between science and technology, between research and development. Science is inherently open-ended and exploratory. Development is a closed loop. Mistakes are imperative in development and are made everyday but each mistake is used for modification, up-gradation or betterment. Probably, the Creator created engineers to make scientists achieve more. For each time scientists come up with a thoroughly researched and fully comprehended solution, engineers show them yet another *lumineu,* yet one more possibility. I cautioned my team against becoming scientists. Science is a passion—a never-ending voyage into promises and possibilities. We had been allocated only limited time and limited funds. Our making the SLV depended upon our awareness of our own limits. I preferred existing workable solutions which would be the best options. Nothing that is new enters into time-bound projects without curse. In my opinion, a project leader should always work for proven technologies in most of the systems as far as possible and experiment from multiple resources".

7
Shift in Career

A few comments by Dr. Kalam in public as well as comments by eminent persons are worth notice. *The Tribune*—a premier newspaper of North India, in its, editorial, "Thus, spake Kalam", gave an assessment of his scientific personality. He himself clarified the point that the nuclear weapons helped avert war and called the Gujarat incidents are very painful. He appears to have a quiet realisation in view of the geostrategic reality today with China as a major nuclear armed nation. His chapter for children in the publication of NCERT is indeed very useful for them. Besides, Dr. Kalam sincerely hoped that every missile launch was just a 'family affair'. He showed a sense of optimism to use science for the new horizons of development of mankind. He sincerely wished that there should be leaders with values for the nation and the humanity.

There were very fine academic comments by most eminent writers—Amita Malik and Inder Malhotra. The comments by the *Hindu* are very commendable, "when he moves into Rashtrapathi Bhavan, Dr. Kalam will, in a way, be the first of his kind". Supriya Roy Chowdhury commented thus, "Since Dr. Kalam is a candidate of the BJP-led NDA, one has to conclude that his politics is at least not fundamentally opposed to what the BJP stands for ideologically".

'Gujarat Incidents Very Painful'

Nuclear Weapons Helped Avert War: Kalam

The man all set to become president, A.P.J. Abdul Kalam, is not quite unfamiliar with politics. At his first press conference, he deftly handled questions ranging from the Gujarat carnage to his "pro-nuclear weapons image"—he fielded them all without faltering and effortlessly. And he was alway politically correct.

Clearly, his own inimitable style was not limited to his hair, he is a man who likes to have "his way", his aim has always been high, and his vision large and wide and he seems determined to leave his stamp on the presidency he is about to enter.

Would his connection with the missile programme send a "wrong signal" as alleged by the Left presidential candidate, Lakshmi Sahgal? How did nuclear India reconcile with the non-violence preached by Mahatma Gandhi? Are India's nuclear weapons "safe"?

"The right signal was the use of technology to develop the nation," he said. He was not simply the bomb man.

He had worked with the space and satellite launch programme for better communications, yes, he had worked on missile technology and, more recently, his ambition was to teach the young.

He wanted people to develop a scientific temper, and he read from the Constitution to prove the point that would be his constitutional duty as President. Why a nuclear weapon? For 3000 years India had been invaded, more lately the English, the French, the Portuguese and even the Dutch were able to set up colonies. "They came with guns, we had only swords, now our neighbours have nuclear bombs, we need a minimum deterrent.. .. no first use, minimum deterrent. .. no further tests, that is our nuclear policy ... and our safety record is very good, safety standards are in position." Why worry about the few nuclear bombs India may have, why not talk about the 10,000 nuclear warheads across the Atlantic, he asked.

He was diplomatic enough not to be drawn on issues such as the recent Indo-Pak tension ("very sensitive issue, we should not discuss this", but he did add that "the last war did not take place because we had nuclear weapons"—nuclear weapons had helped avert a war).

How would a scientist like him cope with politics and his duties in the Rashtrapati Bhavan? It was not a new thing for him, he had worked with six Prime Ministers and, according to him, "a political system should create responsible leadership, empowered citizens, and lead to policies that develop the nation." He hoped technology would be one of the major tools for India's development and as President he could "work with Parliament and the Cabinet" on this.

As for learning politics, that should be easy: "since last Sunday (June 9) my experience with politics has been that it was like trying launch a missile which must correctly hit its target", he said and in the days to come he would learn it. An RSS journal has praised him as a "model Muslim" but clearly he was not impressed saying: "first and foremost, one should be a good human being, every other element—Indian, Muslim, Hindu can be part of that."

On the Gujarat carnage Dr. Kalam said: "What has happened is very painful...We should prevent it at all costs. I can only say religion should graduate into spiritual inquiry, managers must become leaders, and political leaders must have compassion." He refused to be drawn into specific questions on the role of the Modi Government.

He talked of the need for 100 per cent literacy, for development and a higher GDP and implied that they would resolve the problem of communalism. But when it was pointed out that Hitler's Germany was literate and highly developed, and that it was naive to think that fascism could be stopped by development, Dr. Kalam talked of education, health, agriculture and food processing.

Finally, Dr. Kalam related an anecdote: he was a schoolboy on August 15, 1947, the day's newspaper carried two photographs—Nehru unfurling the national flag and Mahatma Gandhi marching barefoot in Noakhali trying to quell the communal disturbances. It was the photograph of Gandhiji that left a lasting impression on him. "Political leadership with compassion" he emphasised again.

The ruling National Democratic Alliance's nominee for the July 15 Presidential election, Dr. A.P.J. Abdul Kalam, was quite impressive during his first encounter with the media. As a learner in the political arena, which he declared as a straightforward person, he handled even difficult and embarrassing questions with the deftness of a hard-boiled practitioner. But throughout the gruelling session he tried to impress upon one and all that India's next President would be a person dedicated to employing science and technology for the good of society. He is not just the father of the country's missile programme. He is a scientific visionary. He would wish to use the position he is soon going to occupy for realising his cherished dream—transforming India into a developed country by 2020. Of course, it is a long and challenging journey, but with Dr Kalam as the moving spirit behind the march forward, the country's efforts may be more focused on achieving the goal. No doubt, science and technology also has a destructive aspect to it. This, however, broadly relates to defence matters. Dr. Kalam looks at India's position as a regional nuclear power from this angle. And he appears to be quite realistic in view of the geostrategic reality today with China as a major nuclear-armed nation. He stated an unalloyed truth when he emphasised at the Press Conference the point that had there been no nuclear deterrent during the India-Pakistan border standoff, the subcontinent would have been on a destructive course by now. What he did not mention was that in the process his vision of using science and technology for faster economic growth of the country would have been shattered.

However, the question had political connotations and therefore, a straight answer should have been avoided. Some critics point out that Dr Kalam's utterances have weakened India's diplomatic offensive against Pakistan. But the fact is that what he has said is not very much wide of the mark. His remarks need to be understood in a larger context. However, it is also true that New Delhi has been trying to make the world believe that Islamabad is an irresponsible possessor of nuclear power and had resorted to blackmailing tactics by threatening to use this ultimate weapon in the event of a full-scale war with India. The NDA presidential nominee's answers on Gujarat and Ayodhya showed that he fully understood the intricacies of the different sensitive problems the country was faced with. He avoided being drawn into a controversy or raising a fresh one. His performance proved that learning how to swim in the sea of politics was not a difficult task for a man of technology of Mr Kalam's stature.

Kalam's Life Brought to Children

It may have been nothing more than sheer coincidence, but the National Council of Education, Research and Training (NCERT) might just have an ace up its sleeve if and when A.P.J. Abdul Kalam is elected the President of India.

An 'up close and personal look at the life of the country's missile man is what the very first chapter of the newly introduced English book for Class IX promises. And even if it was not planned, most at NCERT are keeping their fingers crossed--- for this will probably be the first time that school students will get to read about the personal life of the President during his tenure in office.

The book *Steps to English* is being introduced from this academic session as part of the new books that the Council is introducing till Class IX based on the guidelines suggested by the Curriculum of Framework for School Education 2000.

Although the NCERT maintains that the decision to choose a chapter on Prof. Kalam was based purely on the "scientific expertise of the scientist and the literary value of his autobiographical work

Wings of Fire and not on any assumption of his name coming up for the highest office of the country".

The chapter titled " My Childhood " takes a peek into the life of the Indian scientist and now the Presidential nominee. With excerpts from his book "Wings of Fire " forming the four-page long chapter, students get a rare look into some of the struggling times and rather interesting tales that shaped the life of Prof. Kalam.

"I was one of the many children, a short boy with rather undistinguished looks , bom to tall and handsome parents", reveals the scientist in the book. What makes interesting reading here are the incidents that shaped his life.

Right from the story of a new teacher who during his fifth class made him shift his seat from the first bench to the last because he did not want him to sit with a Brahmin boy to later days when his science teacher who despite being an orthodox Brahmin ways showed Kalam why breaking social barriers was important, the four-page long chapter makes interesting reading by giving some insight into the life of Prof. Kalam.

As NCERT Director, J.S. Rajput, himself describes in the book's foreward, " One important feature of this book is that it contains writings about illustrious Indians. The themes range from age old problems of personality to discussion of contemporary issues like pride in being an Indian and India's rich cultural heritage".

With Kalam, Every Missile Launch was a 'Family Affair'

As A.P.J. Abdul Kalam appears set to be India's next President, former colleagues have been recollecting the humility and low-key style of leadership that permeated his decade-long stint as head of India's missile programme.

Always keen on emphasising the collective effort that went into the successful missile trials, Dr. Kalam once 'used the columns of *The Hindu* to carry his message that many scientists—even their families—had made personal sacrifices to ensure the success of the programme.

A day after the first , epochal flight trial of the 'Agni' Intermediate Range Ballistic Missile on May 22 1989, this correspondent telephoned Dr. Kalam at the test site in Balasore (Orissa) to congratulate him and get his reactions to the successful flight. "Don't write about me," Dr. Kalam insisted. " This is not my success, it is a team effort of 2000 persons. You have no idea, what sacrifices my people have made so that 'Agni ' could fly!"

Learning that a report based on his telephonic talk was being planned, he added: "You tell *The Hindu* readers what quality of people are working with me. Tell them about V.R. Nagarajan." He then proceeded to narrate for nearly 10 minutes an incident that occurred during the long summer campaign of 'Agni", when the flight was postponed again and again.

Mr. Nagarajan, a key member of the electrical integration team, was camping in the Balasore test range, with 500 others for nearly two months, and keeping in touch through telephone every few days with his home in Hyderabad where his young child was not well. Around the middle of April, he discussed with his wife whether he should come home to attend to the child, but they agreed that his work was too important and that she could manage.

A few days later when he rang again, his 82-year-old father answered the call and assured him that all was in control on the home front.

But Mr. Nagarajan sensed from the broken voice, that something was wrong and when he pressed his father, learnt that his brother-in-law, D.L.S. Venkataraman, had died in a train accident on the Kamataka Express a few days earlier and that his body had only now been identified. However, Mr. Nagarajan's wife and parents decided not to inform him the news lest he be distracted from the vital task he was performing for 'Agni'.

With the truth known, Dr. Kalam insisted that Mr. Nagarajan should go home for a few days, but he returned in time to assist with the May 22 flight.

"Compared to such people, my role is nothing", Dr. Kalam said. As he suggested, *The Hindu* next morning highlighted this aspect of the 'Agni' triumph, in a prominent box item opposite the editorial page, headlined:

'Agni did not fuel their emotions'.

Largely due to the efforts of Dr. Kalam and V.S. Arunachanlam, then head of the Defence R&D Organisation, and their mantra of collective achievement, the Government of India took the unprecedented step of presenting a citation and a Rs. 1,000 cash award to every individual, from peon to Mission Director, in over 20 establishments all over India who contributed to that first successful flight of 'Agni'.

Replying to a question whether a man who had been instrumental in making weapons of mass destruction, could be in a position as saviour of the poor and the nation, Dr Kalam said, "Why are you worried about the country having a few nuclear weapons? If you are very particular, you should worry about the 10,000 nuclear warheads across the Atlantic."

He said national security and national development were interrelated and security could not be strong if it was not matched by economic development.

To another question, Dr Kalam said even after being elected as President, he would endeavour to use science as a tool for the development of the country.

Dr Kalam who replied to a majority of the questions with a philosophical note, recalled that as a high school student leader, he was asked on August 15, 1947 to gather 800 students to be present at midnight when the country achieved freedom from British rule.

Marking the historic moment, Pt Jawaharlal Nehru unfurled the Tricolour and spoke in Hindi and English. "At that time, I did not understand both since my mother tongue was Tamil."

The next day, he saw two photographs in newspapers. While one showed Nehru unfurling the Tricolour, the other depicted Gandhiji walking barefoot in riot-hit Noakhali district. "The second photograph changed my life," he said adding, "We have to develop leaders with compassion."

Earlier, Dr Kalam was escorted into the press conference venue—Vithalbhai Patel House—by Parliamentary Affairs Minister Pramod Mahajan.

"Smile does not cost anything" was the first message Dr Kalam gave to the host of mediapersons gathered for his first interaction with the national media.

In his initial remarks, Dr Kalam said he felt "humbled" when he was nominated for the presidential elections and described the top post as "an integrated aspiration of the people." He said, "I will definitely contribute in the nation's vision of prosperity and security". He said his message to the youth of the country was: "Transform the nation into a developed nation."

Citing an anecdote, Dr Kalam said that when he was asked by a young girl whether he was a scientist, technologist or a Muslim or an Indian, his reply was "first and foremost you should be a good human being and then all these elements are inside you."

We Need Leaders with Values: Kalam

"Why are all of you looking so serious? It has been a good rainy day, why don't you smile, it does not cost you anything". And then there was a peal of laughter.

The Presidential candidate, A.P.J. Abdul Kalam, was able to get all the mediamen present to cover has first formal engagement with the press to smile and laugh. But what he did not insist was that they sing the 'Song of Youth' which he has written to inspire young men and women "to sweat and work for a great vision, the vision of transforming India into a developed nation." He was content to distribute copies of the song.

Filing his nomination papers for the presidential race was a humbling experience for him. He was touched by the presence of all the major leaders of political parties and their support for him as the presidential candidate.

The post of head of the Republic symbolised the "integrity and the aspiration of the nation" and even before he takes his official oath, the presidential nominee, certain of winning the election with the support of almost all parties barring the Left, promised to keep in mind, always, the awesome responsibilities of the post.

The key words for him were—and these were peppered in his responses to questions throughout the hour-long interaction—technology as a tool for development, scientific temper, integrity, self-reliance, compassion and humanism. Leaders who do not just "manage" but leaders who bring humanism, compassion and values to politics, a leadership which can conceive policies which can make India a developed nation. Presidentship for him was one more way to serve the country.

Presidential stakes

Dr. Abdul Kalam's shaggy hair style, his white eyebrows, his warm, spontaneous smile, his stiff competition to George Fernandes into matter of sartorial casualness—floppy bush-shirt, loose chappals and total lack of fancy attire. Then, there is our much-loved 88-year old Capt. Lakshmi Sahgal—elegant and trim now in her beautifully starched sari.

We have seen on TV the George Bush-Al Gore shootout complete with all its controversial note fixing. We have seen the warlords of Afghanistan sniping for Karzai during the Loya Jirga. But give me the current Indian presidential dual every time. For colour, for political dirty tricks, for telegenic brevura. And all over two candidates who are respected, loved, as apolitical as people in their professions can be—one is a scientist and the other a doctor—and you have all the ingredients if not for a Mumbai "fillum", at least for a television drama.

Their wonderful backgrounds Dr Abdul Kalam's brother recounting how this poor boy from a fisherman's family had to see his sister sell her gold bangles to pay his school fees. His old teacher at the modest mission school telling us how Kalam shared a hostel room with a Christian and a Hindu. And friends speculating how a rice- and-curd vegetarian would cope with the menus at Rashtrapati Bhavan's official banquets. Then Dr Sahgal attending to a woman patient at her free clinic in Kanpur until the last moment before catching the Shatabdi to Delhi and telling the press emphatically that of course she would return to her practice when her campaign was over. In short, two endearingly natural personally lovable but highly professional people, clearly and openly loving it all and thinking more of the country than themselves. This is the stuff of which presidential drama is made and it simply would not have been the same without television, which does have its uses at moments such as these. For which we must be thankful and forgive TV its constant irritations.

Dr. Kalam as Consensus President

Some are bound to say that all is well that ends well. Indeed, it is gratifying that in the person of the distinguished defence scientist and Bharat Ratna, Dr. A.P.J. Abdul Kalam, the country will have a consensus President. But the tortuous, often messy, manner in which this denouement has been reached does neither the ruling combination nor the Opposition parties any credit.

In fact, the entire polity has been exposed as bumbling and blundering. In the shabby game of one-upmanship a lot has been damaged, most notably and sadly, the prestige and authority of the Prime Minister. This can in no way be covered up, leave alone undone or mitigated, by the crowing chorus within the BJP camp. The sum and substance of this disingenuous noise is that Mr Atal Behari Vajpayee's "masterstroke" has sent the motley crowd in the Opposition into disarray and "nonplussed" the principal opposition party, the Congress, and particularly its leader, Mrs Sonia Gandhi.

Both these claims are true.

Leaders of the Left parties, as so often in the past, are acting as odd men out usually do. Their isolation is far from splendid but they are persisting in their resolve to put up a candidate against the nationally accepted Dr Kalam. This can at best be a quixotic and token gesture much like the challenge in the 1997 presidential poll to Mr K.R. Narayanan by the maverick former Chief Election Commissioner, Mr T.N. Seshan.

It is no secret as that far back as a year ago the BJP's choice for the next incumbent of Rashtrapati Bhawan had focused on the Maharashtra Governor Dr P.C. Alexander. If it were a totally free agent, the saffron party would have liked to select for the presidency a dyed-in-wool member of the Sangh Parivar. But it knew that many of its 23 partners in the National Democratic Alliance (NDA) wouldn't swallow this. It, therefore, decided that Dr Alexander was its best bet, and this view was openly aired at a glittering function at the Prime Minister 's house in the summer of 2001 when Mr Vajpayee released Dr Alexander's book *India in the New Millennium*. Now Dr. Alexander is a first-rate civil servant who had served as Indira Gandhi's Principal Secretary during her second innings in the eighties and later, in Rajiv Gandhi's time, held several high posts. He was also very close to Mr P.V. Narasimha Rao during the latter's five years as Prime Minister. Why then is he in such high favour with the BJP and in such bad odour with Mrs Gandhi and the Congress ? The only explanation is that during his long stint in the Raj Bhawan in Mumbai, he is supposed to have endeared himself to the BJP-Shiv Sena combine, especially to the Sena's supreme commander, Mr Bal Thackeray.

Several BJP stalwarts made no bones about their calculation that sending Dr Alexander, a Christian, to Rashtrapati Bhawan would paint Mrs Sonia Gandhi into a corner because the country would not accept Christians in both highest offices, those of the President and the Prime Minister. This was utter nonsense. It was a Brahmin President, Mr R. Venkataraman, who had sworn in Mr Narasimha Rao, another Brahmin, as Prime Minister. Thereafter no one had said a word when another Brahmin, Dr Shankar Dayal Sharma, became President while Mr Rao was still Prime Minister. It was Dr Sharma who had appointed yet another Brahmin, Atalji, as Prime Minister in May, 1996. That his government then did not last more than 13 days is a different matter.

All this indicates perhaps why, in spite of his awareness of his party's preference for the Maharashtra Governor and his own liking for him, the Prime Minister conveyed to the Congress his proposal that the next President should be elected by consensus. And since Mr Vajpayee had made it clear in advance that a second term for Mr Narayanan was not acceptable to the NDA, he told the Congress that the Vice-President , Mr Krishan Kant, would be the appropriate consensus candidate.

However, even before the Congress leadership—that had some reservations about Mr Kant—could consider the Prime Minister's offer, he apologetically withdrew it. Why? Because hardliners in his party, including some aggressively articulate junior ministers in his government, forced him to do so. To overrule Atalji they argued that the NDA must have its own man in Rashtrapati Bhavan, especially in times when the political situation could be uncertain. Dr Alexander was their man and a "unanimous" decision in his favour was taken. This, incidentally, was the second time the hardliners had railroaded the Prime Minister into reversing his decision on a serious issue. In April they had vetoed Mr Vajpayee's firm resolve to sack Gujarat's Chief Minister, Mr Narendra Modi.

To the Andhra Chief Minister, Mr Chandrababu Naidu, goes the credit for forcing the candidature of Dr Kalam down the BJP's throat after he had read out the Riot Act to Mr Pramod Mahajan, a hardliner who is also the Prime Minister's main trouble-shooter.

It should have been obvious that the Kalam bandwagon had the potential to turn into a juggernaut. But in such poor shape is the once grand old party, the Congress, that it just did not catch on. Its greater failure was that it took on initiative of its own and simply waited for the Prime Minister to make the first move. As an astute analyst has pointed out, the Congress seems to have convinced itself that it has only to sit hand on hand to come to power in the next election because the saffron crowd is doing an excellent job of self-destruction. The Congress leadership has misjudged also in relying on the hope that Mr Narayanan would agree to contest against the NDA's nominee whoever he or she might be.

The ultimate insult to the Congress—after its belated decision to support Dr Kalam, something that could be done more speedily and graciously—has come from the CPM politburo member, Mr Sitaram Yechury. According to him, the Congress has "ceased to be an Opposition party".

of democratic politics is being flouted, in that, a person whose politics is unknown or undefined, is being inducted to play a political role. The President may be the ceremonial head of state, but his role is nothing if not political. The President plays a political role even by his silences.

The induction into the presidency of a technology person, of a manager of science, is a positive development, it is said. For some time now, our politics in general has taken a dualistic turn. In the realms of democratic mobilisation, it is more and more useful to appeal to caste, religious, and ethnic identities.

On the other hand, in the era of liberalisation, policy-making, particularly economic policy-making, has become increasingly a technical exercise, spearheaded by a core group of techno-economist policy intellectuals and led by successive Finance Ministers with a commitment to a technocratic/pragmatic, as distinct from ideological, definition of economic policy making. Economic policy is now shrouded in a technical/technocratic language that is well beyond the understanding of the layman, leave aside the country's large majority of people with no access to basic education.

A President with a high profile in technology management can only accentuate these tendencies, for good or for worse. What is more worrying is that as the erstwhile high priest of the nuclear regimen, the future President may well preside over a process where the Indian state attains a more menacing profile as a nuclear power.

And all the time these processes may be shrouded in a technocratic language inaccessible to the ordinary citizen. Thus, the fact that the Indian state spends as much as 2.38 per cent of its GDP on defence, and a mere 1.58 per cent on social sectors, may be important to the ordinary citizen, but may well be a non-issue as far as techno-managerial considerations of policy are concerned.

As a counter point, there is Lakshmi Sahgal, known for her long association both with the freedom struggle and with the Left movement, particularly the women's movement. As a doctor and a social worker, she is recognised for her service to ordinary citizens. Her credibility as a public figure is beyond question. As she has the support only of the Left Parties, by the CPI (M)'s own admission her candidature is more symbolic than real.

The weakness of her candidature, however, not only drives home the well-known point about the Opposition's fragile unity. The more important consideration here possibly is that given the rushed and unprepared manner in which the Opposition's candidate was put forward, the Left's credibility slipped a little further down in public perception. To whom, then, shall we look?

Having gained the support of key Opposition parties such as the Congress and the Samajwadi Party, A.P.J. Abdul Kalam is set to become the next President of India. The substantial political consensus that has emerged around the candidature of the eminent scientist is matched by popular approval on the ground. The elevation of Dr Kalam to the country's highest and most exalted constitutional post conveys many things. Above all, it is a reaffirmation of the essence of Indian democracy. The fact that a person who hails from such a humble background could rise to occupy the most distinguished position in the land is a testimony to prevalency of opportunity and the capacity to overcome odds through merit and endeavour. Dr Kalam's essential humility and touching simplicity are likely to lend a special character to the majesty of his lofty office.

At another and more immediate level, Dr Kalam's candidature has facilitated a significant but by no means total consensus. Given this, concerns that the presidential election would become a battleground for a fierce and counterproductive political battle have vanished. Of course, with the Left parties having announced Lakshmi Sahgal, a key figure in the Indian National Army, as their candidate for the poll, a contest is inevitable. But with the coming on board of the Congress, the only party with the strength in the electoral college to mobilise the requisite numbers for a keenly fought presidential poll, any contest now is likely to be symbolic rather than real. In the existing circumstances, precipitating a contest cannot provide even a remote hope of victory; however, it may provide an opportunity to record dissatisfaction on matters of principle.

While it is welcome that Dr Kalam's candidature has evoked substantial political support, it is impossible to ignore that this consensus was achieved in far from ideal circumstances. Having found its original nominee, P.C. Alexander, unacceptable to those both within and outside the Government, the NDA's managers went ahead with announcing the candidature of Dr. Kalam rather than doing what they ought to have in the first place—engage in a sincere and wide-ranging consultative process to select a person who is acceptable to all. It is this very lack of a candid search for consensus which, from the very beginning, had lent the presidential election the appearance of a political chessboard, a place on which cynical manoeuvres and cunning stratagems were being played out. Finally, it was the Congress' reluctance to oppose Dr Kalam's candidature which won the day. While there is a justifiable sense of relief that a bitter and fractious presidential election has been averted, the manner in which the consensus was reached wears the unfortunate appearance of one 'enforced' rather than one 'evolved'.

When he moves into Rashtrapathi Bhavan, Dr Kalam will, in a way, be the first of his kind. Previous occupants have either been politicians or administrators with distinct political links. As a scientist who was entrusted with overseeing the country's missile development programme, Dr Kalam's candidature is a departure from an established trend. Not surprisingly, there has been some discomfort with the signal conveyed by the selection of Dr Kalam, seen as the principal architect of India's missile programme, in the wider context of the BJP's pursuit of a militaristic agenda. There is also the question as to whether, given his likely lack of a deep knowledge of the Constitution, he would be able to negotiate the tricky constitutional and political issues that arise. While Dr Kalam's essentially non-partisan nature is not in question, it seems evident that the BJP's seemingly enthusiastic support for his candidature was a result of wholly extraneous factors—underpinned as it was by an element of tokenism and a desire to deflect attention from the horrific and unpardonable communal carnage in Gujarat. The less than straightforward reasons which settled Dr Kalam's candidature however are no reflection either on his integrity or on the undeniable popular support he enjoys as he prepares to become India's next President.

8
Defence, Research and Development

In a fairly comprehensive article on 'Defence R & D : Key to self-reliance', Dr Kalam opined about the need and development of technology. He was confident in his opinion that it generates wealth and power. Whereas he has mentioned that India is self-reliant in armour, armaments and ammunition, surface-to-air and surface-to-surface missiles and a number of technology products. He mentions in detail about the striking power of several technological devices like Arjun, Pinaka, Agni, Prithvi. Trishul, Akash, Nag, Kaveri, Light Combat Aircraft, Remotely Piloted Vehicle System, Advanced Torpedo, Panchendriya, Combat improved, 'Ajeya, Anupam and last but not the least about the technology for industry.

Defence R&D: Key to Self-Reliance

How do we prepare ourselves to become a developed country? Today the important tool of developed countries is technology. Technology generates wealth and power. No country will part with a technology till it enters the next phase of technology development. Thus, we have to create our own technology base. A nation's ability to provide its own security and to conduct an independent foreign policy is dependent on the degree to which the nation is able to underpin self-reliance in defence and defence systems. India is self-reliant in armour, armaments and ammunition, surface-to-air and surface-to -surface missiles, parallel processing supercomputers and a number of technology products. However, technological self-reliance which contributes to our strength and national prosperity also reduces other countries' exports to India. That is why developed countries have invented technology control regimes with the objective of ensuring the continuation of the technological gap and pre-empting our attempts to become a competitor. We have talented manpower, natural resources and a strong technology base. We can combat the control regimes through innovation, partnership, and national will.

The goal of the defence self-reliance plan is to enhance the indigenous content in the weapons and systems from the present 30 per cent to 70 per cent by the year 2005. The Defence Research and Development Organisation (DRDO) is responsible for the design, development and stages leading to production of state-of-art weapon systems, platforms, sensors, allied equipment and life support systems to meet the requirements of the three services of the armed forces. DRDO has grown in multi-disciplinary areas and developed strategic and crucial technologies and systems. Our vision is to transform DRDO into a technological leader with the mission to make the nation technologically independent in critical spheres. DRDO's 52 laboratories have established core competence in Unmanned Aerial Vehicles (UAV), guided missiles, radar in low level aircraft surveillance and multi-target detection and tracking, underwater research, torpedoes, supercomputers, advanced software packages, compact vehicles, assault bridges and certain life support systems. A number of systems developed by DRDO have been produced at the defence public sector units and ordnance factories. These items include the 105 mm light field gun, 5.56 mm INSAS rifle and its ammunition, 130 mm SP gun, 125 mm FSAPDS, influence mine, limpet mine, illuminating ammunitions, a large variety of fuzes, high speed low drag bomb, pilotless target aircraft, INDRA radar for low level surveillance, night vision devices for various applications, a host of sonar systems, an advanced computing system, a number of war game simulation software products, state-of-the-art materials and electronic devices and also Prithvi missile systems. Some of the major programmes are:

ARJUN: This is a state-of-the-art world class tank with superior and accurate fire power suitable for day/night operation, and having high mobility, low sithouette, firing on the move capability and all-round protection including laser warning, NBC, camouflage and low thermal signature. Twelve MK-1 prototypes and 15 preproduction series (PPS) tanks have been manufactured and subjected to extensive user trials including automotive trials over 20,000 km

(11,000 km in desert and 1,000 km on river bed). Mission reliability of 500 km in 48h has been achieved. Integrated weapon system (gun, ammunition, fire control and gun control) has been evaluated by firing trials.

PINAKA : This surface-to-surface multi-barrel rocket system comprising rocket, launcher, replenishment vehicle and command post vehicle including fire control computer is capable of engaging different types of targets up to a range of 39 kms and is capable of destroying areas of 500x700 sqm with a salvo of 12 rockets each fired from a six launchers' battery. A prototype launcher vehicle, command post vehicle and replenishment vehicle have been tested. Prefragmented, incendiary and submunition warheads have also been statically tested. The fire control computer has been tested. PINAKA is expected to contribute about Rs. 600 crores worth of production.

The Integrated Guided Missile Development Programme (IGMDP) cover design, development and production of four missile systems namely PRITHVI, TRISHUL, AKASH and NAG and a technology demonstration project AGNI.

AGNI: This project was undertaken for the development of re-entry, manoeuvrable trajectory and guidance technologies. Flight trials of the system have successfully tested these technologies. This has given the country the capability of delivery of payload with high accuracy at longer ranges.

PRITHVI: PRITHVI is a medium range surface-to-surface tactical battlefield missile, with a range up to 150 km for the army version (P-I) and 250 km for the air force version (P-II). Development of both P-I and P-II has been completed. P-I's production has commenced.

TRISHUL: This is a short range (9 km), low-level, quick reaction, surface-to-air missile for three services. It is also capable of an anti sea-skimmer role. Its subsystems, including three beam guidance have been tested. Integrated flights for army and air force versions and sea-skimming flights have been carried out.

AKASH : This is a medium range (25 km) surface-to-air missile with multiple target handling capability. AKASH with command guidance has been flight tested. AKASH self-propelled launcher, Rajendra phased array radar and other ground systems have been developed. Developmental trials of AKASH are to be completed in 1999.

NAG: This is a third generation anti-tank missile, with 4 km range having fire and forget and top attack capability. It is configured for deployment on a tracked vehicle (NAMICA) or helicopters (CHEETAH & ALH). It has a tandem warhead to defeat explosive reactive armour. Development of launcher vehicle (NAMICA) has been completed, and a helicopter version is under development.

Light Combat Aircraft: This is multi-mission, single engine combat aircraft incorporating state-of-the-art technologies. Full scale engineering development phase-I comprising development of two technology demonstration aircraft with GE engine, flight testing to improve core technologies and parallel development of multi-mode radar, EW equipment and digital avionics are envisaged in the LCA. First LCA (TD-1) was rolled out in November 1995. It is undergoing ground tests to ensure flight safety. Its ground resonance tests have been completed and system integration tests are in progress. In parallel, the second LCA (TD-2) is under integration. Several new technologies like carbon fibre composite structures, control law for unstable aircraft, digital fly-by-wire control system and advanced computing system for avionics have been established. Two prototype vehicles (PV-1 and PV-2) are planned to test full-scale engineering development.

KAVERI: This is an advanced technology gas turbine aero-engine suitable for LCA, having better attributes than the GE 404 engine (of US origin). KAVERI engine and its core engine KABINI have been developed and three KAVERI and two KABINI are undergoing evaluation on multiple test beds and have already been tested for a cumulative period of more than 500 hours.

Remotely Piloted Vehicle System - FALCON : It is to meet the operational requirements for battlefield surveillance and reconnaissance, real-time engagement of targets and damage assessment. The system is ready for user trials.

Advanced torpedo: The navy requires a light weight torpedo for anti-submarine warfare having advanced features comparable with world contemporaries. The system is undergoing user evaluation.

Panchendriya: This is a composite sonar system and tactical weapon control system for F-class submarines. The system has been fitted on-board submarine for sea evaluation.

Combat improved 'Ajeya': The programme is for the upgrading of T-72 tanks with modern features of contemporary main battle tanks such as explosive reactive armour, soft core FSAPDS ammunition, global positioning system, laser warning system and integrated fire detection and suppression system. The tank has been cleared for production.

DRDO has achieved technology breakthrough in certain devices and computing systems.

ANUPAM, with state-of-the art architecture with 0.5 million transistors has been developed at DRDO Lab and this will meet the requirements of strategic programmes. Another breakthrough is the electronic components where production by industry was a problem due to a lack of economy of scale. DRDO, with a cluster of small industries, has led to production of most of the electronic components. Also DRDO established necessary foundries for production of ASICs and MMICS, both silicon and gallium arsenide based. Another important breakthrough was the 32 node parallel processing supercomputer of 2 G. Flop which is being upgraded to 128 nodes. Work is continuing on Tera Flop computing systems. India is self-sufficient in production of all raw materials, special alloys, armour materials, electronic components and devices, computing systems and software.

Technology for Industry

The Non-Ferrous Technology Development Centre has been established as an advanced technology centre, with participation of the Department of Mines, DST, DRDO and public sector undertakings (BALCO, NALCO, HCL, HZL). It has contributed miliform of copper alloys, silver based brazing alloys, titanium implants and master alloys for grain refinement of aluminium. The Advanced Research Centre International is a co-operative venture between India, Belarus, USA and Ukraine. India is represented by DRDO and DST. This centre has been set up for advanced research in powder metallurgy and other special processes leading to exploitation in both defence and civil sectors. This centre has developed coating for the Adour engine turbine blade, exfoliated graphite for high temperature gasket, etc. The Institute of Robotics and Artificial intelligence has been established with the participation of DRDO and DST to develop expertise and products in the areas of robotics and artificial intelligence and to transfer the technologies to industry.

Based on the technologies, a number of spin-off applications have been developed in the areas of bio-medical, industrial and societal sectors. The bio-medical spin-offs include the development of floor reaction orthosis for polio-affected children, cardiac stress test system, pacemaker, Drishti eye laser, carbon-carbon heart valves, hipbone prosthesis and various types of implants based on carbon-carbon materials. A medical data visualisation system called ANAMICA (ANURAG's Medical Data Visualisation and Characterisation Aid) has been developed for 3D surgical visualisation. A low-cost cytoscan system with highly reliable diagnostic capability has been developed for early detection of cancer. The expertise on materials technology has helped in the development of low cost coronary catheters and cardio vascular stent for balloon angioplasty.

Defence technology has many engineering applications such as MMW (millimetric wave) for communication in remote areas, armour materials for bullet proofing, composite material for windmill blade, carbon-carbon for brake discs, robots for NDT (Non Destructive Test) and handling of explosives. Also, the technology has application in remote area development.

Spin-offs

Brackish water in the Rajasthan desert has been converted by cost-effective desalination process into potable water. This will enable remote villages to get potable water by installing the desalination plant linking many villages. The cold desert Leh valley of 1200 square kilometres of arid land has been converted into green and self-sustained vegetable growing land at 4,000 metres high altitude. DRDO has adopted 'Nang' village as a model for other cold desert and high altitude plans of the country.

DRDO projects on tissue conservation, food irradiation, large scale afforestation in DRDO testing ranges, appropriate nutrition for pregnant mothers, micro-watershed approach for local area development and microbial degradation of night soil in very high altitude areas are some of the examples of societal missions. The Society for Bio-Medical Technology (SBMT) was established for development of high-tech bio-medical devices with participation of DRDO, DST, Department of Welfare, Department of Rural Development and the Nizam Institute of Medical Sciences. A number of state-of-the-art bio-medical devices are being developed.

Some countries are seeking to consolidate their technology superiority through technology denial regimes. As a potential major regional power, India is one of the main targets for various export controls or technology denial regimes. Technology denial to India and other developing nations is supported by various regimes such as the NSG NPT, MTCR and the Wassenaar Arrangement for Export Controls as a successor to COCOM. The Government's response to this is a plan for Self-Reliance in Defence Systems for the period 1995-2005, with a goal of progressively enhancing the indigenous content in the annual defence procurement of weapons and systems from around 30 per cent to 70 per cent or more. Clearly this cannot be achieved by DRDO alone without a matching commitment by user services and availability of adequate funds. The plan is being implemented by the three departments of the Defence Ministry as a co-ordinated mission. The main thrust of the Self-Reliance Plan is three-fold: (i) support existing systems and indigenise critical spares; (ii) upgrade existing systems and stretch life and capability; and (iii) induct indigenous systems progressively and minimise import of major systems.

DRDO today has a strong technology base for developing state-of-the-art systems for meeting the needs of the Indian armed forces. No control regime or technology denial can put a hold on DRDO programmes. India is a nuclear weapon state and is a missile power. In the present unipolar world, only strength matters. Technology enables us to build that strength . India's core competence in certain technological areas and scientific and technological manpower have to be harnessed. Through our sustained efforts to enhance this core competence and our drive towards self-reliance in critical technologies, we can transform our nation from a developing to a developed country.

जय विज्ञान जय विज्ञान

जय विज्ञान जय विज्ञान

Nuclear Devices Validated Contemporary Designs in 1998 Tests

After having joined the Nuclear Club in 1974 with a successful underground test with zero fallout, India exercised voluntary restraint and refrained from further testing till 1998 when it conducted five nuclear tests at Pokhran in Rajasthan on May 11 and 13. Dr A.P.J. Abdul Kalam and Dr R. Chidambaram, Chairman of the Atomic Energy Commission, were among those who observed the tests of these three types of devices. According to Dr Chidambaram, a dozen new ideas and systems were tried out in the five tests and the results were satisfactory. The tests were based on the contemporary knowledge of physics, engineering, material science and electronics and were advanced in technique and thus equivalent to several tests carried out earlier by the weapon states. He said these tests of 1998 vintage had given enough data for designing the types of devices need by the country for a credible nuclear deterrent. The computer calculations were exact and yields of the sub-kilotonne devices were predicted accurately. In the case of the thermonuclear device tested by India, the primary stage was a fusion-boosted fission device. In view of the capabilities of India's scientific community, it was not considered necessary to test this device separately. Of course, the nuclear and defence scientists are facing further challenges. The development of a nuclear reactor for submarine has made some progress but it is yet to be delivered. The Sagarika cruise missile is another exciting project and if India does not wish to stop at the intermediate-range ballistic missiles, it will need considerable money and expertise.

9
The Strategic Industries

Dr. Kalam is much engaged in scientific research as it is very clear from his long-drawn chequered career of about five decades. Time and again, he emphasised the point and he, in fact, had deep faith in the fact that science and scientific research should have deep linkage with the development of industry in our sub-continent. This was the advice which he received from Prof. Vikram Sarabhai. After gaining substantial experience in several installations he began to realise the significance to this fact. And day by day, in HAL at Kanpur and Bangalore, and at Trivandrum, his deep identification with science and industry became a glaring pthenomenon in his long scientific career. In fact such an approach brought about novel results which made it clear to the younger generation of the scientists regarding the developmental programme in our industry.

In this scholarly paper, Dr. Kalam has mentioned several points which show his deep involvement in strategic industries. And these are food security, economic security, aritical technologies for India, defence supplies in India, the Indian space programme, the nuclear programme, dual use technology, 1985; Defence technology and industry, 1985-95; the period of stand alone sub-system development, 2005: graduation to systems Engineering; to grawith technology capability, in DRDO, Prithvi missile system, the guided Missile Development Programme, brief description of the Prithvi system, the effectiveness of Prithvi, Prithvi is a cost-effective weapon, the development and production experience of Prithvi, Light Combat Aircraft, DRDO- Navy participation, Action plan for the Army, the future, advanced sensors, National programme in advanced sensors, cryogenic engine for GSLV, where are we in aero propulsion? Hyderplanes of the future, the real proliferators and strategic industries—the future of India.

Strategy means generalship or the art of conducting a campaign and maneouvring an army or execution of a plan of action in business or politics. In modern usage, however, it has come to denote the means used to gain a position of decisive advantage. The word strategy is also used when speaking of planning for the long term; that which is done on a short term basis becomes 'tactical'. Thus, when we use the term strategic industries, we are thinking in the context of industries which give India a decisive advantage over a broad range of areas, and not merely in military terms. In the period following the Second World War, as nations have focussed on the development of their economies, security has come to mean more than just protecting borders with military forces. Other forms of security have come to be of as much importance.

Food Security

The availability of food is a critical factor in the well-being of any nation, one that even developed countries cannot afford to ignore. For a country like India with a large population the task of maintaining a regular supply of food in a stable, consistent and a maner viable to its people, irrespective of the vagaries of the weather and other natural calamities, is itself a stupendous task. Measure aimed at ensuring such unhindered supply fall under steps aimed towards 'food security.'

Economic Security

Economic security or, simply stated, the security of a steady rate of economic growth alongwith a continual spread of benefits to the people is becoming important. It is a complex phenomenon which not merely concerns the fiscal policy or behaviour of financial institutions but also touches upon the very structure of the economy and polity. In the search for economic growth, seek to continuously expand the market for their products. Developed countries achieve this by expanding their activities in several parts of the globe through multinational or transnational companies. They also form visible or invisible cartels to have preferred access to many markets. In addition, they also continually improve their technological strengths and provide machinery and knowhow to others at a very high price. Their knowledge-intensive and technology-intensive activities are called 'high value-added products'. Much of the more routine activities are transferred by these multinational to developing countries in order to derive the advantage of their locations, cheap labour and various other tax incentives. But whenever developing countries have to import technology and knowhow from the developed countries, they often have to pay a huge sum because of the value addition to the already exploited knowledge. There is no easy method to working out this value addition because often data on how this is calculated, or how various costs are apportioned by different multinational companies is confidential.

Thus, developing countries often pay a very high price for old technological imputs and in return have to sell much more goods and services to balance the high price of technology imports. This exerts a continuous pressure to export more often at lower and lower prices, since the impport bills are constantly rising because of the continual input of technological upgradations flowing from the developed countries. This is what is generally called an export-led economy. Some of the foreign exchange required to maintain this import-export balance comes through foreign investors who invest in physical assets in the country such as factories, plants, offices and laboratories, or through investments in stocks and companies. There are also special developmental loans given by bodies like the World Bank or the International Monetary Fund. If for some period the imports greatly exceed the exports or if during the period some withdrawals of foreign investment takes place, fear of the currency crisis ensues. In other words, most developing countries which are basing their strategy of growth on an export-led economy often find themselves maintaining a precarious economic balance. We are witnesssing this in Far Eastern countries, where recent events show how a single developed nation, which has tremendous investment and business in a developing country, can cause its economy to collapse in a matter of weeks.

If transactions were conducted purely on economic and market considerations, even such a tight-rope walk might be possible. One would learn to cope with the rapid changes that such a situation creates. But the reality is far more complicated. There are various commercial pressures and interests, geopolitical considerations besides other disturbances over and above the inherent instabilities of such a situation. A crucial stabilizing factor to tackle such situations is for a country to possess the necessary technological strengths. That is the main insurance against global pressures. Real economic security is assured through technology stengths in areas which are important to the economy.

Critical Technologies for India

A country takes a long time to develop technological strengths. What is important is that it concentrates on a few crucial or critical technologies which can give it a decisive advantage in meeting the kind of economic instability described above. It is interesting to note the list of critical technologies in the report of the USA's National Critical Technologies Panel in March 1991. The criteria used for the selection are given in Table 9.1:

TABLE 9.1

	Criteria	*Description*
National Needs	Industrial competitiveness	Technologies that improve US competitiveness in world markets through new products, introduction and improvements in the cost, quality and performance of existing products
	National Defence	Technologies that have an important impact on US national defence through improvements in performance, needs cost, reliability or productibility of defence systems
	National Security	Technologies that reduce dependence on foreign sources, lower energy costs, or improve energy efficiency
Importance/Criticality	Quality of life	Ability to make strong contributions to health, human welfare and the environment, both domestically and world-wide
	Opportunity to lead markets	Ability to exert and sustain national leadership in a technology that is of para-

Criteria		*Description*
		mount importance to the economy or national defence
	Performance Quality/ productivity	Ability to cause revolutionary or evolutionary improvements over current products or improvement processes in turm deading to economic or national defence benefits
	Leverage	Potential that Government R&D investment will stimulate private sector investment in commercialization or likelihood that success in the technology will stimulate success in other technologies, products or markets
Market Size/Diversity	Vulnerability	Potentially serious damage may be caused if a technology is held exclusively by the other countries and not the United States
	Enabling/pervasive	Technology forms the foundation for many other technologies or exhibits size/ strong linkages to many segments of the economy
	Size of ultimate Market	Ability to exert a major economic impact through the expansion of existing markets, creation of new industries, generation of capital or creation of employment opportunities

Source : Report of the National Critical Technologies Panel, March 1991.

It can be seen from the above that the criteria for selection of critical technologies mentions national defence only as one element. Other criteria include their ability to enhance the quality of life for the American people, industrial competitiveness and energy security. Americans are acutely aware of their dependence for oil on the Gulf countries.

What would be the critical technologies in the Indian context? Would it mean defence technologies alone? Definitely not! Would it mean space or atomic energy alone? Definitely not! Elements related to these areas would be certainly included but there should be much more. Besides, even in the sectors of defence, space or atomic energy there are a number of items which are not that critical in the sense that they would be available relatively easily from several sources. Many of the items would not involve numerous complex operations or be very costly; other items could be relatively easily stockpiled for future consumption. We should then be selective in what we term as critical technologies.

Defence Supplies in India

Let us look at some facts and figures about the nature of the defence equipment and supplies in India. The indigenous production is about 30 per cent and there is a general feeling that this figure ought to be brought up to 70 per cent in the long-term interest of our defence needs in order to achieve this we need to take several steps towards developing certain technological processes in our industries. However, most of these activities would not really qualify as critical technologies. The absence of certain processes in India so far has often been due to the same reasons as it in the commerical sector: insufficient attention to absorb, adapt and to upgrade imported knowhow and equipment. In the process, we have become stagnant technologically and industrially, and have missed out on indigenous improvements to imported systems. In most of these areas, it is possible for us to achieve self-reliance in a relatively short period provided defence R&D, industries, the defence forces and other policy makers work together as a mission. This will not be a cakewalk, but with a concerted effort to build a few prototypes, modify them and subsequently go into production we can meet our needs. We have experience in most of the industries of this sector. There is a tendency even in advance countries to source out defence equipment and products from many assemblies and sub-assemblies drawn from the civilian sector making other similar products. Such an approach can also be adopted to speedily achieve the goal of self- reliance in at least 70 per cent products and systems for the defence forces.

Is that enough? Even while this target is important, there are some critical areas in which India will not be given technologies easily by other countries, irrespective of whether or not India signs some of the existing unequal treaties. That is because they are critical technologies not only for defence, but also for several other purposes, as shown in Table 9.1. Some examples would be submicron level microelectronics or advanced transgenic biotechnology. The countries which possess submicron technologies, for example, can gain a top position globally. Advanced transgenic biotechnology can lead to global markets in agriculture, food products and medicines.

The Indian Space Programme

Let us look at the Indian space programme. Several elements required for launch vehicles including the materials, propellants, guidance and control and so on have been indigenously developed and are manufactured here. India has faced difficulties in achieving all this, as for example, when it attempted to speed up the schedule for the launch of the Geosynchronized Satellite Launch Vehicle (GLSV) through import of cryogenic technology. Some countries were willing to sell it to us. But when one of them agreed to the sale of a full engine, other countries pressurized them into not selling it to India. In a few years India should acquire capability in this field. Nevertheless, as far as satellites are concerned, many of the electronic components and some materials are still sourced outside the country, though India has successfully made many of the assemblies: control system components, guidance systems, sensors, various other electro-mechanical and electronic parts. The dependence for many of the space/ special quality electronic components can, however still be a problem for the Indian satellite programme, especially when it must be competitive internationally.

The end of the Cold War has led to shrinkage of markets for aerospace and defence industries in the developed world. They are in stiff competitions with each other and do not want other countries or companies to emerge as suppliers of satellites as their own market shares would be further reduced. It is in this context, in our endeavour to achieve the commercialization of our strengths in satellite technology, that many components required for Indian satellites may still have to be considered critical.

The Nuclear Programmes

Atomic energy programmes have been subject to severe restrictions for very obvious reasons as the Department of Atomic Energy in becoming self-reliant in areas in which only a few countries have such capability. There are a number of items in the atomic energy programme which are being made indigenously. However, commercial aspects of exploiting nuclear capabilies, especially for power-generation programmes, have been recently given high priority.Given the overall energy situation in India, the use of nuclear power in some measure is inescapable even while thermal and hydropower continue to be the dominant elements. Even to meet these nuclear power requirements, India critically requires a commercial-level power-generation capability, with its commensurate safety and nuclear waste management arrangements. Thus in the Indian context energy security is also crucial, perhaps much more than it is for the USA, because India imports a good part of its crude oil requirements, paying for it with precious foreign exchange. The growth of nuclear technology indeed has become a trend-setter for many high technologists in India.

Dual-use Technology

This discussion of strategic industies mainly concerns defence, space, atomic energy and also critical technology areas which have the potential of multiple uses in the defence and civilian commercial sector in the future. Not that other areas do not have multiple uses. For example, canning or processing of food or preservation of food is equally applicable to the civilian sector, to the export sector or for supplies to the defence forces. But since these are relatively well-stabilized technologies which can be handled by inputs from several sources, including, often, imports in the first instance, we are not covering such dual-use items.

Newly emerging technologies such as robotics or artificial intelligence, which would have a crucial impact on future defence operations and also on many industrial sectors if they have are to be really competitive, merit a closer look. As we look at the emerging manufacturing scenario, it will contain many elements of artificial intelligence and robotics in the medium-term future. If Indian products have to be competitive worldwide and if we aim to substantially through value added products and services, India has to master these technologies. To import them fully from others will often not be cost-effective since the competing foreign companies would not like to part with their best technologies. Often enough not even the better ones will be sold. Thus, even if we do manage to purchase some technologies from them, they will be at a point of technological obsolescence where one has to struggle with very low profit margins which is not good for any business.

The technology areas critical for growth of strategic industries for India, given the above broad considerations, are in the aviation and propulsion sector, high-end electronics, sensors, space communication and remote sensing, critical materials and processing, robotics and artificial intelligence. Before looking into some of these technologies, it is worth understanding something about the defence technologies and industries as they pertain of India.

1985: Defence Techology and Industry

In India, both the Defence Research and Development Organization and defence industries started experiencing certain restrictions on acquisition of technology and products from the developed countries particularly from 1985 onwards. At the same time, developed countries wanted to make India one of their main customers for arms and defence equipment. Obsolescent systems were offered for sale coupled with licensed production for a political price. Liberal credit and deferred payments were provided to propagate the business and make us perennially indebted.

What was the situation in India then? The industrial ambience had led to excellence in fabrication in limited areas. This means that after a design had been converted into fabrication drawings, our industry was in a position to convert it into a finished product. For low-and medium-level technology, there were large industrial complexes where most of the facilities were established under licensed production. In defence production, the private sector played only a limited role. As far as the academic and R&D institutions were concemed, they were interested in working towards self-reliance and to break away from the licensed production syndrome. The DRDO itself was preoccupied with a large number of single discipline projects concentrating on self-reliance through import substitution and/or indigenization. The end users often would like to see full systems.

1985-95: The Period of Stand-alone Sub-system Development

During the next ten years, that is by 1985, certain industries graduated to design and development of subsystems. This was due to the active partnership of the national science and technology agencies such as ISRO, DAE, DRDO and the industries. Many in the private sector who were hesitant to enter this field ten years earlier, started wing with defence PSUs and other public sector companies to take up defence R&D tasks at the subsystem level. For example, private sector industries were in a position to develop phase shifters, displays, tankage, communication systems, certain types of electronic warfare systems, on-board computers, on-board transmitters, thermal batteries and even air frames. This marked a very important step for both the DRDO and Indian industry. Because of such interaction between R&D and industry, the enthusiasm and confidence of industrial esablishments grew and enabled them to design subsystems and to a bsorb the specified sringent processes of technology. Above all it enhanced their willingness to take risks and go through the rigorous quality assurance and certification processes required for military systems.

2005: Graduation to Systems Engineering

During the progress of large R&D projects, there were undoubtedly delays and cost overruns. There was some criticism in the press about this. But here it needs to be underlined that these projects needed support through the dificult phases of their development. In fact, R&D in India survived only because of the efforts of a few visionary scientists and leader. But for them the nation would have been satisfied with making small items surrendering to business interest that would use all means to convert India into a perpetual 'buying nation'. Defence R&D is now taking the lead to reverse this trend through its selfreliance mission in defence systems. In DAE and ISRO too such an impulse for self-reliance is in the forefront.

We forecast that by 2005, more industries will be in a position to take up stand-alone mode systems engineering and systems integration to the specified requirements of R&D organizations. Subsystems like multimode radar, 'Kaveri' class aircraft engines, all composite carbon fibre composite wings, display systems, fly-by-wire systems for Light Combat Aircraft (LCA) and for futuristic aircraft, mission computers and air frames will be developed, engineered, produced and delivered for integration and checkout. Of course, this is the DRDO's vision. We believe that the Indian industry will respond given the national will on other fronts. We believe that when Indian industry becomes strong in systems engineering and systems integration as well as sub-system development and fabrication, the nation will have multiple options on choice of systems and industries to make them competitive and cost effective. In certain sub-systems or technologies we can even compete globally. There would also be a number of civilian commercial spin-off products and services which can be marketed domestically and in foreign markets.

Growth of Technology Capability in DRDO

The DRDO was established in the 1960s. Its major task was to build science-based capability towards making improvements in the available imported systems and weaponry. In the '70s we saw development in ammunition and gun design, leading to production and in the 80's a tremendous thrust was given to major system programmes in design and development which lead to productionization of electronic warfare system, communication systems, missile systems, aircraft, main batte tanks and radars. These programmes gave a new impetus to multiple design and technology development centres resulting in the production of design capability for an integrated weapons system in the nineties. Now the vision for the DRDO is to promote the corporate, strength of the organization. and to make the nation independent of foreign technology in critical spheres. Technology innovation is expected to lead the DRDO and its industrial partners to global competitiveness in systems design and realization. Let us look at the technological growth of a completed missile project, Prithvi and an advanced developmental project, LCA, under. The following observations are drawn from some of my talks on these projects.

Prithvi Missile System

In 1982, a detailed study was carried out for evolving advanced missile systems in order to counter the emerging threats to the security of India. Experts and members of the armed forces took part in this study and it resulted in the Integrated Guided Missile Development Programme comprising five projects. In July 1983, the government approved the programme, whereby a unique management structure as to be established, integrating the development, production, and the user services, with government machinery for expeditious implementation.

The Guided Missile Development Programme

The Guided Missile Development Programme envisaged the design and development of our missile systems, Prithvi, Trishul, Akash and Nag, leading to their production. It also established the re-enty technology capability through Agni. The re-entry technology demonstration was completed by 1992, through flight tests of Agni. Prithvi was the first of the four operational missile systems to be inducted into the armed forces.

The technological goal of the programme is to ensure that the systems will be contemporary at the time of their induction into the armed forces. The systems have been designed to be multi-purpose, multi-user and multi-role in nature. The programme has adopted the philosopy of concurrent development and production to reduce the time-cycle from development to induction.

Brief Description of the Prithvi System

Prithvi is an all-weather, mobile and surface-to-surface guided missile which can engage targets quickly and accurately over a range of 40-250 km. The weapon system is designed to engage targets beyond the range of field guns and unguided rockets. The system is highly mobile with a minimum reaction time and has a capability of being deployed at short notice at desired locations. Its mobility also provides fire and scoot capability.

The Prithvi missile is a single stage system and uses two liquid propulsion engines of three ton thurst capability each. The guidance system of Prithvi is based on a strapdown inertial navigation system along with an on-board computer, which offers integrated solutions to navigation, control and guidance requirements.

It's flight control system allows the missile to follow the desired trajectory, by controlling the vehicle in three mutually perpendicular plances viz. pitch, yaw and control. The electro-hydraulic actuation system is used to control the positioning error. The errors induced due to weather conditions such as wind, shear and gust can be correctedy by the guidance and control systems of the missile. It is also possible to manoeulre the missile in the final phase. The ground support systems is equipped with special vehicles to carry out the mission, command and control, maintenance, logistic support and survey. The modular design and built in check-out and calibration facilities help in equipping the missile in the deployment area with the desired warhead and for carrying out a quick check of the missile's operational readines.

The effectiveness of Prithvi

A manoeuvrable trajectory, its high mobility, low reaction time, its self-contained and self-supporting features and low footprint area make the Prithvi missile system dificult to counter. Besides the high accuracy of its system, its high warhead capabilities and absence of vulnerability to counter-measures, including Electronic Counter Measures (ECM), make the Prithvi missile system potentially dangerous for the enemy. Possession and deployment of a large number of Prithvi missiles can act as a deterrent and prevent a missile attack from our adversaries.

In case of war, the powerful explosive and high accuracy of the Prithvi missile has enormous potential to bring life to a standstill in cities and urban areas, to affect the morale of the enemy. Also, a sizeable portion of the enemy air force would be engaged in neutralizing the mobile missile launchers (as borne out by experience of Allied air forces in the recent Gulf war against mobile Scud sites).

Prithvi is a Cost-effective Weapon

Usually, Vital Areas (VAs) and Vital Points (VPs) which are of high tactical and strategic importance have a high-level of air defence protection. Much of this air cover is multi-layered, with some overlapping redundancy and is net-worked through computer communication links for ensuring effective command and control.

The deep penetration capability of the Prithvi missile, up to 250 km range, will enhance the firepower of the air force against heavily defended target in adverse weather conditions. In addition, the night attack capability of this missile will be useful for attacking targets like factories, petroleum dumps, marshalling yards and other static installations.

The accuracy of the system at 250 km will be further improved upon in Phase II, when terminal homing guidance or anti-radiation systems will be integrated into the Prithvi system. A scheme for retrofit is being contemplated and designed. This capability will be an asset in attacking hard targets like armoured concentrations in their parking sites.

The Development and Production Experience of Prithvi

India had certain strengths in design, materials and engineering when the project was initiated in 1983. However, the development of Prithvi required aerospace quality meterials like magnesium alloys for wings and certain special aluminium alloys for airframe and tankages, and navigational sensors of a certain accuracy, all of which were not available within the country. The Missile Technology Control Regime, though not formally declared , was in effect in some form or the other. All these drove us to deliberately adopt an indigenous route right from the beginning. A number of critical technologies, materials and processes were developed by harnessing the available talents within the country and using innovative management methods. The development of the Prithvi Inertial Navigation System is an example of this. Though we were able to get only the coarse class of sensors for the inertial navigation, our scientists came up with innovations to enhance their accuracy using software. The use of simulation in the design phase, and the hardware in loop simulation to fly the missile on ground, as well as the association of users at every stage, greatly helped in improving the effectiveness of the missile and reduced the number of user trials.

Throughout, the project was driven by goals of excellence in performance and of meeting schedules. Concurrency was built into every activity of the programme to reduce the time from development to induction.

Aside from strengthening the country to face the threats from across our borders, Prithvi has demonstrated that India can develop world-class high technology systems and devices by using its own indigenous strength, and thereby defeating the control regimes. An important benefit of the Prithvi programme is the new breed of technologists and leaders, who can make our country stronger and stronger and self-reliant.

Light Combat Aircraft (LCA)

One of the largest programmes of the DRDO is the Light Combat Aircraft (LCA). It has got all the potential elements of high technology; thirty three R&D establishments, sixty major industries and eleven academic institutions are integrated and working together on this project.

There are two types of fighter aircraft, Light Combat Aircraft and the Medium Combat Aircraft. The Medium Combat Aircraft weighs about 15 tonnes at take-off, whereas the Light Combat Aircraft has 10 tonnes take-off weight. This new generation aircraft has primary structures made of composite materials and advanced avionics. The LCA has technologies of composite wing, fly-by-wire flight control system, multi-processor based mission computer, low RCS, high weapon carrying capability, high manoeuvrability powered by a uniquely designed engine. The LCA design caters for top-class manoeuverability and high performance. In additton, its mission capability and survivability characteristics will be superior to those of the heavier aircaft that would come into the market within the next few years. The LCA will be the most cost-effective aircraft in relations to performance considering the fact that our R&D cost is one-third of that of the developed countries for similar programmes. The LCA the tops lightweight fighters in its capabilities with the unique feature of full-user commitment. The LCA can be marketed at much lower cost than the combat aircraft of similar class.

DRDO-Navy Participation

Let us look at a few other cases of building up strategic technological strength. During 1995, in the Bay of Bengal, despite rough weather conditions, our defence scientists and engineers from Bharat Electronis Limited (BEL) worked with a naval team on a ship to commission the modified electronic warfare system for user trials. In Chandipore-at -Sea, in stormy conditions, DRDO aeronautical and electronics engineers engayed in the final phase of user trials of Pilotless Target Aircraft (PTA) "Lakshya" for the three services. Also during 1995 we had a successful flight of the PTA whose jet engone was designed and developed within the country. The naval ships gave full support in this mission for deploying the simulated missile to encounter IR targets fitted with the PTA. An experimental laboratory on the sea, Sagardhwani, sailed from the west to the east coast with a mission of characterizing the ocean depth with particular reference to temperature gradient.

Another exciting achievement of the Navy is imminent. Work has been completed for the state-of the-art submarine sonar , Panchendriya, by the Naval Physical and Oceanography Laboratory (NPOL) situated on the western coast. The new ships being built will be armed with our Trishul missile system and the hull-mounted sonar Hamsa. It will have its first Modulated Data Bus which is mostly linked by fibre optics. The Government has also approved the Naval Integrated Electronic Warfare Programme (NIEWP) . In four years, ships, submarines and naval aircraft would be provided with the latest electronic surveillance system coupled with electronic counter-measures.

Action Plan for the Army

Strategic technological action by the Army has been equally exemplary. Phased induction of various systems and equipments needs to tbe linked and dovetailed with the defence self-reliance plan. This is a sure way for Indian industries to achieve the goals and the direction for preparing the business plan and for ensuring participation. Likewise, the dependence of our armed forces on imported systems needs to progressively decrease. Also, as is done elsewhere, India has to follow the induction of products in phases like Mark I. Mark II, etc. so that technology capability and production infrastructure are built in a phased way. This situation will cut down the delay of systems readiness. Technological uncertainty will be removed and wiling investment by industries may be possible. The industries should be given clear mandate—will they be developers? Will they be fabricators of an integrated system house and for what possible areas? Once this policy is enunciated industry can fully participate as the financial aspects would be clear. Recently the DRDO opened seven of its laboratories for industry to pick up technologies already developed. These industries have to shape the technologies for commercial application.

User trials of the systems developed is an important part of their induction by the armed forces. Normally, user trials pose a big challenge for the R&D and also the industrial establishments. We are no exception. But the outcome of this exercise could help the country to become independent and self-reliant. If the Army has to gain in self- reliance, rethinking is required in its plans of user trials and also of the mission veyuirements. In view of the onset of the performance evaluation through extensive combined environmental simulation, would it be possible to plan for reduced scale user trial tests for high altitude, and desert conditions? This will result in industries moving over to series production within a short time followed by full-scale production for domestic and international markets. Of course, a series of technological and military considerations would be vital for taking such decisions.

The future

The above has given a glimpse of defence research and its interface with operational systems. Future defence operations are going to be based on multiple networks of Army, Navy, Air Force and space systems. Information technology is going to be used in unprecedented ways, in the planning stages, in various simulation exercises, as well as during actual operations when the need arises,. Continual surveillance is going to be another feature in the years to come. This is done through remote sensing, communications and several other means. Continual improvement of systems with higher precision, speed and maneouvrability would also be a part of this complex picture. All the critical elements are driven by advance in materials electronics advanced sensors, information processing, robotics, and artificial intelligence..

Advanced sensors

Advanced sensor technology has been identified the world over as one of the critical technologies for the future. Advanced sensors require ultra-pure materials and ultra-clean manufacturing conditions. Integrated electonic devices are using microsensors on surface mounted devices. Advanced sensors will be used in every segment of human endeavour covering, agriculture, health services, advanced manufacturing systems, advanced avionics optical communications, space satellites, super smart highways, biotechnology, genetic engineering, pollution control, diagnostics and so on. Molecular and supramolecular systems for sensing and actuation are creating new sensors capable of measuring physical, chemical and biological parameters. In view of the strategic importance of sensors for industrial, aerospace and health applications, it is necessary to have a national mission on advanced sensors. We will lose out in all areas including agriculture or trade if we do not have sufficient national capability in sensors, since quality improvement, productivity enhancemnent and enforcement of standards will require use of advanced sensors. Environmental monitoring is another area based primarily on sensors continually looking at the quality of air, land and water.

A detailed assessment of the state-of-the-art of advanced sensors indicates that the following are major technological trends.

- development of inteligent or smart sensing devices
- emergence of integrated multifunctional sensors
- smart sensors systems capable of performing integration self-compensation and self-correction

- sensors integrated with actuators, and
- development, of artificial noses which can create olfactory images, i.e. sensors can smell and quantify the smell!

It is estimated that the worldwide demand for sensors was of the order of $ 5 billion in 1994; USA has about 55 per cent share of the world market . An analysis of the world market for sensors indicate that industrial control, medical and scientific instruments account for 50 per cent of the global market of sensors. Temperature sensors account for 36 per cent ; pressure sensors 34 per cent and flow sensors 28 per cent of the world demand. The world market for chemical and biochemical sensors is rapidly growing and this is one of the emerging end use applications. The demand for sensors in India will be about Rs. 500 million in 2000 and the dominant use will be in industrial control and automation applications. In spite of the fact that it is strategically important for industrial and defence applications, India has a negligible presence in the advanced sensors market, even in the use of sensors, not to mention in their manufacture and development.

Though there are a large number of institutions active in sensors development programmes in India, most of them have not as yet aimed their efforts at a specific product or service. There is no programme which is oriented towards industry or the health sector. A number of organizations have strong capabilities in one or other element of sensors : for example, for material development or sensor element development or sensor- device integration. There needs to be a sharper forcus for the sensors programme besides closer networking and a joint development programme. Perhaps national teams, as is being done for LCA , could be a model to follow.

National Programme in Advanced Sensors

India has to mount a sharply defined national programme on advanced sensors. If India has to become a major player in advanced sensors there has to be comprehensive national mission implemented in the consortice mode. Several disciplines have to be integrated into developing a focussed product. Among the new capabilities required are micro-fabrication and manufacture. All application segments of advanced sensors need special attentin with specific on focus on market development.

The mission may be implemented through the existing institutions or through a new mechanism. However, the mission has to be very clearly defined and it has to be end-use oriented. It is preferable, if industries take a lead in theis mission. Unless India has strong national capabilities in advanced sensors we may lose out in all areas to newly industrializing countries, since both industrial competitiveness and trade competitiveness are going to depend upon the capabilities in advanced senors. In future, the competitive edge the in manufacturing sector as well as in services is going to be greatly determined by the large-scale use and innovative applications of sensors. Tables 9.2 and 9.3 provide a glimpse of some of strategically and industrially important sensors. It is crucial India develops major industries in these areas. With commercial level operations in the domestic and foreign markets.

Let us now look at a few examples of space systems, which would form a core of strategic sector industries.

Cryogenic Engine for GSLV

For the satellite launch vehicles, all-solid multi-stage rocket systems or solid plus liquid multi-stage rocket systems or all-liquid multi-stage rocket systems can be used. The cost per launch is in a way controlled by the take-off weight of the launch vehicle system for a given payload and type of orbit required. The cost-effectiveness in commercial launch vehicles, that is, the lost of injecting a satellite into a geo-stationary orbit will decide the choice of the propellant system for individual stages. Normally, a liquid rocket system will be of a lower weight and with a cryogenic upper stage further weight reduction is achieved.

TABLE 9.2

Strategically Important Sensors

Area	*Sensor to be developed*	*Trends*	*Action needed*
	Inertial sensors for navigation and avionics	a) laser gyros	Development of ultra noise free and stable lasers
		b) fibre optic gyro	Development of integrated optic chips surface micro machining
	Sensors for submarine	c) micro accelerometer	Development of SQUID sensor

	detection	SQUID based systems	and associated noise-free electonics
Strategically important sensors	Sensors for detecting explosives such as RDX and narcotics	Combining nuclear magnetic resonance	SQUID sensors for sensing ultra and weak electro-magnetic fields nuclear quadrupole arising from nuclear magnetic reso-nance (NMR)/ nuclear quadrupole resonance (NQR) resonance principles
	Piezoresistive microsensors	Surface micro machining of poly-silicon micro-structures	Development of monolithic silicon transducer includcing signal conditioning and calibration

TABLE 9.3
Sensors Needed for Industrial Applications

Area	*Sensor to be developed*	*Trends*	*Action needed*
	Humidity sensors	Polymer electrolytic, heat treated polymer dielectric, inorganic substance distributed polymer (change in resistance due to humidity absorption)	Humidity sensors using changes in permitivity and resistance need to be devel-oped . This will require first development of sensors material and related electronic circuitry
		Cellulose system polymer (change in permitivity)	Metal oxide silicon field effect transistor (MOSFET) using humidity absorption polymer to be developed
Industrial process		Carbon particle distributed	

control and safety		humidity absorption resin (sharp change in resistance with absorption of humidity) MOSFET + humidity absorption polymer (changei in characteristics of transistor)	
		Quartz oscillator + polyamid (change in load of oscillator)	Surface acoustic wave sensors to be developed
Gas sensors for process control		Organic semicon-ductor (increase in conductivity due to absorption of gas) Colouring matter membrane LB membrane (fluorescence quench) Quartz oscillator+ organic thin film (change in load on vibrator) Gas transmission polymer memberane+ electroride (selective perrmiation of gas, electrochemical reaction)	
Sensors for monitoring toxic gases		Artificial noses	Development of multicomponent molecular recognition systems
Industrial process control and safety	Inductive proximity sensors	Non-contact metal detection sensors with wide operating range and fast response	Development of proximity sensors and sensor alignment techniques
	Semiconductor displacement laser sensors	Light emitting diode or semiconductor laser based sensors	Light source and position sensitive detector development

For example, to place a 2.5 ton payload in a geo-transfer Orbit, an all-solid multi-stage launch vehicle will have a take-off weight of 525 tons. This will reduce to 470 tons if the liquid stage replaces the solid upper stages. It will further reduce to 450 tones with all liquid stages and eventually to less than 300 tons when the upper stage is replaced by a cryogenic engine. The major defferences in take-off weight are evident. It is said in the space community that for every additional kilogram of payload, the cost will be reduced by a few lakhs of rupees when utilizing the cryogenic engine. The propellant used in the cryogenic engine is a combination of liquid exygen and liquid hydrogen in specific ratios. The proposed cryogenic engine for India's Geosynchronous Satellite Launch Vehicle, GSLV is of 12-ton thrust class. The engine has to be only 250 kg and has a length of 3.1 metres. The engine has to be very compact with proper insulation, regenerative cooling and sealing for handling liquid oxygen and hydrogen.

The engine has to be closely coupled to the tankages and flow control devices to form the upper stage. The propellant loading, transfer, insulating and pressurizing systems are integrated into one integral system for modular handling and operation. The technological challenges in realizing this stage are many. The materials selected have to work at minus 253°C as well as at high temperatures of 1750°C continuously. The nozzle and thrust chamber have to be regeneratively cooled using the liquid hydrogen itself. For the liquid hydrogen turbo pump, speed has to be maintained above 50000 revolutions per minute (rpm). Compare it with the revolutions of your motor car engine which is 5000 rpm and of a commercial jet aircraft which is almost 15000 rpm. Considering the fabrication, material technology, which is sealing, bearing, insulating technologies and the process of making the various cryogenic sub-systems, the country has yet to develop all these and our industries and R&D laboratories have to work together for this important task. A design and manufacturing database has to be established so that no country can come in the way of our space programmes. In this context it is essential to note that cryogenic cannot be used for any missile engines application as their storage life is limited, the filling operations can be sensed in advance and no mobility is possible. The argument that cryogenic engines can be used for missiles, quoting Missile Technology Control Regime, is non-technical and commercially motivated.

Where are we in Aero Propulsion?

Where are we in aeroengines and propulsion? India with its LCA programme, is now developing a uniquely configured GT engine as described earlier. Similarly, for GSLV, India has to develop within schedule, a cryogenic engine and stand on its own its feet in the area of satellite launching. It can be seen that in both these areas we are lagging behind the developed countries because we did not feel their importance, given the level of aerospace technology missions taken up in the country in the past. Today, the priority given to commercial and military aircraft as well as GSLV cryogenic engines and jet engines has become vital. Bridying the gap in teachnologies to become a part of the leaders in the game is not an impossibe ltask. The partnership between our institutions and industries can accelerate development and our technology acquisition. It will also help tailor the technology acquired to our infrastructure and needs. It can be seen that with the launch of Polar Satellite Launch Vehicle (PSLV), we are almost at par with the developed countries in the area of solid propellant power plants. The PSLV has also established the technologies of storable liquid propellants and related propulsion.

Hyperplanes of the Future

DRDO has entered into ramrocket systems where much higher energy levles (of above 500 sec. with solid propellants and upto 1000 sec with liquid propellants) will be realized. The scramjet engine will give energy level of 3000 sec. Compare this with 450 sec of cryoengines! This is not only for military application. These supersonic combustion engines have application for cruise missiles, launch vehicles and hyperplanes of the future. India's proposed scramjet is designed for operating up to Mach12. In the long term it could become part and parcel of our jet aircraft too. Currently, only a few countries are working in this area. Based on our experience with LCA and GSLV, India should at least take initiative in the elements of the hyperplane programme so that India's hyperplane and future aerospace vehicles can be built around this power plant. The hyperplane can deliver a payload of above 30 tons for a take off weight off 250 tons, giving a quantum jump for the exisiting payload/ take of ratios of max 3 per cent to 15 per cent through mass addition.

A future hyperplane mission can have an integrated power plant complex working in three modes.

- Fan ramjet engine mode in low altitute, low speed flight regimes
- Scramjet engine mode in Mach number range 3 to 12 alongwith in-flight airliquification and mas addition.
- Rocket engine mode till payload launching.

In the critical technology areas of scramjet engines, our aerospace scientists start with the design, development and integration of fixed geometry air intakes for a wide Mach number range supported extensively by analytical tools like Computational Fluid Dynamics (CFD) and experimental set up like hypersonic wind tunnels. The combustor development including the material, fabrication technology and combustion kinetics has just begun. Test and evaluation facilities are to be planned for prototype and full-scale engine testing.

By 2010, commercial jet aircraft, military fighters reusable satellite launch vehicle and the reusable terrestrial payload delivery vehicle will have one common feature, that is, the usage of supersonic combustion egines for flying in hypersonic flight engines.

The Real Proliferators

Recently I addressed diplomats in Delhi on the subject of nuclear proliferation. I offer an extract: 'During my tenure in Delhi, I made a study of the proliferation doctrine initiated by the five nations. The USA for the last four decades, upto 1990, accumulated about 10,000 nuclear warheads and almost an equal number was accumulated by the erstwhile Soviet Union. And this cruel fanaticism was justified in the name of ideology of Capitalism versus Communism! The seeds of nuclear proliferation were thus sown. These two nations used nuclear weapons as a tool to subordinate or influence many national politics by giving so-called nuclear technology for peaceful application or nuclear power stations. For China, nuclear weapon technology was given by the Soviet Union and we have witnessed recently that the same developed countries have ensured that Pakistan will have a certain number of nuclear weapons. This has been reported by a former Prime minister of Pakistan.

The five nuclear weapon countries proclaimed that they were the nations solely approved to possess nuclear weapons. They evolved certain international policies. The total number of warheads they possessed were so many that they created safety and security problems of tremendous magnitude for the world. These two nations driven by the people, negotiated STAR-II (Strategic Arms Reduction Treaty). They signed a treaty for reducing the warheads, including the delivery carriers to 3000. When I asked Dr. William Perry, US secretary for defence, during his visit to India, why 3000 and not zero as Pandit Jawaharlal Nehru had put forth the concept of complete nuclear disarmament in the 1960s, Dr. Perry answered zero nuclear weapons is a dream. He meant that the nuclear weapons should always be with the club of five and be a dream for others. We can assume that at no time will the five nations come to zero level of nuclear weapons. Nuclear weapons are a strong component of the global strategy they visualize. For them they are weapons of political strength and by propagating a non-proliferation doctrine they claim to generate peace. It was a delightful privilege for DAE and DRDO teams, backed up by the political leadership, to break this dangerous and self-centred monopoly of nuclear weapon states.

Similarly, inthe area of chemical or biological weapons or missile systems, the origin of their proliferation is the same. It one opens the Pandora's box of proliferaticn, one would see USA and the former Soviet Union, with the recent addition of China. If there could be an impartial world body, not driven by the superpowers, the developing countries affected by this dangerous proliferation can seek justice and compensation. Can we dream for such a new and just world?

Strategic Industries—the Future of India

We are able to provide only a glimpse of a few important elements of strategic industries to be developed in India. The ones described are well within our reach—technologically, investmentwise and schedulewise. If industries and institutions work together with clear vision and goals in mind and with assiduous build-up of markets right from the word go, Indian industries can reap rich commerical benefits. Also, let us not forget the fact that a strategic technology or industry today, will have day-to-day applications in many walks of life two decades hence. Therefore, it is our duty to build the necessary technologies today so that the future generation of Indians will have new worlds to conquer and not have to struggle with the problems of 'bridging the past gaps' as we are doing today! We owe it to the future generations that we hand them over by 2020 only the excitement and challenges of the future and not the weight of problems of the past or the crises of the present. Only then will India have truly arrived as a developed country populated with proud people confident of their future.

10

Family Tragedies and Professional Pressure

"In 1976, my father passed away. He had been suffering from poor health for quite some time due to his advanced age. The death of Jallaluddin had also taken a toll on his health and spirit. He had lost his desire to live, as though after seeing Jallaluddin return to his divine source, he too had become eager to return to his. Whenever I learnt about my father's indifferent health, I would visit Rameswaram with a good city doctor. Every time I did so, he would chide me for my unnecessary concern and lecture me on the expenses incurred on the doctor. "Your visit is enough for me to get well, why bring a doctor and spend money on his fees?" he would ask. This time he had gone beyond the capabilities of any doctor, care or money. Dust had mingled with dust. My father Jainulabdeen, who had lived on Rameswaram island for 102 years, had passed away leaving behind fifteen grandchildren and one great grandson. This was the Paradise which the righteous have been promised by Allah. Here was all that He had promised. What an exemplary life! My father had lived and died as a role model for every penitent and faithful man, who fears the Merciful though. He is unseen, and comes before Him with a contrite heart.

"He was not a politician, a scholar, or a businessman. He was a man—as plain and transparent as God made him to be. The conventional world judges by appearances instead of judging appearances. My father assuredly pursued the supreme value, the Good, not only because there was no other way to free himself from his endless troubles, but because he must. His life was a process in which all that is evil and bestial in the fallen angel was slowly burnt out, so as to inspire the growth of all that was benign and angelic".

Now Dr. Kalam was to leave for France to test SLV-3 Apogee rocket. But circumstances, once again turned against him when he got the sad news of his mother's death. He immediately rushed to Rameswaram and performed the last rites the next morning.

"The SLV-3 Apogee rocket, developed as a common upper stage with Diamont, Scheduled to be Hight tested in France stuck in a series of knotty problems. I had to rush to France to sort it out. Before I could depart, late in the afternoon, I was informed that my mother was no more. I took the first available bus to Nagarcoil. From there, I travelled to Rameswaram for a whole night in the train and performed the last rites the next morning. Both the souls who took form to give form to me had left for their heavenly abode. What was to be my abode till I reunite with them? The departed had reached the end of their journey. The rest of us had to continue walking the weary road and the game of life had to go on. I prayed in the mosque my father had once taken me to every evening. I told Him that my mother could not have lived longer in the world without the care and love of her husband, and therefore had preferred to join him. I begged His forgiveness. "They carried out the task I designed for them with great care, dedication and honesty and came back to me. Why are you mourning their day of task accomplishment? Concentrate on the assignments that lie before you, and live my glory through your deeds!" Nobody had said these words, but I heard them loud and clear. An inspiring aphorism in the *Quran* on the passing away of souls filled my mind: "Your wealth and children are only a temptation whereas: Allah! with Him is an eternal award." I came out of the mosque with my mind at peace and proceeded to the railway station. I always remember when the call for *namaz* sounded, our home would transform into a small mosque. My father and my mother leading, and their children and grandchildren following".

The next morning he was back at Thumba, physically exhausted, emotionally shattered, but determined to fulfil our ambition of flying an Indian rocket motor on foreign soil.

On his return from France, after successfully testing the SLV-3 apogee motor, Dr. Brahm Prakash informed Kalam about the arrival of Wernher von Braun. Everybody working in rocketry knows of von Braun, who made the lethal V2 missiles that devastated London in the Second World War. In the final stages of the War, von Braun was captured by the Allied Forces. As a tribute to his genius, von Braun was given a top position in the rocketry programme at NASA. Working for the US Army, von Braun produced the landmark Jupiter missile, which was the first IRBM with a 3000 km range. When he was asked by Dr. Brahm Prakash to receive von Braun at Madras and escort him to Thumba, he was naturally excited.

They travelled in an Avro aircraft which took around 90 minutes from Madras to Trivandrum. Von Braun asked Kalam about our work and listened as if he were just another student of rocketry. He never expected the father of modern rocketry to be so humble, receptive and encouraging. He made him feel comfortable right through the flight. It was hard to imagine he was talking to a giant of missile systems, as he was so self-effacing. he observed that the length to diameter L/D ratio of the SLV-3, which was designed to be 22 was on the higher side and cautioned me about the aero-elastic problems which must be avoided during flight.

"Having spent the major part of his working life in Germany, how did he feel in America? I asked this of von Braun who had become a cult figure in the States after creating the Saturn rocket in the Apollo mission which put man on the moon. "America is a country of great possibilities, but they look upon everything non-American with suspicion and contempt. They suffer from a deep-rooted NIH—Not Invented-Here—complex and look down on alien technologies. If you want to do anything in rocketry, do it yourself", von Braun advised me. He commented, "SLV-3 is a genuine Indian design and you may be having your own troubles. But you should always remember that we don't just build on successes, we also build on failures."

On the topic of the inevitable hard work that goes with rocket development and the degree of commitment involved, he smiled and said with a glint of mischief in his eyes. "Hard work is not enough in rocketry. It is not a sport where mere hard work can fetch you honours. Here, not only do you have to have a goal but you have to have tactics to achieve it as fast as possible."

"Total commitment is not just hard work, it is total involvement. Building a rock wall is back-breaking work. There are some people who build rock walls all their lives. And when they die, there are miles of walls, mute testimonials to how hard these people had worked. But there are other men who build rock walls, and all the time they are placing one rock on top of another they have a vision in their minds, a goal. It may be a terrace with roses climbing over the rock walls and chairs set out for lazy summer days. Or the rock wall may enclose an apple orchard or mark a boundary. When they finish, they have more than a wall. It is the goal that makes the difference. Do not make rocketry your profession, your livelihood—make it your religion, your mission".

II

"The pursuit of science gives great happiness, coupled with many hardships and heartbreaks. I went over many such episodes in my mind. Johannes Kepler, whose three orbital laws form the basis of space research, took nearly 17 years after formulating the two laws about planetary motion around the sun, to enunciate his third law which gives the relation between the size of the elliptical orbit and the length of time it takes for the planet to go around the sun. How many failures and frustrations must he have gone through? The idea that man could land on the moon, developed by Russian mathematician Konstantin Tsiolkousky, was realised only after nearly four decades—and that too, by the United States. Prof. Chandrasekhar had to wait nearly 50 years before receiving the Nobel Prize for his discovery of the 'Chandrasekhar Limit', a discovery made while a graduate student at Cambridge in the 1930s. If his work had been recognised then, it could have led to the discovery of Black Hole decades earlier. How many failures must von Braun have gone through before his Saturn launch vehicle put man on the moon! These thoughts helped to give me the ability to withstand apparently irreparable setbacks".

Early in November 1979, Dr. Brahm Prakash retired. He had always been his sheet-anchor in the turbulent waters of VSSC. His belief in the power of team spirit had inspired the management pattern for the SLV project, which later became a blueprint for all the scientific projects in the country. Dr. Brahm Prakash was a very wise counsellor who gave valuable advice whenever Kalam deviated from his mission objectives.

Dr Brahm Prakash not only cemented in him the traits which he had acquired from Prof. Sarabhai, but also helped him give them new dimensions. He always cautioned him against haste. "Big scientific projects are like mountains, which should be climbed with as little effort as possible and without desire. The reality of your own nature should determine your speed. If you become restless, speed up. If you become tense and high-strung, slow down. You climb the mountain in an equilibrium between restlessness and exhaustion.

When each task of your project is not just a means to an end but a unique event in itself, then you are managing the show properly," he would tell me. For the first time in his career, Kalam saw in Dr Brahm Prakash nobility in management.

The Emerson's poem on Brahma:
If the red slayer think he slays,
Or, if the slain think he is slain,
They know not well, the subtle ways
I keep, and pass, and turn again.

On 17 July 1980, 30 hours before the launch of the second SLV-3, the newspapers were filled with all kinds of predictions. One of the newspapers reported, "The Project Director is missing and could not be contacted." Many people preferred to trace the history of the first SLV-3 flight, and recalled how the third stage had failed to burn because of lack of fuel and the rocket had nosedived into the ocean. Some highlighted SLV-3's possible military implications in terms of acquiring the capability for building IRBMs. In fact, the eyes of the whole nation were on them.

In the early hours of the next day, 18 July 1980—at 0803 hours to be precise, India's first Satellite Launch Vehicle, SLV-3 lifted off from SHAR. At 600 seconds before take-off, Kalam saw the computer displaying data about stage IV giving the required velocity to the Rohini Satellite (carried as payload) to enter its orbit. Within the next two minutes, Rohini was set into motion in a low earth orbit. He spoke, in the midst of screeching decibels, the most important words he had ever uttered in his life, "Mission Director calling all stations. Stand by for an important announcement. All stages performed to mission requirements. The fourth stage apogee motor has given the required velocity to put Rohini Satellite into orbit". There were happy cries everywhere. When I came out of the Block House, I was lifted onto the shoulders of my jubilant colleagues and carried in a procession.

The whole nation was excited. India had made its entry into the limited group of nations possessing satellite launch capability. Newspapers carried news of the event in their headlines. Radio and television aired special programmes. Parliament greeted the achievement with the thumping of desks. It was both the culmination of a national dream, and the beginning of a very important phase in our nation's history. Prof. Satish Dhawan, Chairman, SRO, jettisoned his customary guardedness and announced that it was now well within our ability to explore space. Prime Minister Indira Gandhi cabled her congratulations. Everbody felt excited and proud of this hundred per cent indigenous effort.

Personally, Dr. Kalam experienced mixed feelings. He was happy to achieve the success which had been evading him for the past two decades, but he was sad because the people who had inspired him were no longer there to share his joy—his father, his brother-in-law Jallaluddin, and Prof. Sarabhai.

Dr. Kalam visited the Nehru Science Centre in Bombay for a day, on an invitation to share his experiences with the SLV-3. There, he got a telephone call from Prof. Dhawan from Delhi, asking him to join him the next morning. They were to meet Prime Minister Indira Gandhi. He was dressed casually and wearing slippers—not, by any standards of etiquette, a suitable outfit in which to meet the Prime Minister! When he told Prof. Dhawan about this problem, he told him not to worry about his dress. "You are beautifully clothed in your success," he quipped.

Both of them arrived at the Parliament House Annexe the next morning. A meeting of the Parliamentary Panel on Science and Technology chaired by the Prime Minister was scheduled. There were around 30 Members of the Lok Sabha and Rajya Sabha in the room, which was lit with a majestic chandelier. Prof. MGK Menon and Dr. Nag Chaudhuri were also present. Shrimati Gandhi spoke to the Members about the success of the SLV-3 and lauded our achievement. Prof. Dhawan thanked the gathering for the encouragement given by them to space research in the country and expressed the gratitude of the ISRO scientists and engineers. Suddenly, Dr. Kalam saw Shrimati Gandhi smiling at him as she said, "Kalam! we would like to hear you speak".

Dr. Kalam rose and responded, "I am indeed honoured to be in this great gathering of nation-builders. I only know how to build a rocket system in our country, which would inject a satellite, built in our country, by imparting to it a velocity of 25,000 km per hour." There was thunderous applause. He thanked the members for giving them an opportunity to work on a project like the SLV-3 and prove the scientific strength of the country.

Now that Project SLV-3 had been successfully completed., VSSC was to re-organise its resources and redefine its goals. Dr. Kalam desired to be relieved of the project activities, and consequently

Ved Prakash Sandlas from his team was made the Prof. Director for the SLV-3 Continuation Project, which aimed at making operational satellite launch vehicles of a similar class. The Geo Satellite Launch Vehicle (GSLV) was also envisaged, as a distant dream. Dr. Kalam took up the position of Director, Aerospace Dynamics and Design Group, so that he could configure the forthcoming launch vehicles and technology development.

'The next SLV-3 flight, SLV3-D1, took off on 31 May 1981. I witnessed this flight from the visitor's gallery. This was the first time I witnessed a launch from outside the Control Centre. Was I hurt at the coldness of the new environment? Perhaps yes, but I was willing to accept what I couldn't change'.

"I have never lived off the profits of others' minds. My life, as dictated by my nature, has never been the life of a ruthless achiever, a brute boss, an exploiting executive or a dreamy mystic, but that of a thinking being. The SLV-3 was made not through force and manipulation, but through consistent collective effort. Then why this sense of unhappiness? Was it peculiar to the VSSC top level or a universal reality? As a scientist, I was trained to reason out reality. In science, reality is that which exists. And the reality which I had to confront was that my becoming the focus of media attention had created bitterness among my senior colleagues. And because this bitterness was real, I had to reason it out. But can these things be reasoned out? Do not honours come unsought and uninvited?

The meeting with Dr. Raja Ramanna was historic. In January 1981, Dr. Kalam was invited by Dr. Bhagiratha Rao of the High Altitude Laboratory (now the Defence Electronics Applications Laboratory(DEAL), Dehra Dun to give a lecture on the SLV-3. The renowned nuclear scientist, Prof. Raja Ramanna, whom he had always admired, and who was then the Scientific Adviser to the Defence Minister, presided over the function. He spoke on India's efforts in generating nuclear energy and the challenge in conducting the first nuclear test for peaceful purposes. As I had been so closely involved with SLV-3, it was natural that he was soon in full flow while talking about it.

"In fact he has always adnired Prof. Ramanna from a distance, and now he had the opportunity to see him from close. The first thing that struck me when he met Prof. Ramanna was his genuine happiness over meeting him. There was and eagerness in his talk, and immediate, sympathetic friendliness, accompanied by quick, graceful movements.

"He did not take long to come to the point. The *Devil Missile* programme had been shelved in spite of tremendous achievements made by Narayanan and his team at DRDL.The entire programme of military rockets was reeling under a persistent passivity. The DRDO needed somebody to take command of their missile programmes which were stuck at the drawing board and static test bed stages for quite some time. Prof. Ramanna asked me pointblank, if I would like to join DRDL and shoulder the responsibility of shaping their Guided Missile Development Programme (GMDP). Prof. Ramanna's proposal evoked a mixture of emotions in me.

"I felt honoured by the esteem in which Prof. Ramanna held me. He had been the guiding spirit behind the Pokharan nuclear test, and I was thrilled by the impact he had helped create on the outside world about India's technical competence. I know I would not be able to refuse him. Prof. Ramanna advised me to talk to Prof. Dhawan on this issue so that he would work out the modalities of my transfer from ISRO to DRDL.

"I met Prof. Dhawan on 14 January 1981. He gave me a patient hearing, with his typical penchant for weighing everything twice to make sure he didn't miss a point. A markedly pleasant expression came on his face. He said, "I am pleased with their appraisal of my man's work". He then smiled. I have never met anyone with a smile quite like Prof. Dhawan's—a soft white cloud—you could see it in any shape you wanted to.

"I wondered how I should proceed. "Should I formally apply for the post so that DRDL could send the appointment order?" I enquired of Prof. Dhawan. "No. Don't pressurise them. Let me talk to the top-level management during my ensuing visit to New Delhi", Prof. Dhawan said. "I know you have always had one foot in DRDO, now your whole centre of gravity seems to have shifted towards them."

There was a big news for him on Republic Day, 1981. On the evening of 25 January, Mahadevan, Secretary to Prof. UR Rao, rang up from Delhi to inform me about the Home Ministry announcement about the conferment of the Padma Bhushan award on Dr. Kalam. The next important call was from Prof. Dhawan to congratulate him. He felt blissfully elated as it was from his guru. He rejoiced with Prof. Dhawan at his receiving of the Padma Vibhushan. He congratulated him whole-heartedly. He then rang up Dr. Brahm Prakash and thanked him. Dr. Brahm Prakash chided him for the formality and said, "I feel as if my son has got the award. "I was so deeply touched by Dr. Brahm Prakash's affection that I could no longer keep my emotions in check".

"I filled my room with the music of Bismillah Khan's shehnai. The music took me to another time, another place. I visited Rameswaram and hugged my mother. My father ran his caring fingers through my hair. My mentor, Jallaluddin, announced the news to the crowd gathered on Mosque Street. My sister, Zohara, prepared special sweets for me. Pakshi Lakshmana Sastry put a *tilak* on my forehead. Fr. Solomon blessed me holding the holy cross. I saw Prof. Sarabhai smiling with a sense of achievement—the sapling which he had planted twenty years ago had finally grown into a tree whose fruits were being relished by the people of India".

Dr. APJ Abdul Kalam's Speech in Hyderabad

I have three visions for India. In 3000 years of our history people from all over the world have come and invaded us, captured our lands, conquered our minds. From Alexander onwards, the Greeks, the Turks, the Moguls, the Portuguese, the British, the French, the Dutch, all of them came and looted us, took over what was ours. Yet we have not done this to any other nation. We have not conquered anyone. We have not grabbed their land, their culture, their history and tried to enforce our way of life on them. Why? Because we respect the freedom of others. That is why my first vision is that of freedom. I believe that India got its first vision of this in 1857, when we started the war of independence. It is this freedom that we must protect and nurture and build on. If we are not free, no one will respect us.

My second vision for India is Development. For fifty years we have been a developing nation. It is time we see ourselves as a developed nation. We are among top 5 nations of the world in terms of GDP. We have 10 per cent growth rate in most areas. Our poverty levels are falling. Our achievements are being globally recognized today. Yet we lack the self-confidence to see ourselves as a developed nation, self-reliant and self-assured. Isn't this incorrect I have a third vision. India must stand up to the world. Because i believe that unless India stands up to the world, no one will respect us. Only strength respects strength. We must be strong not only as a military power but also an economic power. Both must go hand-in-hand. My good fortune was to have worked with three great minds. Dr. Vikam Sarabhai of the of space, Professor Satish Dhawan, who succeeded him and Dr. Brahm Prakash, father of nuclear material. I was lucky to have worked with all three of them closely and consider this the great opportunity of my life. I see four milestones in my career: one twenty years I spent in ISRO. I was given the opportunity to be the Project Director for India's first satelliter launch vehicle, SLV3, the one that launched Rohine. These years played a very important role in my life of Scientist.

Two: after my ISRO years, I joined DRDO and got a chance to be the part of India's missile programme. It was my second bliss when Agni met its mission requirements in 1994.

Three: The Department of Atomic Energy and DRDO had this tremendous partnership in the recent nuclear tests, on May 11 and 13. This was the third bliss. The joy of participating with my team in these nuclear tests and proving to the world that India can make it, that we are no longer a developing nation but one of them. It made me feel very proud as an Indian. The fact that we have now developed for Agni a reentry structure, for which we have developed this new material. A very light material called carbon carbon.

FOUR: One day an orthopedic surgeon from Nizam Institute of Medical Sciences visited my laboratory. He lifted the material and found it so light that he took me to his hospital and showed his patients. There were these little girls and boys with heavy metallic callpers weighing over three kg.. each dragging their feet around. He said to me: Please remove the pain of my patients. In three week, we made these Floor reaction Orthosis 300 gram calipers and took them to the orthopedic centre. The children didn't believe their eyes. From dragging around a three kg. Load on their legs, they could now move around!. Their parents had tears in their eyes. That was my fourth bliss! Why is the media here so negative? Why are we in India so embarassed to recognize our own strengths, our achievements? We are such a great nation. We have so many amazing success stories but we refuse to acknowledge them. Why? We are the first in milk production. We are number one in Remote Sensing Satellites. We are the second largest producer of wheat. We are the second largest producer of rice. Look at Dr. Sudarshan, he has transferred the tribal village into a self-sustaining, self-driving unit. There are millions of such achievements but our media is only obsessed in the bad news and failures and disasters. I was in Tel Aviv once and I was reading the Israeli newspaper. It was the day after a lot of attacks and bombarments and deaths had taken place. The Hamas had struck. But the front page of the newspaper had the picture of a Jewish gentleman who in five years had transformed his desert land into an orchid and a granary. It was this inspiring picture that everyone woke up to. The gory details of killings, bombardments, deaths, were inside in the newspaper, buried among other news. In India we only read about death, sickness, terrorism. Why are we so negative? Another question: Why are we as a nation so obsessed with foreign things? We want foreign TVs, we want foreign shirts. We want foreign technology. Why this obsession with everything imported. Do we not realize that self-respect comes with self-reliance?

I was in Hyderabad giving this lecture, when a 14 year old girl asked me for my autograph. I asked her what her goal in life is: She replied: I want to live in a developed India. For her, you and I will have to build this develped India you must proclaim. India is not an under-developed nation; it is a highly developed nation. Allow me to come back with vengeance. Got 10 minutes for your country?

You say that our government is inefficient. You say that our laws are too old. You say that the municipality does not pick up the garbage. You say that the phones don't work, the railways are a joke, the airline is the worst in the world, mails never reach their destination. You say that our country has been fed to the dogs and is the absolute pits. You say, say and say.

What do you do about it ? Take a person on his way to Singapore. Give him a name—yours. Give him a face—yours. You walk out of the airport and you are at your International best. In Singapore you don't throw cigarette butts on the roads or eat in the stores. You pay $5 (approx. Rs. 60) to drive through Orchard Road (equivalent of Mahim Causeway or Pedder Road) between 5 PM and 8 PM. You come back to the parking lot to punch your parking ticket if you have over stayed in a restaurant or a shopping mall irrespective of your status identity. In Singapore you don't say anything, Do you? You would't dare to eat in public during Ramadan, in Dubai, would not dare to go out without your head convered inJeddah. You would not dare to buy an employee of the telephone exchange in London at 10 pounds (Rs.650) a month to, "see to it that my STD and ISD calls are billed to some one else." You would not dare to speed beyond 55 mph (88 kph) in Washington and then tell the traffic cop, "Jaanta hai sala main kaun hoon (Do you know who I am). I am so and so's son. Take your two bucks and get lost." You wouldn't chuck an empty coconut shell anywhere other than the garbage pail on the beaches in Australia and New Zealand. Why don't you spit Paan on the streets of Tokyo? Why don't you use examination jockeys or buy fake certificates in Boston? We are still talking of the same you. You who can respect and conform to a foreign system in other countries but cannot in your own. You who will throw papers and cigarettes on the road the moment you touch Indian ground. If you can be an involved and appreaciative citizsen in an alien country why cannot you be the same here in India. Once in an interview, the famous Ex-municipal commissioner of Bombay Mr. Tinaikar had a point to make. 'Rich people's dogs are walked on the streets to leave their afflvent droppings all over the place," he said. "And then the same people turn around to criticize and blame the authorities for inefficiency and dirty pavements. What do they expect the officers to do? Go down with a broom every time their dog feels the pressure in his bowels? In America every dog owner has to clean up after his pet has done the job. Same in Japan. Will the Indian citizen do that here?" He's right. We go to the polls to choose a government and after that forfeit all responsibility. We sit back wanting to be pampered and expect the government to do everything for us whilst our contribution is totally negative. We expect the government to clean up but we are not going to stop chucking garbage all over the place nor are we going to stop to pick up a stray piece of paper and throw it in the bin. We expect the railways to provide clean bathrooms but we are not going to learn the proper use of bathrooms. We want Indian Airlines and Air India to provide the best of food and toiletries but we are not going to stop pilfering at the least opportunity. This applies even to the staff who is known not to pass on the service to the public. When it comes to burning social issues like those related to women, dowry, girl child and others, we make loud drawing room protestations and continue to do the reverse at hoome. Our excuse? "It 's the whole system which has to change, how will it matter if I alone forego my sons' rights to a dowry. " So who's going to change the system? What does a system consist of? Very conveniently for us it consists of our neighbours, other households, other cities, other communities and the government. But definitely not me and you. When it comes to us actually making a positive contribution to the system we lock ourselves along with our families into a safe cocoon and look into the distance at countries far away and wait for a Mr. Clean to come along and work miracles for us with a majestic sweep of his hand. Or we leave the country and run away. Like lazy cowards hounded by our fears we run to America to bask in their glory and praise their system. When New York becomes insecure we run to England. When England experiences unemployment, we take the next flight out to the Gulf. When the Gulf is war struck, we demand to be rescued and brought home by the Indian government. Everybody is out to abuse and rape the country. Nobody thinks of feeding the system. Our conscience is mortgaged to money.

Dear Indians, The article is highly thought inductive, calls for a great deal of introspection and pricks one's conscience too...I am echoing J.F. Kennedy's words to his fellow Americans to relate to Indians...

"ASK WHAT WE CAN DO FOR INDIA AND DO WHAT HAS TO BE DONE TO MAKE INDIA WHAT AMERICA AND OTHER WESTERN COUNTRIES ARE TODAY"

Dr. Abdul Kalam

The Missile Man of India

Did you know Dr. Abdul Kalam was the man behind India's first-ever missile—Prithvi

The recipient of the prestigious Bharat Ratna award Aavul Pakkiri Jainulabiddin Abdul Kalam was brought up in the lush green countryside of Rameswaram in South India. He was the first person to graduate in his family. He began schooling at the Samiyar School in Rameswaram and then completed his basic education from Schwartz School in Ramnathapuram town. He graduated from the St. Joseph's College in Tiruchi. Abdul Kalam was perhaps marked out to be different right from the beginning. As a young boy he was very interested in reading books. In a way, this library which he frequented was the foundation on which Kalam built his career. Kalam is a man of varied interests. He plays the *rudra veena*, has literary leanings—a fan of the Tamil poet Subramania Bharathi. He is religious and a strict vegetarian. He is a rare combination of science, music, and literature! He was fascinated by science and hence found the launch of rockets to be like music to his ears. The flight of missiles was beauty to his eyes. Science seemed to be embedded in him so deeply that it's no wonder that he came to be known as the Missile Man of India

He was the brain behind the launch of Prithvi (the missile). Prithvi had a unique design. They used a particular gyro system, with a unique configured software, which nobody else in the world had tried before. Consequently, when the flight was in progress, the drift could be monitored through the on-board computer. Prithvi had other noteworthy innovations too. The type of thrust termination, was so innovatively configured that for a multiple payload, multiple range scan be achieved. Today, Prithvi is comparable to any world class missile system and probably it is one of the best, in payload capability.

11

A New Feather in the Cap

There was a minor controversy regarding Dr. Kalam's transfer from ISRO to DRDL. At last a decision was made at the highest level in the Ministry of Defence where R. Venkataraman was the Defence Minister and Dr. Arunachalam had replaced Dr. Ramanna.

Meanwhile, Anna University, Madras, conferred the honorary degree of Doctor of Science on him. It had been nearly twenty years since he had acquired his degree in aeronautical engineering. He was happy that Anna University had recognised his efforts in the field of rocketry, but what pleased him most was the recognition of the value of our work in academic circles. To his delight, the honorary doctorate degree was awarded at a convocation presided over by Prof. Raja Ramanna.

"I joined DRDL on 1 June 1982. Very soon, I realized that this laboratory was still haunted by the winding up of the *Devil* missile project. Many excellent professionals had not yet recovered from the disappointment.

I found almost all my senior colleagues living with the pain of dashed hopes. There was a widespread feeling that the scientists of this laboratory had been cheated by the senior officials in the Ministry of Defence. It was clear to me that the burial of the *Devil* was essential for the rise of hope and vision".

"Sometime in the beginning of 1983, Prof. Dhawan visited DRDL. I reminded him of his own advice given to me almost a decade ago. "You have to dream before your dreams can come true. Some people stride out towards whatever it is that they want in life; others shuffle their feet and never get started because they do not know what they want—and do not know how to find either." ISRO was lucky to have had Prof. Sarabhai and Prof. Dhawan at the helm—leaders who generated their goals, made their missions larger than their lives, and then could inspire their entire work-force. DRDL had not been so lucky. This excellent laboratory played out a crippling role that did not reflect its existing or potential capabilities or even fulfil the expectations in South Block".

"Days of debate and weeks of thinking finally culminated in the long-term 'Guided Missile Development Programme'. I had read somewhere, "Know where you are going. The great thing in the world is not, knowing so much where we stand, as in what direction we are moving towards." To draw up a clear and well-defined missile development programme for the production of indigenous missiles, a committee was constituted under my chairmanship. The members were Z.P. Marshall, then the Chief of Bharat Dynamics Limited, Hyderabad, N.R. Iyer, A.K. Kapoor and K.S. Venkataraman. We drafted a paper for the perusal of the Cabinet Committee for Political Affairs (CCPA). The paper was given its final shape after consulting the representatives of the three Defence Services. We estimated an expenditure of about Rs. 390 crores, spead over a period of twelve years".

"Development programmes often get stuck by the time they reach the production stage, mainly because of lack of funding. We wanted to get funds to develop and produce two missiles—a low-level quick reaction Tactical Core Vehicle and a Medium Range Surface-to-Surface Weapon System. We planned to make a surface-to-air medium range weapon system with multi-target handling capability during the second phase. DRDL had been known for its pioneering work in the field of anti-tank missiles. We proposed to develop a third generation anti-tank guided missile having 'fire-and-forget' capabilities. All my colleagues were pleased with the proposal. They saw an opportunity to pursue afresh activities initiated long ago. But I was not entirely satisfied. I longed to revive my buried dream of a Re-entry Experiment Launch Vehicle (REX). I persuaded my colleagues to take up a technology development project to generate data for use in the design of heat shields. These shields were required for building up capability to make long-range missiles in the future".

To get the scheme throgh, Dr. Kalam made a presentation in the South Block. It was presided over by the Defence Minister of the time R.Venkataraman, and attended by the three Service Chiefs: General Krishna Rao, Air Chief Marshal Dilbagh Singh and Admiral

Dawson. The Cabinet Secretary, Krishna Rao Sahib, Defence Secretary, S.M. Ghosh and Secretary, Expenditure, R. Ganapathy were present. Everyone seemed to have all sorts of doubts—about the feasibility and availability of required technological infrastructure, about the viability, the schedule and cost. Dr. Arunachalam stood by Kalam like a rock throughout the entire question-answer session. Members were skeptical and apprehensive of drift—which they felt was common among scientists.

"We spent the intervening time working on permutations and combinations. If they sanctioned only Rs. 100 crores, how would we allocate it? Suppose they gave us Rs. 200 crores, then what would we do? When we met the Defence Minister in the evening, I had a hunch we were going to get some funds at any rate. But when he suggested that we launch an integrated guided missile development programme, instead of making missiles in phases, we could not believe our ears.

We were quite dumbfounded by the Defence Minister's suggestion. After a long pause, Dr. Arunachalam replied, "We beg for time to rethink and return, Sir!" "You be back tomorrow morning please," the Defence Minister replied. I was reminded of Prof. Sarabhai's zeal and vision. That night, Dr. Arunachalam and I laboured together on reworking our plan.

We worked out some very important extensions and improvements in our proposal, taking all the variables, such as design, fabrication, system integration, qualification, experimental flights, evaluation, updating, user trials, productionisation, quality, reliability, and financial viability into account. We then integrated them into a single function of total accountability, in order to meet the needs of the country's armed forces with an indigenous endeavour. We worked out the concepts of design, development, production concurrency and proposed the participation of user and inspection agencies right from the drawing-board stage.

They met Defence Minister Venkataraman and showed him the revised proposal, he was visibly pleased. The proposal of missile development project had been turned overnight into the blueprint of an integrated programme with far-reaching consequences. It would have wide-ranging technological spinoffs, and was exactly what the Defence Minister had in mind the previous evening. Notwithstanding the great respect I had for the Defence Minister, I was not really sure if he would clear our entire proposal. But he did. I was absolutely delighted!

The Defence Minister stood up, signalling that the meeting was over. Turning to me he said, "Since I brought you here, I was expecting you to come up with something like this. I am happy to see your work." In a swift movement, the mystery surrounding the clearance of my appointment as Director DRDL in 1982 was cleared. So it was Defence Minister Venkataraman who had brought him in !

I have always regarded Dr. Arunachalam as a great conversationalist. He has imagination, knowledge and a sense of proportion together with a command over language as he displayed on this occasion, and, an uncanny presence of mind. I was overwhelmed when the Defence Minister located an Air Force helicopter doing sorties between Madras and Madurai later in the day to take me to Madurai as soon as I disembarked at Madras from the regular Indian Airlines flight, which was leaving Delhi in an hour's time. Dr. Arunachalam told me, "You have earned this for your hard work of the last six months".

The Air Force helicopter landed close to the Indian Airlines aircraft as soon as it arrived from Delhi. Within the next few minutes he was on way to Madurai. The Air Force commandant there was kind enough to take me to the railway station, where the train to Rameswaram was just about to roll out of the platform. He was in Rameswaram well in time for Zameela's wedding. He blessed his brother's daughter with a father's love.

The Defence Minister put up our proposal before the Cabinet and saw it through. His recommendations on our proposal were accepted and an unprecedented amount of Rs. 388 crores was sanctioned for this purpose. Thus was born India's prestigious Integrated Guided Missile Development Programme, later abbreviated to IGMDP.

When I presented the government sanction letter before the Missile Technology Committee at DRDL, it was enthused with fire and action. The proposed projects were christened in accordance with the spirit of India's self-reliance. Thus the Surface-to-Surface weapon system became *Prithvi* ("The Earth") and the Tactical Core Vehicle was called *Trishul* (the trident of Lord Shiva). The Surface-to - Air area defence system ws named as *Akash* ("Sky") and the anti-tank missile project *Nag* ("Cobra"). He gave the name *Agni* ("Fire") to his long cherished dream of REX. Dr Arunachalam cam to DRDL and formally launched the IGMDP on 27 July 1983. It was a great event in which every single employee of DRDL participated. Everybody who was somebody in Indian Aerospace Research was invited. A large number of scientists from other laboratories and organisations, professors from academic institutions, representatives of the armed forces, production centres, and inspection authorities, who were our business partners now, were present on this occasion. A closed-circuit TV network had to be pressed into operation to ensure proper communication between the participants for them had no single place to accommodate all the invitees. This was the second most significant day in his career, next only to 18 July 1980, when the SLV-3 had launched Rohini into the earth's orbit.

Wiping Tears

Kalam-Raju Stent

India's first totally indigenous Coronary Stent has been developed by Indian Defence scientists. STents are widely used by cardiologists as a scaffolding device to Dilate constricted arteries for preventing heart attacks. Dr. B. Soma Raju, an eminent cardiologist from Hyderabad, along with scientists from three Defence Labs at Hyderabad developed the "Kalam-Raju Stent" under the aegis of the Society for Bio-Medical Technology (SBMT), under the leadership of the father of the Indian Missile Programme Dr. A.P.J. Abdul Kalam. While an imported stent would cost around Rs. 60,000 its Indian equivalent would be around Rs. 25,000 and projected requirement for the stents is in the order of one million. Apart from saving substantial foreign exchnge, the achievement is expected to bring down the cost advent of coronary stent had almost obviated the need for emergency by-pass surgeries following angioplasty in patients with constricted heart vessels. After clinical evaluation, SBMT proposes to transfer the know-how of Kalam-Raju Stent to a private medical product manufacturing company with a condition that the cost should be affordable. Currently there are seven to eight brands of International stents available and the 'Kalam-Raju Stent' is comparable to the best.

An external cardiac pacemaker for patients suffering from bradycardia (prevalent mainly in mal-nutritioned population). This life saving device need to be available in all Primary Health Care (PHC) centres but its high cost restricts its availability to certain city based hospitals. An Nd-YAG laser for ophthalmic applications for carrying out glucoma treatment and treating cataract. A Web of Life is being created to establish clinical connectivity between remote villages and specialty hospitals in cities thereby making healthcare accessible to all. This will empower local General Practitioners with the benefit of advanced medical know. It will also help in curving distribution of spurious drugs by enabling producer to pre-seribes supplies. An intra-coronary stent which act as a scaffold and helps in reinforcing proper blood flow through artieries narrowed due to atherosclerosis. Due to the high cost of stent its application was restricted to afflment patients. The development of indigenous stent brought down the cost of product by more than 50 per cent and its application has increased three-fold in the first year itsself. The imported expensive stent were prohibiting people, who otherwise when affected by heart problems, they left themselves to fate. The low cost of the indigenous stent could be affordable even for middle class people. Mobile Treatment Units (MTUs) are being developed to tackle life threatening emergency situations integrating the best of environmental engineering, medical equipment and clinical skills. This will take modern healthcare to the doorstep of a common man. These were some of the initiatives taken to see how one can extend the sphere of work. The Almighty has given us power to think and by our thought we create and develop so many products, and by extending the thought a little further there may be new ideas for new applications. It should be our endeavour to see by our work how we could mitigate other's sorrow. It was of immense joy and satisfaction when the indigenous technology made our SLV, Agni and Prithvi took off to great heights, and equally such a joy and satisfaction I could feel when our technologies go in to medical devices and help our people. That be as leg support or protect the heart ! You may also try in your own way how can you wipe the tears of others. Technology is for wiping tears also.

Rockets and missiles are there only for deterring enemy not to harm our country? Technology is universal by nature . The technology that goes into making missiles can also help a polio affected child as real by leg support. The light metal used in missiles help to lift off bearing so much heat, the same light metal helps the polio affected child to work and play like a butterfly. They are spin off from the Defence, Nuclear and Space technologies from which solutions for cost effective medical devices could be developed. Why our people should be forced to buy expensive foreign products during his distress with diseases? Can our indigenous technology provide a solution to common man shielding him from the threat of financial disaster in saving life in an emergency health situation? The answer to such questions led to the adaptation of indigenous technologies from all sectors into creation of an organisation called Society for Biomedical Technology (SBMT). It was created in 1993 bringing together various Engineers and Doctors to work in financially crippled patients with their healthcare problems. The efforts of inter-disciplinary teams cutting across organisational boundaries have fructified in the form of a light weight limb support for polio affected patients called Floor Reaction Orthosis (FRO). The application of ultra-strong fiber reinforced plastic used to make missile nose cones led to the replacement of a 4 kg.conventional caliper into a 400 g FRO. The exquisite material and elegant design made polio affected children ride bicycles, put on usual school uniforms including socks and shoes. When this was tried on with the first child the joy of the child, was inexpressible as the weight from 4000 g FRO to 400 g really made her to feel like a butterfly.

This evening's award function is an important event in my life. I feel honoured to receive the 'Ramanujar Award' given by the Alwars Research Centre. This award was given for my scientific or technological achievements but for inducing my spiritual growth. That is why I consider this award as a special award named after the great spiritual leader 'Acharya Ramanujar'. Spirituality is the door to be opened by everyone in order to attain happiness and prosperity in life. I congratulate the Alwars Research Centre for making people attain a spiritual goal. And also, I am thankful to them for considering me worthy for this great award. I feel very happy to receive the award from the great Tamil scholar Dr. Karunanithi.

Journey Boat and the Power of Prayer

There are two incidents in my life, which I wish to narrate. I joined the Defence Research and Development Organisation in 1964, as a technical assistant. I earned my first salary of Rs. 250. I wanted to go to my home in Rameswaram to give my first earning to my mother and father. I changed so many buses from Bangalore and reached Mandapam. I travelled by train through the only bridge called 'Pamban Bridge' which connected Mandapam and Rameswaram island. There was a heavy downpour mixed with frightening thunder and lightning at Mandapam. I still remember the sea waves hitting the train. It was very doubtful for everyone in the train that it could go ahead or not. After 8 hours delay, the Rameswaram-Dhanuskodi mail crossed through the 'Pamban bridge, at snail's speed. I got down at Pamban and changed to another train and finally reached Rameswaram. My eldest brother came to receive me at the railway station. The whole town Rameswaram submerged in water and looked like a river, flowing and mixing with the sea. We could reach home in 90 minutes which otherwise would take only 10 minutes. I cannot forget that night. The horrible cyclone hit Rameswaram town so badly the roof tops and the thatched leaves could not bear the harsh cyclone and were flown away. Our house instantly became roofless. We were frightened to hear the hissing sound of the air throughout the night. The cyclone was over by next day morning. We found our open house without any roof. My parents finished their namaz in the water filled, roofless room. We just then heard the sorrow news from our island friends. The boat, which was built by my father, was broken into pieces and washed away by the waves. The boat was the only source of livelihood for our family. My father used to take pilgrims in his passenger boat from Rameswaram to Dhanuskodi. The income from the boat only helped our family to survive. That was the only family property, which gave us means to grow up and also helped to get education, had just vanished. Some of you might remember that the same cyclone, also washed away the 'Pamban bridge' and a train on that dreadful night at that sorrowful moment, my father and mother uttered two words 'Insha Allah, Insha Allah' and again immersed themselves in prayer. We could feel the divine power spreading throughout our home and saved our family. The power of prayer was felt by everyone that gave us courage to stand and encounter the problems at that point of time and for ever in future. This experience in my life taught true reality lay beyond the material world, in the spiritual realm, and divine knowledge could be obtained only through such inner experience. As Thiruvalluvar says, such spiritual learning would give 'problems to the problem itself' and drives them away. This is what I learnt, experienced and inherited from my parents. I consider, spiritual life with hard work, gives us true meaning to life. After that cyclone, there were many successes and a few failures in my 40 years of work as a scientist, but I always remembered the Rameswaram cyclone, which gave me and my family enough mental strength to swim through peacefully.

Our Life and Culture

The second incident was a happy and divine one. I have a friend called Mr. Lakshmi Tathachar, who is the Director of Sanskrit Research Centre, Melukote in Karnataka. He is an expert in Tamil and Sanskrit. I have an interest in the Panini grammar, based on that, some research is being done at the Sanskrit Research Centre. He invited me to Melukote, where 'Acharya Ramanujar' walked a thousand years ago. I got an opportunity to go to Melukote on 26 th July.

I felt strange sensation of happiness filling in me as soon as I reached Melukote. As I remembered that this was the same place where Ramanujar walked and showed the spiritual path to the world. While walking, I felt a divine satisfaction filling in me. I saw Tathachar's research centre, his beautiful garen and the famous Sri Narayanar temple in Melukote. I found there is a link between history and the spirituality as that temple, a historical place, tells the story that happened a millennium ago.

After seeing the temple, Tathachar took me to his enchanting garden. I can not forget the scenic beauty and the happiness on seeing it. I saw greenery wherever I turned, with a lot of flowers, trees, herbal plants, vegetables and fruits. There were amazing varieties of flowers with so different colours. The combined nice smell of flowers, the honey bees circling the flowers, bewitching butterflies, singing birds, dancing peacoks, merrily jumping deers and a pond full of anxious fishes popped up on top of water level to see Tathachar and his guests ! All these scenic beauty gave me great happiness. What a wonderful scene! Amidst such wonderful scene, saints from the Sanskrit Research Centre were chanting mantras on 'Purusha Shuktham'. I wondered whether 'was this called a divine paradise'? There was an obvious divine satisfaction at that place where the Almighty and Nature mingle with each other. I saw the vegetables, fruits and flowers were all the result of hard labour and sweat. All plants were grown using natural manure and I soon realised that the hard work and the sweat only bloomed as beautiful flowers and spread the scent everywhere. When the spirituality is mingled with hard work, there we can certainly see such a paradise on earth.

Later I was taken to his library. I spent an hour seeing the old manuscripts on palm leaves, carefully preserved for over thousand years. I had an opportunity to see the rare collections of books both old and new in the same library. I was amazed to see Tathachar using his laptop computer, sitting on rock in a typical 'Kurukal' atmosphere explaining the results of the research on the computer. This is an indication to our generation to preserve our culture and tradition and at the same time to be modern in thoughts and attitude. Our Indian culture keep on growing and refining. While the essence of our culture and tradition is retained, the way of life of modern and future times are adopted. Even after reaching Delhi, the imprints of Melukote did not leave from my heart.

The Divine Light of Melukote

Ramanujar preached a philosophy for the whole mankind. He said everyone should live amicably and not to find any difference with each other. I heard the philosophy reverberating in my ears while at Melukote. I also heard through the saints of Melukote, the incident that happened in Ramanujar's life. Ramanujar was initiated by his Guru with the mantra which would take him to attain the 'Moksha' , but he wanted every one to attain 'Moksha' and unrevealed the same to everyone.

The wonderful scenes I saw at Melukote was also depicted as a song in 'Andal's Thirppavai'. Andal was the only woman among the Alwars, lived much before Ramanujar.

"Let us all sing in praise of the lord who measured this world

With love and affection we bathed the lord in pure water Blessed to have rain thrice every month, our sins washed out

Well grown paddy bore the finest grain,

Fishes jump out, while honey bee slept on lotus flower

Let us all be prosperous and praise the Lord. As depicted about the divine power in the song, I also realised in the temple of Sri Narayanar temple at Melukote, an echo of Ramanujar calling the deity 'my little daughter come', then the deity started walking towards Ramanujar!

Ale Who Looking Beyond

Bread baked without love is a bitter bread that feeds but half a man's hunger, "-those who cannot work with their hearts achieve but a hollow, half-hearted success that breeds bitterness all around Khalil Gibran. All reasonable men adapt themselves to the world; only a few unreasonable ones persist in trying to adapt the world to themselves. All progress in the world depends on these unreasonable men and their innovative and often non-conformist actions.

George Bernard Shaw

I had a rare privilege of working with three great scientific thinkers and fantastic human beings..... Prof. Vikram Sarabhai, founder of space technology in India and a visionary; Prof. Satish Dhawan, former Chairman, ISRO, who gave to the country multiple missions like satellite communication and remote sensing and is a great thinker and teacher; and Prof. Brahm Prakash, Former Director of VSSC and the father of nuclear material in India, who in the later years shaped launch vehicle technology. They were responsible for unifying multiple technologies with management and lead successfully satellite and launch vehicle programmes. Above all they provided many scientific and technological leaders to the country. We all also learnt from these great three, management with nobility. They created together a reliable and efficient leadership in multiple field of science, technology and management. Dr. Kalam

Space Voyager

To the generation now in their 50s Vikram Sarabhai was the father of our space programme. He was the man who not only developed and launched rockets, but who was passionately committed to use all aspects of science and technology in general and space applications in particular as "levers of development". This was particularly the case with regard to satellite-based remote sensing of natural resources, telecommunication and direct-to-village community "Development TV". Sarabhai was much more than a highly talented scientist. He was a dreamer, creator and innovator, not only in science and technology, or in its organization and management but also in a huge range of developmental institutions ranging from the Space Science & Technology Centre, Trivandrum, to the Indian Institute of Management, Ahmedabad, and the Nehru Foundation for Development. I first met Vikrambhai in 1967 on one of his frequent visits to the Boston-Cambridge area in the US to pursue collaborative project with MIT. He told me he had taken over as chairman, Atomic Energy Commission, and was looking for a special assistant. Would I be interested? I Jumped at the offer. Over the next three years I assisted him on a host of policy and management issues relating to atomic energy, space and electronics. Vikrambhai has often been typified as a dove on nuclear weapons and missiles. This was not true. As far back as 1956, at a meeting of the governing body of the Coucil of Scientific and Industrial

Research of which he was a member, he had called for the country to start R&D on "rockets and missiles". In the area of atomic energy he mounted programmes for capability and capacity building all across the chain from the mining of uranium ore at the Jaduguda mines in Bihar to the building of atomic power stations. He was disillusioned with the Non-proliferation Treaty well before the government decided in 1968 not to sign it, and strove hard to make our atomic programme self-sufficient. Sarabhai had very definite views about the kind of role which scientists could and should play in building an independent and modern India. In a broadcast over AIR on August 4, 1965 he spoke of three goals. First, to foster creativity, an interest in getting to the core of problems and dedication to what one may call the "scientific method". Second, to provide experience on a wide scale whereby man can evolve values and ethics consistent with the real constraints imposed by his environment. Third, to apply their skills and knowledge to the diverse practical tasks of society like building of the economy, creating of a desirable social environment of policymaking in the areas of defence, development and social change.

However, Vikrambhai was eqully forthright about the reciprocal responsibility of society towards scientists. As he put it, "We look down on our research scientists in national laboratories or our academics in universities if they engage themselves in outside consultation or if they choose to augment their income from task-oriented projects of a practical nature. We implicitly promote the ivory tower, the alienation of the persons of insight from those who do thing." Sarebhai advocated a more dicisive role for scientists in the promotion and application of science and technology to contribute to the attainment of socio-economic goals set by planners. indeed, he called for and worked for scientists and technologists to be heavily involved in the policy and management aspects of science and technology intensive areas of national endeavour, other than science and technology in a narrow sense. For instance he felt scientists and engineers, rather than judges, should be roped in to solve inter-state river water disputes. A similar proposal of his was the marshalling of resources to design an integrated development programme for the Brahmaputra-Ganga river system and to make this the basis of a new relationship between India and the then East Pakistan. He also gave us tools and techniques and above all a philosophy for organizing and managing scientific institutions. To him these were not just the R&D agencies of atomic energy, space, electronics, CSIR, etc, but all organizations in which science and technology was involved. His testament was the document entitled "Approaches to the Administration of Scientific Organizations". This document should be a primer not only for every R&D and science and technology manager but all civil servants. So far it has been Vikrambhai, the scientist, R&D manager, science and technology policymaker and planner. But he was a Renaissance man with interests in music, painting and architecture. He was a great creator—of motivated people, of institutions and programmes. He was a scion of a wealthy business family but never let a peon carry his briefcase. "It is against my principles," he used to say. "We have to be constantly alert to see that long-inherited feudal reflexes do not seep back into our veins." That would be the greatest travesty of the new India.

12
Need for Dedicated Leadership

At this point of time, several countries of the world were waiting to see how far India could go in the direction of Missile Technology. The magnitude of the IGMDP was really unprecedented in the country and the schedules projected were quite quixotic by the norms and standards prevailing in the Indian R&D establishments. Dr. Kalam was fully aware that obtaining sanction for the programme could at best be seen as only ten per cent of the work done. To get it going with success would be quite a different matter altogether. The more you have, the more you have to maintain. Now that they had been given all the necessary money and freedom to proceed. He had to take my team forward and live up to the promise he had made.

That manpower was available; money has been sanctioned; and some infrastructure was also there. What was lacking then? What else does a project need to succeed apart from these three vital inputs? The crux was going to be the mastery over missile technology by our establishments in the country.

As a dedicated scientist, Dr. Kalam expected nothing from abroad. Technology being a group activity, we would need leaders who could not only put their heart and soul into the missiles programme, but also carry along with them hundreds of other engineers and scientists. We knew we had to be prepared to encounter numerous contradictions and procedural absurdities that were prevalent in the participating laboratories. We would have to counteract the existing attitudes of our public sector units which believed that their performance would never be tested against solid reality. The whole system—its people, procedures, infrastructure—would have to learn to extend itself. We decided to achieve something that was way beyond our collective national capability and I had no illusions about the fact that unless our teams worked on the basis of proportion or probability, nothing was going to be achieved.

"The most remarkable thing about DRDL, was its large pool of highly talented people, many of whom were, unfortunately, full of egotism and rebelliousness. Unfortunately, there was not even enough accumulated experience with them to make them confident about their own judgement. On the whole, they would discuss matters very enthusiastically, but would finally accept what a few said. They would unquestioningly believe in the knowledge and powers of outside specialists."

In this context, Dr. Kalam managed him to seek the able services of A.V. Ranga Rao, an experienced scientist in his establishment—an avoidable inconvenience. With his thick white beard and a pipe clutched between his teeth, there was a certain aura around this extremely gifted, but slightly egocentric individual.

He consulted Ranga Rao on revamping the existing management system to achieve an optimum utilization of human resources. Ranga Rao had a series of meetings with scientists sharing their vision of developing indigenous missile technology and explaining to them the different aspects of the IGMDP. In less than four months, literally four hundred scientists began to work on the missile programme.

During this period, the most important task before Dr. Kalam was the selection of the Project Directors who would lead individual missile projects. There were several talented persons. In this regard. I had a detailed discussion with a large number of prospective scientists and engineers. He wanted five Project Directors to train another twenty-five Project Directors and team leaders of tomorrow. Many of his senior colleagues tried to establish friendships with during this period. He respected their concern for a lonely man, but avoided any close contacts. Through loyalty to a friend one could be easily led into doing the wrong things, something that was not in the best interest of the organisation.

Perhaps the main motive behind my living in isolation was my desire to escape from the pain of loving, which I consider very difficult in comparison to making rockets. All I desired was to be true to my way of life, to uphold the science of rocketry in my country and to leave with my head held high and with a clean conscience. I took quite some time and did a lot of hard thinking to decide who should lead the five projects. I examined the working styles of many scientists before making my decision. I think some of my observations will interest you." Dr. Kalam believed firmly.

A basic aspect of a person's working style is how he plans and organises tasks. At one extreme is the cautious planner, who carefully spells out each step before making any move. With a sharp eye for what can possibly go wrong, he tries to cover all contingencies. At the other end is the fast mover, who weaves and dodges without a plan. Inspired by an idea, the fast mover is ever ready to take action.

His search for someone to lead the *Prithvi* project ended with Col Sundaram who had deep connections with EME Corps of the Indian Army. With a post-graduate degree in Aeronautical Engineering and expertise in mechanical vibrations, Sundaram was head of the Structures Group at DRDL. He found in him a readiness to experiment with new ways of resolving conflicting points of view. He was an experimenter and innovator in team work. He had an extraordinary capability for evaluating alternative ways of operating.

For *Trishul,* he was looking for a man who not only had a sound knowledge of electronics and missile warfare, but who could also communicate the complexities to his team in order to promote understanding and to earn his team's support. He found in Cmde SR Mohan, from the Indian Navy, a talent for detail and magical power of persuasion.

For *Agni,* my dream project he needed somebody who would tolerate his occasional meddling in the running of this project. In RN Agarwal he found the right blend. He was an alumnus of MIT with a brilliant academic record and had been managing the Aeronautical Test Facilities at DRDL with keen professional acumen.

Due to technological complexities, *Akash* and *Nag* were then considered missiles of the future; their activities were expected to peak about half a decade later. Therefore, I selected the relatively young Prahlada and NR Iyer for *Akash* and *Nag* respectively. Two other young men, VK Saraswat and AK Kapoor were made deputies to Sundaram and Mohan respectively.

In those days, there was no forum in DRDL where issues of general importance could be openly discussed and decisions debated. Scientists, it must be remembered, are also basically emotional people. Once they stumble, it is difficult for them to pull themselves together. Setbacks and disappointments have always been and always will be an inherent part of any career, even one in science. However, I did not want any of my scientists to face disappointments that made them take any irreversible, negative decisions. To avoid such eventualities a Science Council was created—a sort of *panchayat* where the community would sit together and take common decisions. Every three months, all scientists—juniors and seniors, veterans and freshers—would sit together and let off steam.

"The very first meeting of the Council was eventful. After a spell of half-hearted enquires and expressions of doubt, one senior scientist, MN Rao, shot a straight question: "On what basis did you select these five Pandavas (he meant the Project Directors)?" I was, in fact, expecting this question. I wanted to tell him that I found all these five Pandavas married to the Draupadi of positive thinking. Instead, I told Rao to believe in the future. I had not selected these Project Directors to merely perform today, I had picked them to take charge of a long-term programme where new storms would arise everyday".

"Every tomorrow, I told Rao, will give opportunities to these enthusiastic people—the Agarwals, Prahladas, Iyers, and Saraswats—to gain a fresh grip over their goals and get a strong hold on their commitments".

Dr. Kalam gave a very five definition of a leader. In my opinion, a productive leader must be very competent in staffing. The leader should continually introduce new blood into the organisation. He must be competent in handling complexities and problems and in dealing with new concepts. Skill in handling these complex entities is an important asset for achieving high productivity. The leader must be capable of instilling enthusiasm in his team.

"We drew up a proposal to establish a model high technology research centre with very advanced technical facilities like an inertial instrumentation laboratory, full-scale environmental and electronic warfare (EMI/EMC) test facilities, a composites production centre, high enthalpy facility, and a state-of-the-art missile integration and checkout centre. By any standards, this was a gigantic task. An altogether different brand of expertise, grit and determination were required to realise this project. Goals and objectives had already been created here. Now they had to be understood and shared with a large number of people from various agencies, through the problem-solving and communication processes that the leader of the team must build up and maintain. Who would be the most suitable person to do so? I saw almost all the required leadership qualities in MV

Suryakantha Rao. Then, as a large number of agencies would participate in the creation of RCI, someone had to protect hierarchical delicacies. I selected Krishna Mohan, who was in his mid-thirties, to complement Suryakantha Rao, who was in his late fifties at that time. Krishna Mohan would encourage involvement rather than relying on obedience and patrol of people at their work locations."

Now Col SK Salwan joined the team. A mechanical engineer, he brought with him abundant energy, working like a faceless soldier in a winning troop. In the final phase of construction, with SHAR also in Andhra Pradesh, the search for a suitable site spread towards the eastern coastline and finally terminated at Balasore in Orissa. A site along the north-eastern coast was identified for a National Test Range. Unfortunately the entire project ran into rough weather because of the political issues raise around the evacuation of people living in that area. We decided therefore to create an interim infrastructure adjacent to the Proof Experimental Establishment (PXE) at Chandipur in Balasore District of Orissa. A funding of Rs 30 crores had been made to construct the range, called the Interim Test Range (ITR). Dr HS Rama Rao and his team did an excellent job of working out innovative and cost-effective specifications for electro-optical tracking instruments, a tracking telescope system and an instrumentation tracking radar. Lt Gen RS Deswal and Maj Gen KN Singh took charge of creating the launch pad and range infrastructure. Defence Minister R Venkataraman visited DRDL in September 1983 to appraise himself of the activities of IGMDP. He advised us to list all the resources we needed to achieve our goals, overlooking nothing, and then include in the list our own positive imagination and faith. "What you imagine, is what will transpire. What you believe is what you will achieve," he said. Both Dr Arunachalam and I saw a horizon of endless possibilities stretching before IGMDP; and our enthusiasm proved infectious. We were excited and encouraged to see the best professionals in the country getting attracted towards IGMDP. Who would not want to associate with a winner? The word got around that the IGMDP had been born to succeed.

Dr. A.P.J. Abdul Kalam, the father of India's integrated guided missile program, states three visions for India based on the achievements and progress that he has witnessed in the history of the nation and during his own career as a missile scientist. Dr. Kalam's three visions for India are FREEDOM, DEVELOPMENT, and STAND

UP. The focus of his presentation is on developing India its fullest potential, while standing up to the rest of the world with fully validated self-respect for the achievements that have been obtained in the modern time.

If we are not free, no one will respect us

I have three visions for India. In 3,000 years of our history, people from all over the world have come and invaded us, captured our land, and conquered our minds. From Alexander onwards, the Greeks, the Portuguese, the British, the French, the Dutch—all of them came and looted us and took over what was ours. Yet we have not done this to any other nation. We have not conquered anyone. We have not grabbed their land, their culture, and their history, nor tried to force our way of life on them, Why? Because we respect the freedom of others.

That is why my first vision for India is FREEDOM. I believe that India and its first vision of freedom in 1857, when we started the War of Independence. It is this freedom that we must protect and nurture and build on. If we are not free, no one will respect us.

My second vision for India is Development. For 50 years, we have been a developing nation. It is time to see ourselves as a developed nation. We are among the top five nations of the world in terms of gross domestic product (GDP); we have 10 per cent growth rate in most areas.

Our poverty levels are falling, and our achievements are being globally recognized today. Yet we lack the self-confidence to see ourselves as a developed nation-self-reliant and self-assured. Isn't this right? I have a third vision, that India must STAND UP to the world, because I believe that unless India stands up to the world, no one will respect us. Only strength respects strength. We must be strong not only as a military power, but also as an economic power—both must go hand-in-hand.

India Must Stand-up to the World

My good fortune has been to work with three great minds: Dr. Vikram Sarabhai of the Department of Space, Professor Satish Dhawan, who succeeded him, and Dr. Brahm Prakash, father of nuclear material. I was lucky to have worked with all three of them closely, and consider this the great opportunity of my life.

I see four milestones in my career. One is the 20 years I spent in ISRO. I was given the opportunity to be the Project Director for

India's first satellite launch vehicle, SLV-3, the one that launched Rohini. These years played a very important role in my life as a scientist. Two: After my ISRO years I joined DRDO and got a chance to be part of India's guided missile program. It was my second bliss when Agni met its mission requirements in 1994.

Three: The Department of Atomic Energy and DRDO had this tremendous partnership in the recent nuclear tests, on May 11 and 13, 1998. This was the third bliss, the joy of participating with my team in these nuclear tests and proving to the world that India can make it, that we are no longer a developing nation but one of them. It made me feel very proud as an Indian the fact that we have now developed for Agni a re-entry structure for which we have developed this new material, a very light material called carbon-carbon.

Why is the Media here so Negative?

One day an orthopaedic surgeon from Nizam Institute of Medical Sciences visited my laboratory. He lifted the material and found it so light that he took me to his hospital and showed me his patients. There were these little girls and boys with heavy metallic callipers weighing over 3 kg each, dragging their feet around. He said to me, "Please remove the pain of my patients. "In three weeks we made these floor reaction Orthosis 300 g callipers and took them to the orthopaedic centre. The children didn't believe their eyes—from dragging around a 3 kg load on their legs, they could now move around. Their parents had tears in their eyes—that was fourth bliss.

Why is the media here so negative? Why are we in India so embarrassed to recognize our own strengths, our achievements? We are such a great nation. We have so many amazing success stories but we refuse to acknowledge them. Why? We are the second largest producer of wheat in the world. We are the second largest producer of rice. We are the first in milk production. We are number one in remote sensing satellites. Look at Dr. Sudarshan, he has transformed the tribal village into a self-sustaining, self driving unit. There are millions of such achievements, but our media is obsessed only with bad news and failures and disasters.

13

Patronage of Prime Ministers

After several sessions, they decided to improvise a *Devil* missile to test the system. A *Devil* missile was disassembled, many modifications made, extensive subsystem testing was done and the missile check-out system was reconfigured. After installing a make-shift launcher, the modified role and extended range *Devil* missile was fired on 26 June 1984 to flight test the first indigenous Strap down-Inertial Guidance system. The system met all the requirements. This was the first and very significant step in the history of Indian missile development, which had so far been restricted to reverse engineering, towards designing our own systems. A long-denied opportunity was at last utilized by missile scientists at DRDL. The message was loud and clear for everyone to hear. We could do it! It did not take long for the message to reach Delhi. Prime Minister Indira Gandhi expressed her desire to personally apprise herself of the progress of the IGMDP. We were charged with enthusiasm. Everyone wanted to do his best. The entire organisation was filled with an aura of excitement. On 19 July 1984, Shrimati Gandhi visited DRDL. She was a person with a tremendous sense of confidence—in herself, in her work and in her country. I felt it was an honour to receive her at DRDL as she had instilled some of the own pride into my otherwise modest frame of mind. She was immensely conscious that she was the leader of eight hundred million people. Every step, every gesture, every movement of her hands was made to look its best. The esteem in which she held our work in the field of guided missiles served immensely to boost our morale.

During the one hour that she spent at DRDL, she covered wide-ranging aspects of the IGMDP, from flight system plans to multiple development laboratories. In the end, she addressed the 2000-strong DRDL community. She asked for the schedules for the flight system that we were working on. " When are you going to flight test *Prithvi*?" Shrimati Gandhi asked. I said, "June 1987." She immediately responded, "Let me know what is needed to accelerate the flight schedule?" She wanted scientific and technological results fast. "Your fast pace of work is the hope of the entire nation," she said. She also told me that the IGMDP should be not only on schedule but also in pursuance of excellence. "No matter what you achieve, you should never be completely satisfied and should always be searching for ways to prove yourself," she added. Within a month, she demonstrated her interest and support by sending the newly appointed Defence Minister, SB Chavan, to review our projects. Shrimati Gandhi's follow-up approach was not only impressive, it was effective too. Today, everyone associated with aerospace research in our country knows that excellence is synonymous with the IGMDP.

Dr. Kalam's meeting with T.N. Seshan was very interesting, TN Seshan was on the review board. Between SLV-3 and now, we had developed a mutual fondness. However, this time as the Defence Secretary, Seshan's queries about the schedules and viability of financial propositions presented were much more pointed. Seshan is a person who enjoys using communication to bring adversaries to their knees employing sharp-edged humour. Although he is prone to be loud and can turn argumentative on occasions, in the end he would always ensure maximization of all available resources towards a solution that was within implementation.

The team was particularly pleased to answer his questions about the advanced technology employed in the IGMDP. I still remember his uncanny curiosity about the indigenous development of carbon-carbon composites. And to let you into a small secret—Seshan is perhaps the only person in the world who enjoys calling me by my full name which contains 31 letters and five words—Avul Pakir Jainulabdeen Abdul Kalam.

"The missile programme had been pursued concurrently in and had partners in design, development and production from 12 academic institutions and 30 laboratories from DRDO, the Council of Scientific and Industrial Research (CSIR), ISRO and industry. In fact, more than 50 professors and 100 research scholars worked on missile-related problems in the laboratories of their respective institutes. The quality of work achieved through this partnership in that one year had given me a tremendous confidence that any development task could be undertaken within the country so long as we could have our schedules focused. Four months before this review, I think it was during April—June 1984, six of us in the missile programme visited academic campuses and enlisted promising young graduates. We presented an outline of the missile programme before the professors and the aspiring students, about 350 of them, and requested them to participate. I informed the reviewers that we were expecting around 300 young engineers to join our laboratories."

Shrimati Gandhi's death was a tremendous loss to the scientific community. She had given impetus to scientific research in the country. But India is a very resilient nation. It gradually absorbed the shock of Shrimati Gandhi's assassination. Her son, Rajiv Gandhi, took over as the new Prime Minister of India. He went to the polls and obtained a mandate from the people to carry forward the policies of Mrs. Gandhi, the Integrated Guided Missile Development Programme being a part of them. By the summer of 1985, all the groundwork had been completed for building the Missile Technology Research Centre at Imarat Kancha. Prime Minister Rajiv Gandhi laid the foundation stone of the Research Centre Imarat (RCI) on 3 August 1985. He appeared very pleased with the progress made. There was a child-like curiosity in him which was very engaging. The grit and determination displayed by his mother when she visited us a year ago was also present in him, although with a small difference.

Madam Gandhi's personality was that of a taskmaster, whereas Prime Minister Rajiv Gandhi had a charisma which could charm anybody into accomplishing the results. He told the DRDL family that he realised the hardships being faced by Indian scientists and expressed his gratitude towards those who preferred to stay back and work in their motherland rather than go abroad for comfortable careers. He said that nobody could concentrate on work of this type unless he was free from the trivialities of daily life, and assured us that whatever could be done would be done to make a scientist's life more comfortable.

Within a week of his visit Dr. Kalam left for the USA with Dr Arunachalam on an invitation from the United States Air Force. Roddam Narasimha of National Aeronautical Laboratory and KK Ganapathy of HAL accompanied us. After finishing their work at the Pentagon in Washington, they landed in San Francisco on their way to Los Angeles to visit Northrop Corporation. He utilized this opportunity to visit the Crystal Cathedral built by his favourite author, Robert Schuller. He was amazed by the sheer beauty of this all-glass, four-pointed star-shaped structure that is more than 400 feet from one point to another. The glass roof which is 100 feet longer than a football field seemed to float in space. This Cathedral has been built at the cost of several million dollars through donations organised by Schuller. "God can do tremendous things through the person who doesn't care about who gets the credit. The ego involvement must go," writes Schuller. "Before God trusts you with success, you have to prove yourself humble enough to handle the big prize." He prayed to God in Schuller's church to help me build a Research Centre at the Imarat Kancha—that was to be his Crystal Cathedral.

Interview with APJ Abdul Kalam

I have three visions for India. In 3000 years of our history, people from all over the world have come and invaded us, captured our lands, conquered our minds. From Alexander onwards the Greeks, the Portuguese, the British, the French, the Dutch, all of them came and looted us, took over what was ours. Yet we have not done this to any other nation. We have not conquered anyone. We have not grabbed their land, their culture, their history and tried to enforce our way of life on them. Why? Because we respect the freedom of others. That is why my first vision is that of Freedom. I believe that India got its first vision of this in 1857, when we started the war of independence. It is this freedom that we must protect and nurture and built on. If we are not free, no one will respect us. My second vision for India is Development. For fifty years we have been developing nation. It is time we see ourselves as a developed nation. We are among top 5 nations of the world in terms of GDP. We have 10 per cent growth rate in most areas. Our poverty levels are falling, our achievements are being globally recognized today. Yet we lack the self-confidence to see ourselves as a developed nation, self reliant and self assured. Isn't this right? I have third vision. The India must stand up to the world. Because I believe that unless India stands up to the world, no one will respect us. Only strength respects strength. We must be strong not only as a military power but also as an economist power. Both must go hand-in-hand. My good fortune was to have work with three great minds. Dr. Vikram Sarabhai of the Deptartment of Space, Professor Satish Dhawan, who succeeded him, and Dr. Brahm Prakash, father of nuclear material. I was lucky to have worked with all three of them closely and consider this the great opportunity of my life. I see four milestones in my career:

(1) Twenty years I spent in ISRO. I was given the opportunity to be the project director for India's first satellite launch vehicle, SLV-3. The one that launched Rohini. These years played a very important role in my llfe of scientist.

(2) After my ISRO years, I joined DRDO and got a chance to be the part of India's guided missile programme. It was my second bliss when Agni met its mission requirements in 1994.

(3) The Deptartment of Atomic Energy and DRDO has this tremendous partnership in the recent nuclear tests, on May 11 and 13.

This was the third bliss. The joy of participating with my team in these nuclear tests and proving to the world that India can make it. That we are no longer a developing nation but one of them. It made me feel very proud as an Indian. The fact that we have now developed for Agni a re-entry structure, for which we have developed this new material. A very light material called carbon-carbon. One day an orthopedic surgeons from Nizam Institute of Medical Sciences visited my laboratory. He lifted the material and found it so light that he took me to his hospital and showed me his patients. There were these little girls and boys with heavy metallic callipers weighing over three Kgs. each, dragging their feet around. He said to me: Please remove the pain of my patients. In three weeks, we made these Floor reaction Orthosis 300 gram calipers and took them to the orthopedic centre. The children didn't believe their eyes from dragging around a three kg. load on their legs, they could now move around: Their parents had tears in their eyes. That was my fourth bliss! Why is the media here so negative? Why are we in India so embarrassed to recognise our own strengths, our achievements? We are such a great nation. We have so many amazing success stories but we refuse to acknowledge them. Why? We are the second largest producer of wheat in the world. We are the second largest producer in rice. We are the first in milk production. We are number one in Remote Sensing Satellites. Look at Dr. Sudarshan, he has transformed the tribal village into a self-sustaining, self driving unit. There are millions of such achievements but our media is only obsessed with the bad news and failures and disasters. I was in Tel Aviv once and I was reading the Israeli newspaper. It was the day after a lot of attacks and bombardments and deaths had taken place. The Hamas had struck. But the front page of the newspaper had the picture of a Jewish gentlemen who in five years had transformed his desert land also an orchid and a granary. It was this inspiring picture that everyone woke up to. The gory details of killings, bombardments, deaths, were inside in the newspaper, buried among other news. In India we only read about death, sickness, terrorism, and crime. Why are we so negative? Another question : why are we, as a nation so obsessed with foreign things? We want foreign TVs, we want foreign shirts. We want foreign technology. Why this obsession with every imported? Do we not realize that self-respect comes with self-reliance? I was in Hyderabad giving this lecture, when a 14 year old girl asked me for my autograph. I asked her what her goal in life is: She replied: I want to live in a developed India. For her, you and I will have to build this develop India. You must proclaim.

The Road to Missile Development

India's interest in missiles dates back to the time of Tipu Sultan, the ruler of the Karnataic during the medieval period. As early as in 1958, the year the Defence Research and Development Organisation (DRDO) was formed, the then Scientific Advisor to the Defence Minister, D.S. Kothari, declared unambiguously that ballistic missiles were "undoubtedly (one of) the greatest and most portentous problems..."

The reason for anxiety was the great reach that ballistic missiles have. Tipped with a nuclear warhead, the dangers only multiplied. Even at that time missiles and rockets formed one of the areas in which defence R&D was planned to be conducted.

The first clear indication that India was seriously considering the idea of launching the Integrated Guided Missile Development Programme came in 1979, when a committee was established, under the Ministry of Defence, with the then DRDO Director General, Raja Ramanna, as the Chair. The committee is popularly known as 'Missile Policy Committee'. Besides recommending the launching of an 'integrated missile development programme', the Committee recommded the "procurement, development and production of missiles for the three Services, in the short term, as also to build up the infrastructure in certain areas so as to take up projects for development of more sophisticated missiles in the long term."

It was almost around the time that the Missile Policy Committee was set up that the Devil Project was wound up. The Defence Research and Development Laboratory (DRDL), the lab responsible for developing missile, was in need of an accomplished project manager with this in view, the then DRDO Director General, Raja Ramanna, suggested in 1981 that Abdul Kalam be appointed director of DRDL, to run the missile development project.

Eighteen months later Abdul Kalam was appointed Director DRDL. Abdul Kalam led the team that successfully concluded the SLV-3 project. By this time, a considerable amount of technological and industrial and human resource were also available.

At the DRDL, a high level committee called the 'Missile Technology Committee' was formed. Deliberations in this body resulted in the formulation of the basic plan, which was later fine tuned, for the development of guided missiles. Abdul Kalam recently wrote that the IGMDP is a product of a 'detailed study' conducted in 1982 "for evolving missile systems in order to counter the emerging threats to the security of India". A team was formed under the chairmanship of Abdul Kalam, with Z.P. Marshal, N.R. Iyer, A.K. Kapoor and K.S. Venkataraman as members, which drew up a paper, with inputs from the three services, for the Cabinet Committee on Political Affairs (CCPA) on the development of indigenous guided missiles.

Subsequently, the proposal was discussed at a presentation presided over by the then Defence Minister, Venkataraman, and finally cleared by the Cabinet. Consequently, the programme was launched on 27 July, 1983 at DRDL, Hyderabad, by the then DRDO Director General, V.S. Arunachalam, amidst fanfare, in the presence of a large gathering of scientists, academicians, officers of the armed forces and production agencies.

Five projects leader were selected, one for each of the missile projects, with Abdul Kalam as the head of the entire programme.

Agni

Agni is an intermediate range ballistic missile (IRBM). Classically a ballistic missile is one that travels outside the earth's atmosphere, during most part of its flight, before re-entering. The missile is set into a ballistic path to prevent deflection. For most part of the missile's flight, the only external force that acts on it is the gravitational pull of the earth.

Guidance : Like the Prithvi, Agni I also relied on strap down inertial navigation. Agni II uses a more stable closed loop inertial navigation system.

Propulsion: It is a three-stage missile, with the third stage being the warhead. In the first three tests, the first stage used solid propellant rocket motor and the second stage used liquid propulsion. In the fourth and fifth tests, both the stages used solid propulsion. In solid propulsion, the propellant grain, the oxidises and the fuel, whose physical state is solid, is stored in a chamber. When ignited, by means of an electric charge, it burns out completely at a predetermined rate, and is expelled through a nozzle in the form of gases. The third stage is the missile's warhead.

Warhead: It can carry a conventional warhead and can also carry a nuclear warhead. The warhead is enclosed in a heat shield to protect it from burning as the missile re-enters the earth's atmosphere. The four types of conventional warheads are incendiary, fragmentary, unguided munitions and guided submunitions. The warhead would have a maximum weight of one ton.

Range: With a warhead of one ton, the missile would be able to reach targets 1,500 km. away. With the weight of the warhead reduced, the missile has a maximum range of 2,500 km. Some reports claim that Agni has a CEP of 60m.

Prithvi: Is a tactical, battle-field-support missile. It is planned in three versions—for the army, air force and navy. Prithvi is 8.56 m long and has a thickness of one metre.

Guidance: The missile has the latest on-board computers operating with real time software as well as an advanced strap down inertial navigation and guidance system. The inertial guidance system "does not rely on outside reference like heat, light or electromagnetic radiation (but) measures the distance between two points (launch and impact points) over a period of time".

Propulsion: Prithvi is a single stage missile that has a two-chamber rocket motor with storable liquid propellants. Prithvi uses fifty per cent xylidene—the fuel—and the remaining fifty per cent triethylamine and nitric acid—the oxidiser—as propellant. The missile has a shelf life of five years with the propellant loaded and twenty-five years without the propellant being loaded. Prithvi-III is a "Boosted liquid properllant version, to generate more thrust-to-weight ratio".

Range: The missile has a minimum range of 40 km As stated earlier, Prithvi is planned in three versions. While the army has opted for the shorter 150 km range version, the air force has gone in for the 250 km extended range-version. The naval version, now in the drawing board stage, has a reported range of 350 km.

Warhead: Five variants of the missile's warhead have been planned. They are: incendiary, fragmentary, unguided munitions and guided sub-munitions. While the first three variants have already been developed, the status of the fourth is uncertain. The fifth type of warhead is a nuclear warhead, whose development status, too, is uncertain.

Akash

The Akash is a mobile area defence surface-to-air missile (SAM) system being developed for the exclusive purpose of the Indian Air Force (IAF).

Guidance: Akash uses both command guidance and active homing—the latter is used in the terminal phase. In active homing, the homing head is switched after which it starts searching for the target. Once the target is located, it is traced and active homing commences.

Tracking: The Akash missile system has multiple-target handling capability. The targets are tracked by Indra phased array radar, which can track one hundred targets at a time and is, thus, critical for the missile system.

Propulsion: The missile uses an integrated solid rocket propellant system.

Speed: The missile moves at a speed of 600 metres per second-mach 2, which means that the missile would reach the target at its full range of 30 km in fifty seconds, and in a much lesser duration if the target were located within a distance of 30 km.

Trishul

Trishul is a quick-reaction SAM "designed to counter a low level attack". The missile will be used by all the three services. The missile becomes operational at an altitude of 500 metres. It has been described as India's answer to the U.S. Patriot missiles that have been used to counter the Iraqi Scuds.

Guidance: The missile operates on command-to-line of sight guidance. In this method the guidance signal is transmitted from launch site to the missile, giving the missile its deviation from the pathline pointing from the launcher to the target, also called the line of sight (LOS). The missile has a computer on board to actuate its control mechanism to turn it towards the line of sight.

Propulsion: Trishul used a solid dual thrust rocket motor for propulsion.

Materials: Trishul is made of aluminium alloy structures, fibre glass composites and maraging steel.

Range and Warhead: The missile has a minimum range of 500 metres and a maximum range of nine km and can carry a warhead of 15 kg. weight. Trishul has sea skimming capability when launched from ships. Sea skimming missiles travel at a very low height, just a few metres above the sea level, actually skimming the waves. Hence the name. The utility of such missiles lies in the fact that the low height and high speed of movement render them high single shot kill probability, besides being significantly immune to electronic counter measures (ECMs), given their small radar cross section.

While the army version of Trishul has already undergone user trials, the airforce version was flight tested, using the Pilotless Target Aircraft (PTA) as the target, and trails of the surveillance radar and fire control system of the naval version have commenced.

Nag

Nag is a third generation Anti-tank Guided Missile (ATGM) that possesses an all-weather capability and also has top attack capability. In other words, it targets the turret of the tank, where the armour is the thinnest.

Nag's airframe is made of composite materials, which make the missile light, without comprosing its strength, while its foldable wings enalbe it to be launched by a tube, like any other third generation ATGM.

While the first generation ATGMs are wire guided, the second generation is semiautomatic. The third generation is a fire and forget type.

Nag has been designed to be launched from 'either the Namica (BMP-2) vehicle or the Army Aviation version of the Advanced Light Helicopter (ALH). However, the exact status of the latter this version is not known. Trial launches of the missile using the Namica have been conducted.

Propulsion: Nag uses solid propulsion. A smokeless high energy solid propellant is used in Nag. The advantage of using such propellant is that it would not leave tell-tale trials behind, and would, thus, enable the launcher to make good its escape.

Guidance: Nag uses homing guidance. In this type of guidance, a homing head also called a seeker head locks on to the target, after receiving the target co-ordinates from the tracking radar, in its infrared or millimetric sights, before being fired. A seeker head is vital to the missile because it enables it to reach the target (home in). The seeker has already been tested.

Range and Warhead: Nag has a range of four km. The missile uses a tandem warhead. Warheads for various missiles.

This year's convocation was special in the sense that it saw the degree of Doctor of Science, Honoris Causa, being conferred on Dr. APJ Abdul Kalam, Dr. Kalam a genius, a brilliant scientist and Science Administrator as one of the leading visionaries of India, is responsible for the creation of India's first indigenous Satellite launch Vehicle (SLV III), and the Integrated Missile Development Program of the country. His efforts towards India's self sufficient in advanced weapons systems are well known to all. He identified five major areas of importance namely: agriculture and food economy; education and health care; Information Technology; infrastructure and critical technologies. India to be a developed nation needs to satisfy three criteria. It should be economically strong, self reliant in military technology and have a standing in the world forum. To the young people present he said, "do not get discouraged to belong to one of the hundreds of developing nations of the world and not the developed G8 (countries). Think of the billion ignited Indian minds which is the most powerful resource compared to any resource on the earth, above the earth and below the earth. Our sweat will transform developing India into a developed India".

14

New Horizons and Challenges

Working with a team of young and energetic scientists required tact, wisdom and proper handling of the ambitious young men. At first, they were free to argue with their scenarios without any kind of difficulty. Their opinion was valued and it did give out effective results. To seek the academic support of several educational institutions was an uphill task, particularly to keep tract of the research work during undertaken by these institutions. Such a style did pay rich scientific dividends which were used in the on-going new rocket researches in our sub-continent in this direction. Moreover, seminars and academic interaction did play a significant role

The young engineers, numbering 280, changed the dynamics of DRDL. It was a valuable experience for all of us. We were now in a position to develop, through these young teams, a re-entry technology and structure, a millimetric wave radar, a phased array radar, rocket systems and such other equipment. When we first assigned these tasks to the young scientists, they did not grasp fully the importance of their work. Once they did, they felt uneasy under the burden of the tremendous faith placed in them. He remembers one young man telling him, "There is no big shot in our team, how will we be able to break through?" He told him, "A big shot is a little shot who keeps on shooting, so keep trying." It was astonishing to see how in the young scientific environment, negative attitudes changed to positive and things that were previously thought impractical began happening.

At the review meetings, I would insist that the youngest scientists present their team's work. That would help them in visualising the whole system. Gradually, an atmosphere of belief grew. Young scientist started questioning senior colleagues on solid technical issues. Nothing would daunt them, because they were afraid of nothing. If they had doubts, they rose above them. They soon became persons of power. A person with belief never kneels before anyone, whining and whimpering that it's all too much, that he lacks support, that he is being treated unfairly. The first launch of the Missile Programme was conducted on 16 September 1985, when *Trishul* took off from the range at Sriharikota (SHAR). It was a ballistic flight meant for testing the in-flight performance of the solid propellant rocket motor. Two C-Band performance of the solid propellant rocket motor. Two C- Brand radars and Kalidieo- theodolite (KTLs) were used to track the missile from the ground. The test was successful. This was followed by the successful test flight of the Pilotless Target Aircraft (PTA). Our engineers had developed the rocket motor for the PTA designed by the Bangalore- based Aeronautical Development Establishment (ADE). The motor had been type-approved by DTP&P(Air). This was a small but significant step towards developing missile hardware that not only functions but is also acceptable to the user agencies. A private sector firm was engaged to produce a reliable, airworthy, high thrust-to weight ratio rocket motor with technology input from DRDL. We were slowly graduating from single laboratory projects to multi-laboratory programmes to laboratory-industry exercises. The development of PTA symbolised a great meeting point for four different organizations. I felt as if I was standing at a meeting point and looking at the roads coming from ADE, DTD&P (Air) and ISRO. The fourth road was the DRDL, a highway to national self- reliance in missile technology."

Let me highlight a few contributions of academic institutions to the various missile systems. *Prithvi* had been designed as an inertially guided missile. To reach the target accurately, the trajectory parameters have to be loaded into its brain—an onboard computer. A team of young engineering graduates at Jadavpur University under the guidance of Prof. Ghoshal developed the required robust guidance algorithm. At the IISc, postgraduate students under the leadership of Prof. IG Sharma developed air defence software for multi- target acquisition by *Akash*. The re-entry vehicle systems design methodology for *Agni* was developed by a young team at IIT Madras and DRDO scientists. Osmania University is Navigational Electronics Research and Training Unit had developed state-of-the art signal processing algorithms for *Nag*. I have only given a few sample cases of collaborative endeavour. In fact, it would have been very difficult to achieve our advanced technological goals without the active partnership of our academic institutions.

Let us consider the example of the *Agni* payload breakthrough. *Agni* is a two - stage rocket system and employs re-entry technology developed in the country for the first time. It is boosted by a first-stage solid rocket motor derived from SLV-3 and further accelerated at the second stage with the liquid rocket engines of *Prithvi*. For the Agni, the payload gets delivered at hypersonic speeds, which I calls for the design and development of a re- entry vehicle structure. The payload with guidance electronics is housed in the re-entry vehicle structure, which is meant to protect the payload by keeping the inside temperature within the limit of 40°C, when the outside skin temperature is greater than 2500°C. Another challenge involved in the *Agni* payload design was related to the tremendous speed with which it would re-enter the atmosphere. In fact, *Agni* would re- enter the atmosphere at twelve times the speed of sound (12 Mach , as we call it in science). At this tremendous speed, we had no experience of how to keep the vehicle under control. To carry out a test, we had no wind tunnel to generate that kind of speed. If we sought American help, we would have been seen as aspiring to something they considered their exclusive privilege. Even if they consented to co-operate, they world be certain to quote a price for their wind tunnel greater than our entire project budget. Now, the question was how to beat the system. Prof. SM Deshpande of the IISc found four young bright scientists working in the field of fluid dynamics and, within six months, developed the software for computational Fluid Dynamics for Hypersonic Regimes, which is one of its kind in the world.

Another achievement was the development of a missile trajectory simulation software, ANUKALPANA by Prof. IG Sharma of IISc to evaluate multi-target acquisition capabilities of an *Akash*-type weapon system. No country would have given us this kind of software, but we developed it indigenously.

As work on the project spread horizontally, performance appraisal became more and more difficult. DRDO has an assessment -linked policy. Leading nearly 500 scientists, I had to finalize their performance appraisals in the form of Annual confidential Reports (ACRs). These reports would be forwarded to an assessment board comprising outside specialists for recommending promotions or otherwise. Many people used to look at this part of my job with an uncharitable bias. Missing a promotion was conveniently translated by many into a so-called dislike I had towards them. Promotions of other colleagues were also seen by many as subjective favours granted by me. Entrusted with the task of performance evaluation, I had in fact to be an alert judge of scientific effort. The 1983 reorganisation was done with the objective of renewal: it was indeed a very complex exercise handled agilely by AV Ranga Rao and Col R Swaminathan. We created a team of newly joined young scientists with just one experienced mind and hurled at them the big challenge of building the strap-down inertial guidance system, an on-board computer and a ram rocket in propulsion system. These exercises were being attempted for the first time in the country, and the technology involved was comparable with world-class systems. The guidance technology is centred around the gyro and accelerometer package, and electronics to process the sensor output. The no-board computer carries the mission computations and flight sequencing. A ram rocket system breathes air to sustain its high velocity for long duration after it is put through a booster rocket. The young teams had not only designed these systems but also developed them into operational equipment. Later *Prithvi* and then *Agni* used similar guidance systems, with excellent results. The effort of these young teams made the country self-reliant in the area of protected technologies. It was a good demonstration of the 'renewal factor'. The intellectual capacity renewed through contact with enthusiastic young minds had achieved these outstanding results.

Now, besides the renewal of manpower, emphasis had to be laid on augmenting the strength of project groups. Often people seek to satisfy their social, egoistic, and self-actualisation needs at their workplaces. A good leader must identify two different sets of environmental features. One, which helps a person's need-satisfaction and the other, which creates dissatisfaction with his work. We have observed that people look for those characteristics in their work that relate to the values and goals which they consider important in giving meaning to their lives. If a job meets the employees' need for achievement, recognition, responsibility, growth and advancement, they will work hard to achieve goals.

Once the work is satisfying, a person looks at the environment and circumstances under which work is performed. He observes the policies of the administration, qualities of his leader, security, status and working conditions. Then, he correlates these factors to the inter-personal relations he has with his peers. He examines his personal life through these maintenance factors. It is the net effect of all these aspects that decides the degree and quality of a person's effort and performance.

The matrix organization evolved in 1983 proved excellent in meeting all these requirements. So, while retaining this structure of the laboratory, we undertook a task-design exercise. The scientists working in technology directorates were made system managers to interact exclusively with one project. To deal with the public sector undertakings (PSUs) and private sector firms associated with the development of the missile hardware, an external fabrication wing was formed under PK Biswas, a developmental fabrication technologist of long standing. This reduced pressure on the in-house fabrication facilities, enabling them to concentrate on jobs which could not be undertaken outside, which in fact occupied all the three shifts.

Work on *Prithvi* was nearing completion when we entered 1988. For the first time in the country, clustered Liquid Propellant (LP) rocket engines with programmable total impulse were going to be used in a missile system to attain flexibility in payload range combination. Now, besides the scope and quality of the policy decisions Sundaram and I were providing to the *Prithvi* team, the project/s success was dependent on creative ideas being converted into workable products and the quality and thoroughness of the team members, contribution. Saraswat with Y Gyaneshwar and Pvenugopalan did a commendable job in this regard. They instilled in their team a sense of pride and achievement. The importance of these rocket engines was not restricted to the *Prithvi* project; it was a national achievement. Under their collective leadership, a large number of engineers and technicians understood and committed themselves to the team goals, as well as the specific goals which each one of them was committed to accomplish personally. Their entire team worked under a self-evident sort of direction. Working together with the Ordnance Factory, Kirkee, they also completely eliminated the import content in the propellant for these engines.

Since the Interim Test Range at Balasore was still at least a year away, we had set up special facilities at SHAR for the launch of *Prithvi*. These included a launch pad, block house, control consoles and mobile telemetry stations. I had a happy reunion with my old friend MR Kurup who was the Director, SHAR Centre by then. Working with Kurup on the *Prithvi* launch campaign gave me great satisfaction.

Kurup worked for *Prithvi* as a team member, ignoring the boundary lines that divide DRDO and ISRO, DRDL and SHAR, Kurup would spend a lot of time with us at the launch pad. He complemented us with his experience in range testing and range safety and worked with great enthusiasm in propellant, making the maiden *Prithvi* launch campaign a cherished experience.

Prithvi was launched at 11:23 hrs on 25 February 1998. It was an epoch-making event in the history of rocketry in the country. *Prithvi* was not merely a surface-to-surface missile with a capability of delivering a 1000 kg conventional warhead to a distance of 150 km with an accuracy of 50 meter CEP; it was in fact the basic module for all future guided missiles in the country. It already had the provision for modification from a long-range surface to an air missile system, and could also be deployed in a ship for the ship role.

The launch of *Prithvi* sent shock waves across the unfriendly neighbourhood. The response of the Western bloc was initially of shock and then of anger. A seven-nation technology embargo was clamped on India forbidding it to buy anything even remotely connected with the development of the guided missiles. The emergence of India as a self-reliant country in the field of guided missiles upset the entire developed world.

Two centuries of subjugation, oppression and denial have failed to kill the creativity and capability of the Indian people. Within just on decade of gaining independence and achieving sovereignty, Indian Space and Atomic Energy Programmes were launched with a perfect orientation towards peaceful applications. There were neither funds for investing in missile development nor any established requirement from the Armed Forces. The bitter experiences of 1962 forced us to take some basic first steps towards missile development.

The *Agni* team was comprised of more than 500 scientists. Many organisations were networked to undertake this huge effort of launching *Agni*. The *Agni* mission had two basic orentations—work and workers. Each member was dependent on others in his team to accomplish his target. Contradiction and confusion are the two things most likely to occur in such situations. Different leaders accommodate concern for workers while getting work done, in their own personal ways. Some shed any concern for workers in order to get results. They use people merely to reach goals. Some will give less importance to work, and make effort to gain the warmth and approval of people working with them. But what this team achieved was the highest possible integration in terms of both quality of work and human relationships. Involvement, participation and commitment were the key words to functioning. Each of their team members appeared to be performing by choice. The launching of *Agni* was the common stake not only for our scientists, but for their families too. VR Nagaraj was the leader of the electrical integration team. Dedicated technologist that he is , Nagaraj would forget basic requirements like food and sleep while on the integration jig. His brother-in-law passed away while he was at ITR. His family kept this information from Nagaraj so that there was no interruption in his work towards the launching of Agni.

All activities preparatory to the launch went according to schedule. It was decided to move the people living in nearby villages to safety at the time of the launch. This attracted media attention, and led to much controversy. By the time 20 April 1989 arrived, the whole nation was watching us. Foreign pressure was exerted through diplomatic channels to abort the flight trial, but the Indian Government stood behind us like a rock and thwarted any distraction to our work. We were at T-14 seconds when the computer signalled "Hold", indicating that one of the instruments was functioning erratically. This was immediately rectified. Meanwhile, the down-range station asked for a "Hold". In another few seconds, multiple *Holds* were necessitated, resulting in irreversible internal power consumption. We had to abort the launch. The missile had to be opened up to replace the on-board power supplies. A weeping Nagaraj, by now informed about the tragedy in his family, met to promise that he would be back within three days. The profiles of these courageous people will never be written in any history book, but it is such silent people on whose hard work generations thrive and nations progress. Sending Nagaraj off, I met my team who were in a state of shock and sorrow. I shared my SLV-3 experience with them. "I lost launch vehicle in the sea but came back with success. Your missile is in front of you. In fact you have lost nothing but few weeks of rework". "This shook them out of their immobilisation and the entire team went back to retrieve the sub-systems and re-charge them.

The press was up in arms, and made various interpretations of the postponement of the flight to suit the fancies of their reader ship. Cartoonist Sudhir Dar sketched a shopkeeper returning a product to the salesman saying like *Agni* it would not take off. Another cartoonist showed one *Agni* scientist explaining that the launch was postponed because the press button did not make contact. The *Hindustan Times* showed a leader consoling press reporters, "There's need for any alarm... it's a purely peaceful, non-violent missile".

After a detailed analysis conducted virtually round the clock for the next ten days, our scientists had the missile ready for launch on 1May 1989. But, again, during the automatic computer check- out period at T-10 seconds, a *Hold* signal was indicated. A closer inspection indicated that one of the control components, SI-TVC was not working as per the mission requirements. The launch had to postponed yet again. Now, such things are very common in rocketry and quite often happen abroad too. But an enthusiastic nation was into mood to appreciate our difficulties. The *Hindu* carried a cartoon by Keshav showing a villager counting some currency notes and commenting to another, "Yes, it's the compensation for moving away from my hut near the test site—as few more postponements and I can build a house of my own.." Another cartoonist designated *Agni* as "IDBM-Intermittently Delayed Ballistic Missile." Amul's cartoon suggested that what *Agni* needed to do was use their butter as fuel.

I took some time off, leaving my team at ITR to talk to the DRDL- RCI community. The entire DRDL-RCI community assembled after working hours on 8 May 1989. I addressed the gathering of more than 2,000 persons, "Very rarely is a laboratory or an R and D establishment given an opportunity to be the first in the country to develop a system such as *Agni.* A great opportunity has been given to us. Naturally major opportunities are accompanied by equally major challenges. We should not give up and we should not allow the problem to master us. The country doesn't deserve anything less than success from us. Let us aim for success". I had almost competed my address, when, found myself telling my people, "I promise you, we will be back after successfully launching *Agni* before the end of this month." Finally, the launch was scheduled for 22 May 1989. The previous night, Dr Arnachalam, Gen KN Singh and I were walking together with Defence Minister KC Pant, who had come to ITR to witness the launch . It was a full- moon night . It was high tide and the waves crashed and roared, as if singing of His glory and might. Would we succeed with *Agni* launch tomorrow? All of us had this question at the back of our minds, but none of us was willing to break the spell produced by the beautiful moonlit night, Breaking a long silence, the Defence Minister finally asked me, "Kalam! What would you like me to do to celebrate the *Agni* success tomorrow ? " It was a simple question, to which I could not think up a answer immediately. What did I want? What was it that I did not have? What could make me happier? And then I found the answer. "We need 100,000 saplings to plant in RCI," I said . His face lit up with a friendly glow. "You are buying the blessings of Mother Earth for *Agni*," Defence Minister KC Pant quipped. "We will succeed tomorrow", he said.

Next day *Agni* took off at 0710 hrs. It was a perfect launch . The missile followed a text-book trajectory. All flight parameters were met. It was like waking up to a beautiful morning from a night marish sleep. We had reached the launch pad after five years of continuous work at multiple work centres. We had lived through the ordeal of a series of snags in the last five weeks. We had survived pressure from everywhere to stop the whole thing.

Prime Minister Rajiv Gandhi called the Agni launch "a major achievement in our continuing efforts to safeguard our independence and security by self-reliant means. The technology demonstration through *Agni* is a reflection of our commitment to the indigenous development of advanced technologies for the nation's defence ." "The country is proud of your efforts ," he told me. President Venkataraman saw in the *Agni* success the fulfilment of his dream. He cabled from Simla, "It is a tribute to your dedication, hard work, and talent."

Agni marked the completion of five years of IGMDP. Now that it had demonstrated our competence in the crucial area of re-entry technology and with tactical missile like *Prithvi* and *Trishul* already test-fired, the launches of *Nag* and *Akash* would take us into areas of competence where there is little or no international competition. These two missile systems contained within themselves the stuff of major technological breakthroughs. There was a need to focus our efforts sharply on them.

In September 1989, he was invited by the Maharashtra Academy of Sciences in Bombay to deliver the Jawaharlal Nehru Memorial Lecture. He used this opportunity to share with the budding scientists my plans of making an indigenous Air-to-Air missile—*Astra*. It would dovetail with the development of the Indian Light Combat Aircraft (LCA). He told them that our work in Imaging Infra Red (IIR) and Millimetric Wave (MMW) radar technology for the *Nag* missile system had placed us in the vanguard of international R and D efforts in missile technology. He also drew their attention to the crucial role that carbon- carbon and other advanced composite materials play in mastering the re-entry technology. *Agni* was the culmination of a technological effort that was given a start by Prime Minister Indira Gandhi when the country decided to break free from the paralysing fetters of technological backwardness and the dead skin of subordination to industrialised nations.

The second flight of *Prithvi* at the end of September 1988 was again a great success. *Prithvi* has proved to the best surface to-surface missile in the world today. It can carry 1000 kg of warhead to a distance of 250 km and deliver it within a radius of 50 metres.

15

Academic Honours

Almost four busy and well- engaged decades passed by. Each day meant work—indeed a new type of work—for Dr. Kalam. For him there was no holiday and no family commitment. He had adopted a kind of habit which meant some useful work. He witnessed several Republic Days. But the Republic Day falling in January 1990 was unique in his career. He was conferred the Padma Vibushan along with Dr. Arunachalam. Two of his colleagues, J.C. Bhattacharya and R.N. Agarwal were awarded Padma Shri.

With this great honour, there seemed to be no change in the life style of Dr. Kalam. He lived in a room 12 by 10 feet which contained some books, papers and a few pieces of furniture. At this point of time, he realised the fact that several scientists leave the country for betters perks, but Dr. Kalam now liked this kind of decision. His own country was more important for him. Dr. Kalam received the old memories of several years when he spent his busy career in the company of several affectionate personalities. I sat alone for quite some time in silent contemplation. The sand and shells of Rameswaram: the care of Iyadurai Solomon in Ramanathapuram; the guidance of Rev Father Sequeira in Trichi and Prof. Pandalai in Madras, the encouragement of Dr. Mediratta in Bangalore: the hovercraft ride with Prof. Menon, the pre- dawn visit to the Tilpat Range with Prof. Sarabhai; the healing touch of Dr Brahm Prakash on the day of the SLV-3 failure; the national jubilation on the SLV-3 simmering at VSSC, Dr. Ramanna's faith in inviting me to DRDO; the IGMDP, the creation of RCI, *Prithvi*, *Agni*... a gust of memories swept over me. Where were all these men now? My father, Prof. Sarabhai, Dr. Brahm Prakash? Could I meet them and share my joy with them? The Madurai Kamaraj University requested him to deliver their convocation address. When I reached Madurai, I enquired about my high school teacher Iyadurai Solomon, by now a Reverend and 80 years old . I was told that he lived in a suburb of Madurai. I took a taxi and searched for his house . Rev. Solomon knew that I was going to give the convocation address that day. He, however, had no way of getting there. There was an emotional reunion between teacher and pupil. Dr. PC Alexander, the Governor of Tamil Nadu, who was presiding over the function, was deeply moved on seeing the elderly teacher who had not forgotten his pupil of long ago, and requested him to share the dais.

"Every convocation day of every University is like opening the floodgates of energy which, once harnessed by institutions , organ isations and industry, aids in nation-building, "I told the young graduates. Somehow I felt I was echoing Rev. Solomon's words, spoken about half a century ago. After my lecture, I bowed down before my teacher. "Great dreams of great dreamers are always transcended, "I told Rev. Solomon, "You have not only reached my goals, Kalam! You have eclipsed them," he told me in a voice choking with emotion.

We celebrated the nation's forty- fourth Independence Day with the test firing of *Akash*. Prahlada and his team evaluated a new solid propellant booster system based on a composite modified double base propellant. This propellant with its unprecedented high energy properties was crucial in assuring the long- range surface-to-air missiles. The country had taken an important step in ground-based air defence of vulnerable areas.

The Missile Council declared 1991 the Year of Initiative for DRDL and RCI. When they chose the route of concurrent engineering in IGMDP, we selected a rough track. With the completion of developmental trials on *Prithvi* and *Trishul*, our choice was on test now. He exhorted my colleagues to user trials within the year. He knew that it was going to be a tough task, but that was not going to inhibit them. Rear Admiral Mohan retired and his deputy Kapoor, was to take over *Trishul*. I had always admired Mohan's understanding of missile command guidance . This sailor- teacher -scientist could outwit any other expert in the country in this field . His candid exposition of various aspects of the Command Line of Sight (CLOS) guidance system during the *Trishul* meetings will always linger in my memory.

The year 1991 started on a very ominous note. On the night of 15 January 1991, the Gulf War broke out between Iraq and the Allied

Forces led by the USA . In one stroke , thanks to satellite television invading Indian skies by that time, rockets and missiles captured the imagination of the entire nation. People started discussing Scuds and Patriots in coffee houses and tea shops. Children began flying paper kites-shaped like missiles, and playing war game on the lines of what they heard on American television networks. The successful test firing of *Prithvi* and *Trishul* during the course of the Gulf War was sufficient to make an anxious nation relax. The newspaper reports of the programmable trajectory capability of the *Prithvi* and *Trishul* guidance system, using microwave frequencies in virtually unjammable bands, created widespread awareness. The nation was quick to draw parallels between the missiles operational in the Gulf War and our own warhead carriers. A common query I encountered was whether *Prithvi* was superior to a Scud, whether *Akash* could perform like a Patriot, and so on. Hearing a "Yes " or a " Why not?" from me, people's faces would light up with pride ad satisfaction. After the Gulf War concluded with the victory of the technologcally superior Allied Forces, over 500 scientists of DRDL and RCI gathered to discuss issues that had emerged. He posed a question before the assembly: was technology or weapon symmetry with other nations feasible, and if yes, should it be attempted? The discussion led to many more serious questions such as, how to establish effective electronic warfare support? How to make missile development proceed apace with the development of equally necessary systems like the LCA; and what were the key areas where a push would bring progress?

At the end of a lovely discussion spread over three hours, the consensus emerged that there was no way to redress asymmetry in military capability except to have the same capability in specific areas as your potential opponent. The scientists vowed to achieve a reduced CEP in the accuracy of *Prithvi's* delivery , perfecting the ka band guidance system for *Trishul* and realising all carbon carbons-entry control surfaces for *Agni* by the end of the year. The vow was later fulfilled.

The same year, Dr. Kalam received an honorary degree of Doctor of Science from the IIT, Bombay. In the citation read by Prof. B Nag on the occasion, he was described as "an inspiration behind the creation of a solid technological base from which India's future aerospace programmes can be launched to meet the challenges of the twenty first century." Well, perhaps Prof. Nag was only being polite, but he believes that India will enter the next century with its own satellite in geo-stationary orbit 36,000 km away in space, positioned by its own launch vehicle. India will also become a missile power. India is a country with tremendous vitality . Even though the world may not be seeing its full potential or feeling its full power, no one dare ignore it any more.

On 15 October, Dr. Kalam turned sixty. He looked forward to superannuating and planned to open a school for less privileged , but talented children. My friend, Prof. P Rama Rao , who was heading the Department of Science and Technology in the Government of India , even struck a partnership with me to establish what he called a Rao- Kalam school. We were unanimous in our opinion that carrying out certain missions and reaching certain milestones, however important they may be or however impressive they might appear to be, cannot be the final sum of human life. But we had to postpone our plan as neither of us was relieved by the government of India.

It will be a tall claim to opine that my life can be a role model for anybody ; but some poor child living in an obscure place, in an underprivileged social setting may find a little solace in the way my destiny has been shaped. It could perhaps help such children liberate themselves from the bondage of their illusory backwardness and hopelessness? "Assessing the human temperament Dr. Kalam made an observation that most Indians suffer unnecessary miseries all their lives because they do not know how to manage their emotions. They are paralysed by some sort of a psychological inertia. Phrases like 'the next best alternative; the only feasible option or solution; and till things take a turn for the better' are commonplace in our business conversations. Why not write about the deep-rooted character traits which manifest themselves in such widespread, self-defeatist thought patterns and negative behaviour? I have worked with many people and organisations and have had to deal with people who were so full of their own limitations that they had no way to prove their self- worth than by pushing him around.

Abraham Maslow was the first person to moot the new psychology of self -actualisation at a conceptual level . In Europe, Rudolf Steiner and Reg Revans developed this concept into the system of individual learning and organisational renewal. The Angeo-German management philosopher, Fritz Schumacher introduced Buddhist economics and authored the concept of "Small is Beautiful." In the Indian subcontinent Mahatma Gandhi emphasised grass- root level technology and put the customer at the centre of the entire business activity. JRD Tata brought in progress -driven infrastructure. Dr. Homi Jehangir Bhabha and Prof. Vikram Sarabhai launched the high, technology -based atomic energy and space programmes with a clear-cut emphasis on the natural laws of totality and flow. Advancing the developmental philosophy of Dr. Bhabha and Prof. Sarabhai, Dr. MS Swaminathan ushered in the Green Revolution into India working on another natural principle of integrity. Dr Verghese Kurien brought in a powerful co-operative movement through a revolution in the dairy industry. Prof. Satish Dhawan developed mission management concepts in space research.

When IGMDP was sanctioned in 1983, we did not have an adequate technology base. A few pockets of expertise were available, but we lacked the empowerment to utilize that expert technology. The multi-project environment of the programme provided a challenge, for five advanced missile systems had to be simultaneously developed. This demanded judicious sharing of resources, establishing priorities, and progressive induction of manpower. Eventually, the IGMDP had 78 partners, including 36 technology centres and 41 production centres spread over public sector undertakings ordinance factories, private industries, and professional societies, besides a well- knit bureaucratic structure in the Government. In the management of the Programme , as much as in the technological inputs, we attempted to develop a model that was appropriate, even tailor- made, for our very specific needs and capabilities. We borrowed ideas that had been developed elsewhere, but adapted them in the light of what we knew were our strengths and what we recognised as the constraints we would be compelled to work under. All in all, appropriate management and our cooperative endeavours helped to prove what talent and potential lay in our research laboratories, government institutions and private industries.

To successfully pursue these goals, they have to learn elaborate rules of etiquette and familiarize themselves with customs, traditions, protocols and the like. The youth of today must de-learn this self-defeating way of living life. The culture of working for material possessions and rewards must be discarded. When I see wealthy, powerful, learned people struggling to be at peace with themselves, I remember people like Ahmed Jallaluddin and Iyadurai Solomon. How happy they were with virtually no possessions!

On the coast of Coromandel where the earthy shells blow ,
In the middle of the sands

Lived some really rich souls. One cotton lungi and half a candle

One old jug without a handle

These were all the worldly possessions of these kings in the middle of the sands.

You, I, everyone on this planet is sent free by Him to cultivate all the creative potential within us and live at peace with our own conscience. We differ in the way we make our choices and evolve our destiny. Life is a difficult game. You win it only by retaining your birthright to be a person. And to retain this right, you will have to be willing to take the social or external risks involved in ignoring pressures to do things the way others say they should be done. What will you call Sivasubramania Iyer inviting me to have lunch in his kitchen? Zohara, my sister, mortgaging her gold bangles and chains to get me into engineering college? Prof. Sponder insisting that I should sit with him in the front row for the group photography? Making a Hovercraft in motor- garage setup? Sudhakar's courage? Dr Brahm Prakash's support? Narayanan's Management? Venkataraman's vision? Arunachalam' drive? Each is an example of a strong inner strength and initiative . As Pythagoras had said twenty-five centuries ago, "Above all things, reverence yourself."

I am not a philosopher . I am only a man of technology. I spent all my life learning rocketry. But as I worked with a very large cross-section of people in different organizations, I had an opportunity to understand the phenomenon of professional life in its bewildering complexity. When I look back upon what I have narrated so far, I feel it gives a dogmatic appearance to propositions which were really nothing more than my own observations and conclusions. My colleagues, associates, leaders, the real heroes of the drama I lived; the complex science of rocketry; the important issues of technology management; all seem to have been treated in a diagrammatic manner. The pains and cheers, the achievements and the failures—markedly differing in context, time, and space—all appear grouped together.

This is the story of the period ending with the first *Agni* launch—life will go on. This great country will make great strides in all the fields if we think like a united nation of 900 million people. My story—the story of the son of Jainulabdeen, who lived for over a hundred years in Mosque Street in Rameswaram island and died there ; the story of a lad who sold newspapers to help his brother; the story of a pupil reared by Sivasubramania Iyer and Iyadurai Solomon; the story of a student taught by teachers like Pandalai; the story of engineer spotted by MGK Menon and groomed by the legendary Prof. Sarabhai; the story of a scientist tested by failures and setbacks; the story of a leader supported by a large team of brilliant and dedicated professionals. This story will end with me, for I have no inheritance in the worldly sense. I have acquired nothing, built nothing, possess nothing—no family, sons, daughters.

16

Secular India's Convenient Choice

APJ Abdul Kalam - The Super- Scientist with the Common Touch. The choice of the father of the Indian missile programme for the presidency will mark the return of an intellectual to the Rashtrapati Bhavan, says Raman Swamy.

His full name is Dr. Avul Pakir Jainulabdeen Abdul Kalam. With his trade-mark hairstyle of shoulder-length silver-gray locks, he will fit the role that destiny seems to have in store for him—India's only truly intellectual president after Sarvepalli Radhakrishnam.

Abdul Kalam belongs to a rare breed of those who dream lofty dreams, and work hard to transform vision into reality. The man who guided India into the global "Space Club", has a favourite quotation that could inspire his countrymen if, and when, he enters Rashtrapati Bhavan: "We must think and act like a nation of a billion people and like that of a million people . Dream, dream, dream! Conduct these dreams into thoughts, and then transform them into action."

Above all he is quinessentially Indian. Never allowing his astounding success as a scientist to diminish his humanity and humility. Despite having had an unparalleled career as a defence scientist and been crowned with the highest civilian award of India, the Bharat Ratna, he retains the common touch.

The father of Missile Technology still conducts himself as the man next door. He has not forgotten his humble roots in Rameshwaram, where he was the first graduate in the family, with his brothers not even finishing school.

Born in 1931, Kalam's education began at the Samiyar school in Ramewaram, and moved to the Schwartz School in Ramnathapuram town. Graduation was from St. Joseph's College engineering at the Madras Institute of Technology.

As the scientific and technology advisor to the prime Minister he propelled India into the select club of missile powers. He recently resigned from the post to take up a more ambitious programme of teaching and creating scientific temper in the minds of young inquisitive and knowledge thirsty Indians.

Kalam's father Jainulabiddin Marakayar was a panchayat board president. He also owned a few boats which ferried pilgrims between Rameswaram and Dhanushkody. But after a cyclone ravaged Dhanushkody in 1964, the operations were limited to ferrying passengers between Rameswaram and ships anchored off the coast. Kalam's father had an excellent relationship with the main Ramnathasamy temple in the town. According to Muthumeeran, in return for supply of small boats every year, his father was accorded certain honours by the temple authorities during temple festivals.

Kalam , according to his family, is a strict vegetarian. Adept at playing the 'rudra veena', he is a fan of the Tamil poet Subramania Bharathi. A teetotaler and deeply religious, he recites the *Qur'an* and the *Bhagwad Gita* with equal familiarity and devotion.

Kalam never did marry. He once told a friend, half jocularly, that if he had married, he would never have achieved even half of what he has managed to.

Choosing Mr. Right

Nuclear scientist A.P.J. Abdul Kalam has benefited from some negative fallout—Prime Minister A.B. Vajpayee and Home Minister L.K. Advani's lack of keenness for another term for President K.R. Narayanan: the antipathy of the Congress Left parties and Telugu Desam to Maharashtra Governor P.C. Alexander, who was Vajpayee's original choice, and the lukewarm sentiment in the National Democratic Alliance (NDA) and opposition parties for Vice- President Krishan Kant. And Kalam emerged as the most acceptable name.

As the consultations began in May over the next presidential candidate, the political disarray over Gujarat which had clouded parliament continued to grip the parties. The divisions which had marked the voting continued with Telugu Desam supremo Chandrababu Naidu creating tense moments for Vajpayee, while Samajwadi Party chief Mulayam Singh Yadav remained out of syne first with the Congress and then with the entire opposition. The Prime Minister had made up his mind that the new President, though not belonging to BJP, will have no links with the opposition, especially the Congress. Thus Alexander was Vajpayee's first presidential choice. But Vajpayee felt that other constituents like Trinamool Congress and Janta Dal (U) might go with Naidu's choice of Kant, making it a very close contest. Vajpayee also worried about the call for a conscience vote among the minor allies and independents throughout the country that could send his nominee tumbling to a shock defeat.

Then Naidu made his master sweep and proposed Kalam's name. While the suggestion united the NDA, there was some disarray among the opposition. But on the whole, there was wide spread approval of the choice of a high achiever in the fields of science and technology.

Kalam seems a good choice because he is not a politician, but has worked as a scientist, with governments run by different parties. He wore a hero's mantle when there was a short supply of iconic figures. He also belongs to a minority community, though he refuses to wear his religion of the sleeve. He prefers being just an Indian.

There are, however, some questions on whether Kalam has the experience for the job. Like Rajendra Prasad, Fakhruddin Ali Ahmed, Neelam Sanjiva Reddy and Giani Zail Singh, Kalam has not served as the Vice- President. But unlike him they had served in Parliament and were ministers. Kalam has only been to the officers gallery of the Lok Sabha and Rajya Sabha as Secretary of Defence Research.

Though he will have a clutch of competent advisers, there are doubts about whether he is prepared for the complexities of life in Rashtrapati Bhavan. As the custodian of the Constitution, the President has to make many hard decisions without being guided by the cabinet. For instance, Presidents have raised critical queries on the suitability of candidates, recommended by the Chief Justice and the Centre, for the post of judges in the Supreme Court and High Courts. Also, the President has to approve appointments of heads of various bodies . Some of the tricky areas are constitutional issues like Centre- State relations, tussles between the executive, Parliament and judiciary, and a coalition government in the state or at the Centre losing majority.

But Kalam's admirers are not worried. Since he has worked in the government and attended innumerable cabinet meetings as an official, he knows how the system works. He is, after all, a man who has practised the highest standard of ethics and probity in public life. Vajpayee went to the Congress President Sonia Gandhi to thank her for endorsing his candidature, even if very grudgingly.

As a consensus candidate Kalam's credentials are impeccable. A Muslim in Rashtrapti Bhavan may be politically correct , but he is seen as a man of honour besides being one of the great scientific minds of our time. What was jarring was the backstage intrigue.

Act One Elimination

Vajpayee and his colleagues were desperately searching for a nominee who would suit the NDA bill and enjoy wide political acceptance. Unwittingly, Kalam became the weapon of a devastating political strike. In a matter of six days. Kalam's candidature saw the People's Front breaking up and the Congress sheepishly toeing the great consensus.

By picking a rank outsider, the NDA stymied the opposition, but not before a drama of bluff, double cross and palace intrigue. When a conclave of senior NDA ministers at Vajpayee's 7 Race Course Road residence agreed on the evening of June 9 that Kalam should be the ruling coalition's nominee, the hunt for the scientist's mobile number began. A joint secretary in the PMO was tasked to trace Kalam. When the architect of India's missile programme graciously accepted Vajpayee's offer, a sense of relief washed over those present at the prime minister's residence.

The game began when Vajpayee ruled out a second term for Narayanan. For the past four years, Narayanan had not exactly endeared himself to the NDA .The prime minister was upset with the President almost since he staked claim in 1998. Narayanan has been periodically raising uncomfortable questions over selection of Judges. Use of Article 356 and appointment of various constitutional authorities. The President's ideological distaste for the Vajpayee Government was no great secret.

With a bare 55 per cent of the 11 lakh votes with the NDA , the Prime Minister was not willing to run risks. Yet, both Vajpayee and Home Minister L.K. Advani were clear about their fundamentals—the next president should not be part of either the Left or baptised in Congress culture.

The decision would be taken by a cabal which comprised, besides Vajpayee, Advani, Defence Minister Fernandes, External Affairs Minister Jaswant Singh, Parliamentary Affairs Minister Pramod Mahajan and Rural Development Minister M. Venkaiah Naidu. When the group first met on June 5, the shortlist included K.C. Pant, L.M. Sighvi, Dr. Kalam and Viren Shah. The favourite was Maharashtra

Governor P.C. Alexander, the choice of Mahajan, Shiv Sena chief Bal Thackeray and Nationalist Congress Party leader Sharad Pawar. The group was virtually unanimous about Alexander but awaited further consultation with the allies and opposition leaders.

Events gathered momentum on June 6 when Advani hosted a lunch which was attended by Vajpayee and Andhra Pradesh Chief Minister N. Chandrababu Naidu. Also present was NDA's troubleshooter Mahajan. Naidu made his preference for kant quite obvious and indicated that if the NDA persisted with Alexander, the vice president should be considered for a second term. He expressed his difficulty in accepting Alexander. However, after forceful arguments by Advani, Naidu suggested they look for a consensus candidate. He had one condition: no name should be finalised without consulting him. By the evening Vajpayee and Advani began to actively consider Kant, Fernandes was asked to sound out allies.

For the next 16 hours Fernandes talked to all the NDA allies. Not a single constituent, from Mamata Banerjee to Naveen Patnaik, favoured Kant. Thackeray even threatened to withdraw support to the Government. At a noon meeting at Race Course Road on June 7, the wise men decided to talk to Naidu. Soon after the meeting, the Prime Minister spoke to Naidu, who after initial opposition fell in line.

The stage is set for A.P.J. Abdul Kalam, the presidential candidate of the ruling National Democratic Alliance and almost all the Opposition parties barring the Left, to file his nomination papers in the Parliament House tomorrow.

On arrival in Delhi he was escorted by he Parliamentary Affairs Minister, Pramod Mahajan, who had gone to Chennai to accompany him here, and greeted by several Ministers on arrival at the airport. He had a number of engagements, including a lunch hosted for him by the Prime Minister, Atal Behari Vajpayee, and a call on the President, K.R. Narayanan. During the day he also had separate meetings with the Leader of the Opposition, Sonia Gandhi, the Defence Minister, George Fernandes, and the Samajwadi Party leader, Mulayam Singh Yadav, who was the first to suggest his name for the top post, and who even today appealed to his "friends" in the Left to desist from opposing Dr. Kalam. Perhaps to emphasise that Dr. Kalam was a candidate of not only the ruling NDA but also the main opposition party, Mr. Vajpayee invited the Congress president and Manmohan Singh to the lunch he hosted for Dr. Kalam. Dr. Singh attended but Sonia Gandhi could not as she was occupied elsewhere.

It seems that separate sets of nomination papers will be filed for Dr. Kalam by the NDA, the Congress and the Samajwadi Party. Ms. Gandhi is certain to be the main proposer in the form to be submitted on behalf of her party and other senior leaders. Dr. Singh, some Chief Ministers and others would also sign the papers. Mr. Vajpayee himself will be the main proposer for the NDA.

Even at this late stage, parties such as the PMK have appealed to the Left not to force a contest, and several smaller parties, including the Republican Party of India and the Indian National League, have pledged support for Dr. Kalam.

A Wrong Signal: Sehgal

And Lakshmi Sehgal the Left parties' candidate, who is expected to file her nomination papers on June 21, told a press conference that the nomination of the nuclear scientist, Dr. Kalam, had sent a "wrong signal," especially at a time when Indian and Pakistani armies were standing face to face on the border and for her (an old Indian National Army soldier) there would be no running away from the battlefield (even if the outcome was known).

Capt. Sehgal said the carnage in Gujarat would be the focal point of her campaign" Gujarat is a case (for President's rule).... May be many lives would have been saved (if this had been done)", she said in response to a question.

At her press conference , Capt. Sehgal was flanked by the CPI (M) general secretary, Harkishan Singh Surjeet, and the CPI (M) politburo members, Prakash Karat and Sitaram Yechury, the CPI general secretary, A.B. Bardhan, the CPI national secretary, D. Raja, Abani Roy of the RSP, and S.C. Gaud of the Forward Bloc.

She said she saw the Presidential contest as a political battle, part of the struggle she had been part of all her life. Today, the four foundation pillars of the Constitution—secular democracy, economic self- reliance, federalism and social justice—were under severe stress. Indians were together in the freedom struggle, and today more than ever the "synergisting of our pluralistic society or rich diversity" was needed to safeguard and strengthen the future.

With the changing global situation, particularly when China and Pakistan are our bordering countries, it would be a right decision on the part of our government that we develop enough deterrence so that they do not become adventurous and wander into our borders, Hence it would not be wrong to say that our nation should be strong. At various quarters it has been well- opined that the choice of Dr. Kalam is a matter of pride and rejoicing for our country. Undoubteetty, with a very rich scientific background, we have selected a scholar of international fame in the field of nuclear and space sciences. It is derogatory to say that such an eminent person like Dr. Abdul Kalam was selected because of his religion. Indeed to uphold our secular values and constitutional tenets, we do not necessary need a constitutional expert or a politician but a person who is proud of our secular fabric and has firm faith in our constitution—qualities which the NDA presidental condidate possesses in abundance.

That Dr. Abdul Kalam made nuclear deterrence a point in favour of averting a conflict between India and Pakistan appears to be some what disturbing. Being associated with nuclear energy and missile development, the scientist in him was quite apparent. However relevant question arises whether a President should involve himself in formulating policies when an elected Prime Minister, answerable to Parliament, is charged with such responsibility. In fact, the convention is that a Rashtrapati talks less and listens more.

Of 'Kalam Iyer'

I have serious reservations about Prof. A.P.J. Abdul Kalam as President. His enthusiasm for the nuclear bomb is a major drawback. It shows the mind of a man who is not only apolitical but also plainly amoral.

Does he think of missiles and nuclear weapons as playthings with which to amuse himself and the nation? As advisor on defence, he should have given a little thought to the matter . Instead he coins a phrase, 'Strength respects strength, as though nuclear bombs give a nation strength'.

Kalam regards May 11 and 12, 1998 as his crowning achievement. One of his favourite slogans is, 'The nation is bigger than the individual'. He might add, 'The bomb is bigger than the nation'.

As one devoted to the *Bhagvad Gita*, Kalam, no doubt , must be familiar with the description of the divine force: 'Were the splendour of a thousand suns to shoot forth all at once in the sky that might perchance resemble the splendour of that Mighty One. 'Great scientists like Oppenheimer and Einstein were fascinated by this passage, but it also filled them with awe and fear. For Abdul Kalam , the nuclear weapons seem just another technological achievement. Its human dimension, its social and political consequences seem to have escaped his attention. He is in essence a technocrat who would do any job assigned to him diligently. Almost all the projects he has worked on are of a military nature , his spiritual inclinations notwithstanding . Kalam, himself has said , 'I'm not a philosopher. I'm only a man of technology. I spent all my life learning rocketry.'

It's obvious that the nuclear connection has a lot to do with his voice for Presidentship. In the context of Gujarat, his being a Muslim has helped too. He is also taken to be a Hindu because he reads the *Gita* and the Upanishads, is a vegetarian (but eats eggs) and has frugal habits. When he lived in Thiruvananthapuram, he was known to his friends as 'Kalam Iyer' because he moved around with the Brahmins and copied their ways. His closeness to various saints across the country, including the Shankaracharya of Kanchi is well-known. The sangh parivar has been enthusiastic, thinking of him as a role model for the minorities, the kind of person who fits in well with the RSS philosophy of meekness towards the Hindu majority.

His remark to reporters that any time is good for him to file his nomination was taken to signify his rationality and scientific temper. But then what is one to make of this remark of his in an interview with a newspaper? 'Materialistic things in life don't matter—whatever happens, happens for our good. One must leave things to the mercy of the Almighty'. Such fatalism doesn't behove a true scientist. Scientists are not supposed to leave things to 'the will of God'.

'National Interest Favours Kalam'

Jaipur, 19. The Union Labour Minister, Sharad Yadav, today asserted that the "considered" decision of the National Democratic Alliance (NDA) to field A.P.J. Abdul Kalam for the President's post was in the larger national interest and hoped that the Left parties would withdraw their nominee to avoid a contest.

Speaking to reporters after inaugurating the new building of the Regional Vocational Training Institute for Women here, Mr. Yadav said Dr. Kalam's name did not appear abruptly out of nowhere, but was given a "careful thought" jointly by all the constituent parties of NDA.

"The NDA will maintain a similar unity even in the selection of the Vice President, the process for which is yet to start," Mr. Yadav said, while denying that the BJP was imposing its agenda on other parties of the ruling combine. "It is the NDA agenda that governs all of us, " he affirmed.

The Labour Minister disagreed with the charge that Dr. Kalam would be a novice in politics and pointed out that he had held sensitive positions that involved constant interactions with the top political leadership. "As a person in charge of defence technology, he has interacted with Prime Ministers Indira Gandhi and Morarji Desai," Mr. Yadav said.

"Looking to the consensus built in favour of Dr. Kalam across the political spectrum, it will be good if the Left Front withdraws its nominee," he said. He added that Dr. Kalam's appointment as President would inculcate scientific temper among people and inspire the youtn to make strides in science and technology.

Mr. Yadav did not comment on whether his party, Janata Dal (United), would be asking for more seats in the Union Cabinet expansion and reshuffle expected shortly. "As far as Rajasthan is concerned, Janata Dal (United) is the third force here and we will strengthen our base in the tribal areas," he said.

Earlier, while inaugurating the new building of Regional Vocational Training Institute for Women (established under the Union Labour Ministry) at Jhalana Doongari Institutional area here, Mr. Yadav said the women's training and empowerment had been a priority area of the Central Government. "The increased participation of women in education and vocational training is essential to ensure a greater role for them in the economy, " he said.

The Rajasthan Chief Minister, Ashok Gehlot, speaking on the occasion, underlined the need to associate women with the fields of advanced information technology, management and electronics; and said the trained women would play a significant role in these sectors and accelerate the pace of development. RSS's economic ideologue S. Gurumurthy, Arun Jaitley and the late Ramnath Goenk tried to dismiss Rajiv Gandhi form the office of Prime Minister. But for Arun Shourie's intervention , who was then the editor of the *Indian Express* and waging a particularly vituperative campaign against Rajiv Gandhi over the Bofors issue, the hotheads would have prevailed over Zail Singh and would have plunged India into a constitutional crisis.

If Kalam becomes President, he would be unlike any of the men who held this largely ceremonial office. Radhakrishnan, Zakir Hussain and Shanker Dayal Sharma were highly educated and had earned doctorates from highly regarded universities abroad. Radhakrishnan authored several books on Indian philosophy and lectured on that at Oxford before becoming Vice-Chancellor of Andhra University. He went on to become our first ambassador to the then Soviet Union, where he was reputed to have even charmed Joseph Stalin.

Shanker Dayal Sharma followed up his PhD from Cambridge University in Constitutional Law School. Over dinner at the Raj Bhavan at Hyderabad when he was the Governor of Andhra Pradesh, he told me about how he used to play squash late in the night at Harvard's Lower house, where I was a tutor. I told him that the midnight squash tradition continued in the basement squash courts of Loell House and that I bore the brunt of it many a night as my rooms were in the same wing as the courts! But he was industries minister in Indira Gandhi's first government before being chosen as her nominee for President in preference to Dr Hidayatullah. Sanjeeva Reddy whose earlier nomination for President had divided the Congress made it to that office after the Janata wave of 1977. He was the first Chief Minister of Andhra Pradesh before moving on to national politics. He was Congress president before becoming a Union minister and was a member of the infamous Syndicate that had unsuccessfully tried to make Indira Gandhi a puppet Prime Minister.

R. Venkatraman was a highly regarded Congress leader who had served with distinction as Industries Minister in Tamil Nadu and later in the Union Government . In between he was the editor of *Swarajya* which was founded by C. Rajagopalachari who succeeded Lord Mountbatten as Governor-General of India. Venkatraman was also defence minister and it was during his time that the Bofors case came on the surface.

Kalam has little in common with his predecessors. He does not have the educational attainments of Radhakrishnan, Zakir Hussain and Sharma who were genuine Ph.D.s. from top -notch institutions. Kalam just has an engineering degree from Madras University.

"I once met President Narayanan at a small reception at the Rashtrapati Bhavan. For lack of something more intelligent to say, I complemented him on his nice house. The President was very embarrassed and assured me that his actual living quarter were quite small and ordinary. Kalam would need even less. He has a reputation for living in guesthouses or Army mess rooms.

Missile Man's Mission: A Prosperous India

Minutes after Dr. A.P.J. Abdul Kalam had delivered an inspiring lecture, a ten-year-old girl came up to him and requested for his autograph. What is your ambition, asked Dr. Kalam now all set to become the President of India. Without blinking her eyes the young girl replied: I want to live in a developed India. The remark struck the father of India's missile programme like lightning; this has been his dream too. Precisely at that time, Dr. Kalam was writing, along with his colleague, Y.S. Rajan, his new book *India 2020: A vision for the New Millennium.* He dedicated the book to the girl with the words: "This book is dedicated to her and the millions of Indians who share her aspiration". So impressed was Dr. Kalam by the resoluteness of the young girl that he wrote in the preface: Ignited young minds, we feel, are a powerful resource . This resource is mightier than any resource on the earth in the sky and under the sea.

Stepping in of Dr. Kalam in the Rashtrapati Bhavan, almost a month from now, appears a certainty. Guess what would be his first message to the nation? It may be on these lines: We must work together to transform our developing India into a developed India and the revolution required for this effort must start in our minds . His vision relates to a prosperous India without poverty—an India strong in trade and commerce; an India strong in many fields of science and technology and an India with health and education to all. His space technology vision has come true and reaching out to the people . The achievements include communication through networks in remote areas; disaster warning system; quick resource surveys to target ground water and save forest cover campaign.

The man, who has spent all his life learning rocketry and will now occupy the highest office of the land knows well how to manage men, matters and materials. Dr. Kalam is now well-known in India and abroad but there are still little known facets of his life. His full name is Avil Pakir Jalauddin Abdul Kalam and he hails from the southern most tip of India. Coming from a poor family of Rameswaram, he has come up hard way in life. His father Jainulabiddin Marakayar was a panchayat board President and owned a few boats which ferried pilgrims between Rameswaram and Dhanuskhody. Come the 1964 cyclone and Dhanushkody was ravaged, limiting the operation of boats to ferrying passengers between Rameswaram and the ships anchored off the coast. Marakayar had excellent relations with the holy temple of Rameswaram and during the temple festivals special hours were bestowed on him.

Youngest in his family, Dr. Kalam was the first to graduate; none of his brothers and sisters could even complete their school stage. His schooling was done in Rameswaram and at a missionary school in Ramanathapuram town. He did his graduation from St. Joseph College in Tiruchi. There was a time when his father could not afford his school fee and his sister had sold her ornaments to send him for higher education. As a young boy Kalam even sold newspapers at the behest of his elder brother who was a newspaper agent. The prodigy in Kalam came to the fore since his school days but proliferated when he joined aeronautical engineering at the Madras Institute of Technology. Kalam is now 71 but remained a bachelor.

He once told his friend jocularly: "Had I married, I would have never done even half of what I have managed to do". It is just a coincidence that, for the first time , both the President and the Prime Minister of India will be bachelors.

Dr. Kalam is a strict vegetarian, well- versed in the works of Tamil Poet Subramania Bharathi, likes to play "rudra veena" and recites verses of the "Geeta". When he was awarded Bharat Ratna in 1997, he lived in the Defence Research and Development Organisation (DRDO) guest house in Delhi and his accommodation comprised a bed room, a sitting room, a makeshift visitor's room and an attached bath. Books have been only Dr. Kalam's worldly possession. He did not have even a TV set and tuned to AIR bulletins to keep himself abreast of developments. His frugal meal was cooked by the guest house's cook and included boiled *rasam, sambhar* and a vegetable.

Those who have worked closely with Dr. Kalam say he is the happiest person when a research in scientific field is put to use for the mankind, particularly the poor and the disabled. He was emotionally moved when polio- affected children stood on their feet with the help of calipers made out of carbon- carbon material developed by the team of scientists working with him. Carbon-carbon material developed for Agni missile , made calipers one tenth of their original weight of four kilos.

In remote villages of snow-clad Ladakh, not a blade of grass grew and vegetables were transported with great difficulty. On a visit to the area, Dr. Kalam asked the DRDO unit there to explore the possibility of growing plants. A research was carried out and now the villages grow enough vegetables not only to meet their requirements but also of the needs of neighbouring villages. Kalam is a "work-alcoholic" and works seven days a week . There are no holidays and weekends for him.

When Kalam Made a Secret Wish to KRN

It is a strange mix : missiles and moon, nuclear bomb and nature. But that is what A.P.J. Abdul Kalam is. The NDA'S candidate for the post of President is an ardent lover of nature . Consider this. In February this year , the Bharat Ratna scientist went to the Rashtrapati Bhavan for a private dinner with K.R. Narayanan. The President came upto the Western Gate to see off his distiguished guest.

Presiden's ADC sits in a room close to this gate. As KRN and Kalam came out in the open, Kalam stopped, his gaze fixed on the sky. The President asked him what he was thinking about. Pat came the answer from Kalam that he wanted to have a walk " here " in a moon- lit night. When moon in shining up in the sky and myriads of flowers are down below, the walk would be beautiful.

KRN was apparently flummoxed for a moment. Perhaps because taking a walk in a moon- lit night in the Rashtrapati Bhavan can be the prerogative of the President only. But the President replied courteously that Kalam should feel free to visit Rashtrapati Bhavan any time to have his moonlight walk. The topic ended there only. Kalam probably never thought or even dreamt that providence had a bounty in store for him . No prizes for guessing where in Rashtrapati Bhavan Kalam would be found after July 24, particularly on moonless nights.

Who's the Hostess?

History of sorts will be created with the two top positions in the country being held by bachelors. Dr A.P.J. Abdul Kalam as the presidential nominee of the BJP- led NDA has never been married as is the case with Prime Minister Atal Behari Vajpayee. However, in Mr. Vajpayee's case he has a loving foster family. His foster daughter Namita is always at hand and plays the hostess. This is where Dr. Kalam might be handicapped given his status of a confirmed bachelor once he occupies Rashtrapati Bhavan next month.

Nitish Proposed

With several leaders taking credit for throwing up the name of

Kalam for the high office of President, it now appears that Railway Minister Nitish Kumar was the first to make the suggestion . It caught the fancy of the BJP leaders and others because of Dr. Kalam being an apolitical scientist besides belonging to the minority community. At the end of the day after Dr. Kalam's name for the post of President had been clinched, there were several claimants who patted their own acumen publicly that the missile men was their choice. Among these busy- bodies who claimed that they had propped up Dr Kalam's name included TDP supremo and Andhra Pradesh Chief Minister Chandrababu Naidu and Samajwadi party leader and former defence minister Mulayam Singh Yadav.

Ram and Kalam

Ram Jethmalani is one of those men who always remain in the news. The likes of him can never remain away from the media glare. He had made it clear months ago that he was going to contest the post of President and that he should be taken as a serious candidate. He was then probably hoping for Shiv Sena's support . But much changed in between. Sena 's support never came. Bal Thackeray plumped for Maharashtra Governor P.C. Alexander. But when the opposition parties did not favour Alexander, the BJP unleashed a tactical missile on the opposition by zeroing in on Kalam .

Last Laugh

Dr Kalam's candidature for the post of President was a political masterstroke of the BJP leadership that left the opposition high and dry. It led to the dissolution of the People's Front and created differences between the Congress and the Left. Congress leaders privately admitted that the party was outsmarted in the presidential sweep-stakes and it was finally left with no alternative but to back Dr. Kalam.

The Congress was hoping against hope that President K.R. Narayanan would agree to be the Opposition candidate. Had the BJP persisted with P.C. Alexander, the Congress and the Opposition would have surely forced a contest.

The Congress leaders were uncomfortable with Alexander as he was seen close to Shiv Sena leader Bal Thackery. They say that Mr. Narayanan might still have considered contesting had Mulayam Singh Yadav not walked out of the People's Front.

In the event of contest between NDA and a unified opposition, the fight would have been tough. Now of course, the BJP is having the last laugh and it is now certain that the Vice President would be a BJP man. The BJP three- time Rajasthan Chief Minister Bhairon Singh Shekhawat is the front runner.

A Trump Card for the Prime Minister

With the Left coming up with the name of Captain Lakshmi Sehgal as its presidential candidate, here's at least a sense of diversion. Asked why this delay in forwarding Sehgal's candidature, a CPI(M) spokesperson said, "why this talk that we are late. In the first place itself we didn't want to support A.P.J. Abdul Kalam's name for the simple reason that he is an NDA candidate and that would mean going along with the NDA agenda."

Two other names—Justice A.M. Ahmedi, the former Supreme Court Chief Justice and Ms Fathima Beevi, former Supreme Court Judge (who later became Tamil Nadu Governor and was later recalled)—were doing the rounds as the Left's choice for the highest office till Friday evening when Captain Sehgal's name came up. Captain Sehgal has a number of points in her favour—she is the daughter of the legendary activist Ammu Swaminathan, a former comrade of Netaji Subhas Chandra Bose and is presently based in Kanpur, immersed in social work along with her daughter Subhashini Ali. However with the Congress' support to Kalam, she will be on the losing end.

Professor Kalam's name is a virtual trump card for the Vajpayee government in the sense that after the Gujarat carnage, a Muslim name for the highest office in the country could supposedly work a balm for members of the minority community and could send positive signals to the Middle Eastern countries. But a social analyst commented, "Muslims have begun to see through these political games and if you talk of the Middle Eastern countries , they hardly matter in today's political scenario because even whilst the Gujarat carnage was at its peak, not one Muslim nation spoke out and the pressure on the Vajpayee government came in only from the European countries."

Perhaps, not enough pressure because Gujarat Chief minister Narendra Modi sits not just untouched but he even addressed a press conference in Delhi on Thursday, outlining his moves for the ensuing Assembly elections in that State. It's of course for the Election Commission to decide whether there can be free and fair polls in that state with Modi having firmly saddled in that seat and making adequate 'arrangements' for the elections.

KRN for Kerala?

Speculation is already ripe whether the outgoing President Mr. K.R. Narayanan will head for his home state , Kerala, where his wife, Usha, has already made a base. For the last several years , she has been regularly visiting a particular Kerala village and looking after several projects for the socio-economic development of the residents. The other option for the Narayanans would be to live in a bungalow in Lutyen's Delhi or in the Media Centre (Gurgaon) house owned by his diplomat daughter, Chitra. One could say that the campus and the building of the Presidents lodge are in the best and most beautiful setting compared to the lodging of any Head of the state on the work. With 345 rooms, several lawns, tennis courts, polo ground and variety of chambers chance the prestige of the Rashtrapati Bhawan. Earlier Dr. Kalam occupied an accomondation of 4-room apartment.

From a 4-Room Apartment to 345-Room Rashtrapati Bhavan

For over a decade, apartment 833 in a south Delhi guest house housed a long-haired scientist in shirtsleeves who ate frugally and rarely missed his daily walks.

Now its guest A.P.J. Abdul kalam seems set to savour the splendours of living in Rashtrapati Bhavan, the sprawling 345- room presidential citadel in Delhi.

India's president-in-waiting Abdul Kalam occupied four room flat in the Defence Research and Development Organisation (DRDO) guesthouse during his career as one of the nation's top scientists. Finally, it seems his dream of walking by the moonlight in the Mughal Gardens—the exquisite garden adjoining the presidential palace—will come true.

If elected President in the July 15 poll, he will stay in apartments originally planned for the vicereine's ladies- in-waiting in the regal mansion.

Rashtrapati Bhavan, an imposing four- floored British built mansion, stretches across 18,580 square metres and is set in the midst of a 400-acre garden. Three million cubic feet of stones and 700 million bricks have gone into the structure and some 23,000 workers have sweated over it.

Edwin Lutyen, the British architect of the viceregal palace—for that was its original purpose—was inspired by British and Mughal architecture. A key feature is the array of canals and fountains of water that keep the air cool and lend a soft liquid murmur to the campus.

Walking- enthusiast Abdul Kalam may find it interesting to note that it takes three hours to cover the building on foot.

It takes Rs. 90 million annually to maintain the red brick and sand stone building that contains with in its pillars and walls a variety of chambers anterooms, courts, galleries, saloons, staircases, corridors, kitchens, pantries and ironing rooms.

Though it has generally seen Presidents well past their prime and usually too involved with matters of state, the palace also has nine tennis courts, two theatres, a squash court, a polo ground and a golf course.

If elected President, Abdul Kalam will have to host visitors in the Durbar Hall at the heart of the building where the country's civilian and military honours are handed over.

A 2,300- year- old stone bull, believed to have been sculpted during King Ashoka's reign in the third century B.C. stands guard outside the hall, called the "throne room" by the British.

The west wing or the guest wing comprises two suites ,Dwarka and Nalanda, for visiting dignitaries and their entourage.

The Council Room is a repository of several historic events during Indian independence and afterwards. It is where the decision to divide the sub- continent into India and Pakistan in 1947 was taken.

The six-acre Mughal Garden is the staqe for many open -air receptions. It has a large variety of roses, bougainvilleas, tulips and dahlias, apart from lesser- known exotic species.

Trees thrive in the man-made forest created around the palace, and it is easy to spot the mango, Neem, Jamun, Peepal and banyan among the 600-odd varieties.

Few citizens can ever hope to witness the palace in its full glory, but they nevertheless cause the inevitable traffic jam in the centre of the capital to catch a glimpse of the magnificent, fully lit Rashtrapati Bhavan on special days .

Kalam Enters Poll Fray

The 71-year old noted scientist, Dr. A.P.J. Abdul Kalam, who is virtually the country's President-in-waiting ,today entered the ring when his nomination papers were filed by all major political formations, baring the Left.

Accompanied by Prime Minister Atal Behari Vajpayee, Telugu Desam Party Chief and Andhra Chief Minister Chandrababu Naidu and Samajwadi Party chief Mulayam Singh Yadav, Dr. Kalam, attired in a light blue shirt and dark blue trousers, reached the chamber of Rajya Sabha Secretary- General and Returning Officer R.C. Tripathi at 11.45 a.m. Where Leader of the Opposition Sonia Gandhi was waiting thus hopefully auguring the phase of consensus.

Mr. Vajpayee handed over the first set of nomination papers. It had Home Minister L.K. Advani, TDP supremo N. Chandrababu Naidu, Samajwadi Party President Mulayam Singh Yadav, BSP leader Mayawati AIADMK leader O Panneerselvam, Samata leader and Defence Minister George Fernandes and DMK leader Murasoli Maran, Shiv Sena leader Suresh Prabhu, BJD chief Naveen Patnaik and Trinamool Congress chief Mamta Banerjee among the 60 proposers and equal number of seconders.

Three Chief Ministers Chandrababu Naidu of Andhra Pradesh, Mayawati of Uttar Pardesh and Naveen Patnaik of Orissa were also present at the chamber of the Rajya Sabha Secretary General.

Parliamentary Affairs Minister Pramod Mahajan said the first page of the nomination carried 23 signatures which included all NDA and other non-Congress supporters.

Congress President Sonia Gandhi filed the second set of papers on behalf of her party. Those who signed these papers included Leader of the opposition in the Rajya Sabha Manmohan Singh, Lok Sabha Deputy Speaker P.M. Sayeed, Rajya Sahba Deputy Chairperson Najma Heptullah, Mr Arjun Singh, Mr Natwar Singh, Mr Pranab Mukherjee, Mr Shivraj V. Patil a d Congress spokesman S. Jaipal Reddy. As per the election rules, a nomination paper must be proposed by at least 50 members and 50 seconders, belonging to the electoral college comprising the members of Parliament and Legislative Assemblies.

Dr. Kalam's nomination is the first filed on behalf of any political party. The only other candidate of some consequence, Capt. Lakshmi Sehgal being fielded by the Left parties is expected to file her nomination on June 21.

There was a slight delay in filing of the papers as Dr Kalam insisted on withdrawing Rs 15,000 from his bank account to pay for the security deposit for the election. Sources said Dr. Kalam preferred to pay his own money rather than accept it from anyone else.

In a lighter vein, Parliamentary Affairs Minister Pramod Mahajan told newspersons that he paid the money, the media would have made much out of it.

The press conference by Dr Kalam scheduled for after the filing of nominations was postponed till tomorrow to the dismay of host of mediapersons who had gathered well in advance.

The Congress spokesman said his party filed a separate set of papers as "we have taken a positive decision favouring Dr. Kalam independently as a party. Therefore , we have signed the nomination separately".

Mr Reddy said the nomination papers filed by Congress on behalf of Dr Kalam carried more than 120 signatures.

After reaching Parliament House, Dr Kalam went to the Prime Minister's Office from where he was taken in a procession to the Returning Officer's chamber as news lensmen jostled with one another for a vantage position to photograph Dr Kalam who is all set to become the next President.

Earlier, Dr. Kalam had a meeting with Andhra Pradesh Chief Minister N. Chandrababu Naidu here this morning. Dr Kalam spent half -an - hour with Mr Naidu who was believed to have played a significant role in his nomination as NDA candidate.

Dr Kalam whose name is synonymous with India's technological development in missiles, rockets, battle tanks and light combat aircraft, had a rousing welcome as he landed here from Chennai, accompanied by Mr Mahajan. The choice of Dr. Abdul Kalam was made convenient at one voice by all to parties except the Left Parties which took sometime to select one against the consensus condidate Dr. Lakshmi Sehgal of the INA fame, a dedicated patriot and disciplined soldier was requested to be their condidate. She agreed to their request.

A Convenient Choice

India's No.1 scientist and technologist, Dr A.P.J. Abdul Kalam, is all set to become the President. And, once again, Andhra Pradesh Chief Minister, Mr. N. Chandrababu Naidu, has pulled off a political *coup*, instrumental as he was in Dr. Kalam's emerging as the NDA's candidate for the post. For the BJP-led NDA, it was a good opportunity to placate its disgruntled ally, sulking over the BJP's refusal to concede his demand to remove the discredited Gujarat Chief Minister, Mr Narendra Modi, from his post. So total was Mr Chandrababu Naidu's displeasure that he had spurned the Speaker's post which should have gone to the Telugu Desam Party after the death of G.M.C. Balayogi in an air- crash.

But after the NDA turned down his support to the Vice-President, Mr Krishna Kant, who was also acceptable to the Congress (I), and came out with the candidature of the Maharashtra Governor, Dr P.C. Alexander, who was unacceptable to the Congress (I) and the Left Parties, the TDP supremo plumped for Dr Kalam.

Though one would love to believe that Dr Kalam was selected for his scientific temper, his passion for making India self-sufficient in every aspect of life—from nuclear technology to food security—his gentle temperament and his people skills, the truth obviously lies elsewhere. At this point in time, it suits almost all political parties to support the candidature of Dr Kalam, one of the most non-controversial public figures ever.

For Mr Chandrababu Naidu, the crucial election to the Andhra Pradesh state Assembly is at hand next year, and he hopes that, while going to vote, the Muslims will forget that he had supported a BJP -led NDA government in Delhi and remember- and appreciate-that he was instrumental in sending Dr Kalam to Rashtrapati Bhavan. After all, had he not refused to endorse Dr Alexander's candidature, with certain support from Ms. Mayawati's Bahujan Samaj Party and Ms Jayalalithaa's AIADMK. The NDA could have thrown the gauntlet at the Congress (I) and other Opposition parties, and would not have shied away from an election for the Presidential post.

A jubilant Chandrababu Naidu recalled on Tuesday how there was no unanimity on the presidential candidate among the NDA constituents and its friends, including the TDP "On June 8, when this was conveyed to me by the Defence Minister Mr. George Fernandes, I asked if there was a chance of a new candidate and then I suggested to him the name of Abdul Kalam, which came to me spontaneous".

But for all the spontaneity that he claimed in suggesting Dr Kalam's name, what he said next during his chat with journalists certainly let the cat out of the bag. Urging the Opposition parties to play a constructive role in evolving a national consensus and looking beyond 'routine politics", he added significantly, that the choice of Dr Kalam as India's President would send "the right signal to the nation and international community at this hour of turmoil". He need not have said more.

However much anybody might like to claim that the highest

office in the land is above politics, one knows that, in reality, this is not so. Of course, Dr Kalam would be one of the few Presidents who will not take any political baggage to Rashrapati Bhavan—Dr S. Radhakrishnan was another such president. But several occupants of Rashtrapati Bhavan have played politics. Those who know Dr Kalam or have worked with him are all praise for the simplicity, integrity, brilliance and vision of the man who has always wanted to see India self-reliant. Indigenisation has been the burden of his song during his various avatars in the DRDO, ISRO and later , as Chief Scientific Advisor to the Prime Minister.

But perhaps the best and the most enduring quality of Dr Kalam is his ability to dream—dream about a strong, vibrant and self- reliant India, which can hold its own in the comity of nations.

An interview with an eminently senior leader of the CPI , A.B. Bardhan. He opines that it is not necessary for the President to be a political figure but the person has to be familiar with contemporary political issues facing the country and constitutional problems that may arise during his tenure.

Presidency: The Issue Goes Beyond Personalities

The Left parties, decision to challenge the NDA nominee for the presidential election has forced a contest . The stand taken by the Left has perplexed many and confused some but CPI General Secretary A.B. Bardhan is clear on the issue as he asserts that "the election of President is always a political contest." In a frank conversation, Mr Bardhan went into the reasons for the impending contest.

Excerpts

Q Why a contest for the nation's 12th President when it is clear that the nominee of the Left parties is sure to be defeated?

The election of the President has always been a political contest. The President is the protector of the Constitution. It is not necessary for the President to be a political figure but the person has to be familiar with political issues facing the country and constitutional questions that may arise.

Q: Are you suggesting that NDA nominee A.P.J. Abdul Kalam is not familiar with the political issues?

I am not discussing the personality but I am on issues . In India today we are facing serious problems involving Pakistan. We have faced the Gujarat situation and Ayodhya can disrupt the national unity and brotherhood of our people. At the same time, we are faced with a serious economic crisis involving millions of kisans and agricultural workers and employees.

We would like a President who is aware and sensitive to all these questions so that in a climate of coalition governments he can take a proper decision when called upon to do so. It is worth recalling here that it is we who had first suggested that it would be good if we can decide the issue by consensus. Unfortunately, the NDA did nothing. After putting forward and ditching their own nominee twice, they chose to nominate Dr A.P.J. Abdul Kalam. This was also not done through consensus .

It is in this kind of political environment and circumstances that the Left parties had to decide and we reached a conclusion that a political contest should take place. The question, here ,is not of choosing between personalities or supporting any personality. The issue transcends personalities . After all, a nominee for the President is bound to be an eminent person of great intergrity and learning. But connected political questions would still remain to be focused and debated. It is in this context that the Left parties have chosen to nominate Lakshmi Sahgal.

Knowing fully well that you can't make your candidate win, you are still opting for a symbolic contest

No, no this is not a symbolic contest. Symbolism does not arise from the possibilities of victory or defeat, but from the serious nature of political issues in a given situation. Otherwise, it would mean that every time you fight an election and there is no possibility of a success then it is a symbolic fight. I disagree with this kind of description. Though his (Dr Kalam's) eminence as a scientist is beyond question but I am not aware of his having expressed view on any of the issues that have faced the country or affected the nation.

Q: But in this political process, opposition unity has been wrecked?

No, it is not correct to say that . At least the Left parties are together and not getting disarrayed. In a storm, some ships must keep afloat and not get swept away. The Left has a political identity, howsoever, big or small.

Q: But then the People's Front has come as under.

Who has walked out of the Front? Only one party has done so and tomorrow others might join it. Therefore, the People's Front as a third front is not the question. Those who walked out of the Front have to answer, not the Left parties. They chose to be on the side of the BJP . One should not think that the Front is something where one can walk in or walk out as it suits your convenience. If their idea was to be with the BJP, the BSP and the Congress against whom they have always voiced strong opposition, then it is for them to decide. It so happens that they share the same views on Dr Kalam.

Q: You were pressing for a second term for President K.R. Narayanan and the ruling alliance was harping on the tradition of President having served a second term

There is no such tradition or convention. This was a discovery by the BJP to suit its purpose. The Vajpayee government says that barring the first President, Dr Rajendra Prasad, no other President has served a second term. Why bar Dr Prasad? It arose only in the case of Mr Narayanan because of special circumstances that are here today. There is no point of talking of traditions here and if they are so particular then why the same logic is not applied in the case of the Vice- Presidents. Vice-Presidents have been elevated to the position of President. I think five or six Vice-Presidents got elevated. Why then this tradition was not thought of? I mean conventions and traditions are used selectively by some parties like the BJP when it suits their purpose and abandoned when it doesn't.

Congress for Kalam

The Congress declared that it would support A.P.J. Abdul Kalam, the ruling National Democratic Alliance's proposed presidential candidate. While the Congress decision virtually ensures Dr. Kalam's victory, the prospects of a contest—even if a token one— have not dissipated altogether as the Left Front remains unchanged in its commitment to put up a fight against the NDA nominee.

Within an hour of the Congress going public with its decision, Dr. Kalam rang up the Congress president, Sonia Gandhi, to thank her. From among the non- NDA political forces, the Samajwadi Party had already announced itself in favour of Dr. Kalam.

The Congress decision, arrived after "extensive consultations", is being described as the triumph of "realism" over "romanticism". That the political realists, headed by the Kerala Chief Minister, A.K. Antony, began making themselves heard; and the "Antony line" prevailed once Ms. Gandhi indicated her preference for it. Her own role in the three days of prolonged decision-making was described by one senior CWC member as one of "sensitivity and maturity".

The Congress spokesperson Jaipal Reddy, cited the "totality of circumstances and the candidature of Kalam" as the crucial elements in the final decision; nonetheless, he expressed "respect" for the viewpoint of the Left. The decision, Mr. Reddy said, was unanimous.

Asked whether the decision would sour the party's relations with the Left, Mr. Reddy answered in the negative and said: "Our relations with the Left have always been ideologically- oriented ; and our difference are tactical." He pointed out that Manmohan Singh and Natwar Singh, both senior CWC members, called on the CPI (M) general secretary, Harkishan Singh Surjeet to apprise him of the decision.

However, the party informed the Prime Minister, Atal Behari Vajpayee, and the NDA through the media. "They informed us perfunctorily; we'll inform them through this press conference". The decision to support Dr. Kalam's candidature was apparently firmed up this morning at an "unofficial CWC" which was attended by Mrs Gandhi, her two political secretaries, Ambika Soni and Ahemd Patel, Dr. Manmohan Singh and Natwar Singh.

As soon as the Congress indictated that it was going to go its separate way, the Left parties went into a huddle and decided to take a final view tomorrow at a formal meeting of the Left Front.

The basic position to oppose Dr. Kalam's candidature remains and tomorrow's meeting would decide the form and fashion in which this could be carried out.

The possibility of fielding a candidate from among the Left parties is high with at least two of the four constituents—The Revolutionary Socialist Party (RSP) and All -India Forward Bloc (AIFB)—favouring the move. The CPI (M) politburo member, Prakash Karat, said the party would consult the politburo members ahead of tomorrow's meeting. "Our stand to oppose the candidature of NDA nominee remains".

Overwhelmed, Says Kalam

The Presidential candidate, A. P. J. Abdul Kalam, has thanked the " leaders, political parties and the nation for the confidence and faith" they have reposed in him. "The post of President of India indeed reflects the integrated aspiration of the nation," he said in a statement today.

Initially Dr. Kalam was scheduled to meet the press this morning, but the meeting was called off. Instead, the former Principal Scientific Adviser to the Union government released a statement, which he later read out to the media at Anna University.

Dr. Kalam was "really overwhelmed" at the many phone calls, e- mails and media reports which were "pouring in continuously from Monday onwards," after the announcement of his candidature. Since then everyone had been asking for a message from him. He recalled a "famous Indian thought" that "whatever happened has happened for the good, whatever is happening is happening for the good and whatever will happen, will happen for the good".

Sharing a personal anecdote, Dr Kalam said that while he was recently addressing a student group at Porbandor, he was asked by a ClassX girl what his message was for the young people. He told that everyone should grow with the thought that " the nation is bigger than the individual".

Lakshmi Sehgal Makes the Contest Interesting

It is now evident that the fight for the Presidential office between two persons of divergent background is an unequal contest.

There is nothing common between the missile man Dr. A.P.J. Abdul Kalam and octogenarian Capt. Lakshmi Sehgal. While Dr. Kalam has been basking in the glory of his achievements, Capt. Sehgal was a heroine of the days gone by. Dr. Kalam has a vision of developed India but Capt. Sehgal's dream of seeing triumphant INA soldiers marching to the Red Fort was shattered long ago. The fight between the country's top scientist and a freedom fighter of yesteryears is uneven indeed. The only thing common between the two contestants is that both are Tamilians and born in the same state. The contest is more ideological and, given the wide support extended to Dr. Kalam in the electoral college, the challenge appears to be symbolic.

Resurrecting Capt. Sehgal from virtual retirement, the left parties have, unfortunately, sought to make her cadidature a fight between secularism and communalism, focussing on the gruesome happenings in Gujarat. She proposes to launch her campaign in Ahmedabad and visit the nearby relief camps. Dr. Kalam has virtually demolished the main plank of the left by stating emphatically "What has happened in Gujarat is very painful. We should prevent it at all cost. I can only say religion should graduate into spiritual inquiry, managers must become leaders, and political leaders must have compassion".

Dr. Kalam is not BJP's candidate nor does he subscribe to that party's ideology. A welcome aspect of the campaign is that both Dr Kalam and Capt.Sehgal have no personal rancour against each other and have demonstrated mutual respect. Mark her words: "I admire him for his scientific achievements. I do not know him personally and have nothing against him." She does not agree with her sponsors that long political experience and sound constitutional knowledge is needed to occupy the highest office of the land. What is needed is a political and social perspective.

Capt. Sehgal was virtually bewildered when the left parties approached her and requested her to become their Presidential candidate. She was away from the limelight for long years since the INA guns fell silent, barring a few occasions, like the one when she was honoured with Padma Vibhushan. She was influenced by the Communist movement rather late in life after she herself saw the plight of labourers and, subsequently, joined the CPI-M but her first allegiance continued to be Netaji and the INA. Though in late eighties, she still works for the welfare of the poor and the needy.

Maj-Gen. Shahnawaz Khan known to be the right hand man of Netaji, has described her in his book "INA and its Netaji" published in 1946 with a foreword by Jawaharlal Nehru, in these words: "Dr. Lakshmi Swaminathan, a young energetic and outstanding brave lady was selected by Netaji to be the commander of the Rani Jhansi regiment." Within a brief period of six months the member of the regiment mastered all their training and every bit as well trained and disciplined as any soldier of the Azad Hind Fauz. The girls were particularly good in bayonet fighting and all of them were eager to use the weapon against the British forces,

Maj-Gen Khan wrote : Early in 1944 when other units of the Azad Hind Fauz were moving to Burma for an assault on Imphal, the girls of Rani Jhansi Regiment submitted an application written in their blood to Netaji telling him that they were as anxious as any male member to proceed to the front and lay down their lives for the liberation of their country". Netaji conceded to their request and the regiment was moved from Singapore to Rangoon. No wonder, Netaji appointed Dr. Lakshmi as a minister in his 14 member provisional government.

Daughter of the brilliant lawyer, Swaminathan, Lakshmi opted for medical education when sending girls to college was considered a taboo. Her mother, hailed from Kerala and was a known Congress leader, Lakshmi joined the freedom movement inspired by Sarojini Naidu. Her first marriage did not last long and soon after separation she left for Singapore.

That was the year 1940 and the second world war was gathering momentum. Lakshmi came across a band of Netaji's followers in Singapore and she formally joined the INA in 1942. She raised a high motivated force of women volunteers which later came to be known as Rani Jhansi regiment. Initially the strength of the brigade was only 15 women. While working with Netaji, she came across a dedicated and handsome young man, Col. P.K. Sehgal, and INA hero.

He was a confidant and ADC of Subhas Bose.

She subsequently married Col Sehgal and their daughter Subhashni Ali, is a dedicated CPI warker and a former member of the Lok Sabha. Subhashni has played a key role in persuading her mother to be the left parties candidate in next month's presidential election.

She Fights a Losing Battle, but Without Bitterness

Focus has been on the two Presidential candidates—the Left's Capt. Lakshmi Sehgal and the NDA's Dr. Kalam. In last week's column, I had mentioned about Sahgal's glorious nationalist past and her equally glorious present—even at 88 years she runs a charitable clinic, tending of hundreds patients in Kanpur's industrial belts.

No, she doesn't talk much, keeps a low profile and though she's fighting a losing battle, there's no bitterness. In fact, she has addressed just one Press meet so far and soon after filing her papers, she rushed back to Kanpur to get back to the routine. She would be back here on June 26 to address several women's groups.

And focus shifts from wahwahing to Dr Kalam's nuclear the

ories (thank fully none have been tried out so far) to some other aspects—his self- proclaimed, bramacharya' status, his preference for veggie fare, his love for going for long winding walks, his mastery to deviate from giving direct answers to even simple queries on the Gujarat carnage..I could go on but the question of his hairstyle seems to distract. Till date Jagmohan' hairdo is said to be the ultimate in terms of style and effort but Dr. Kalam's strands seem to stand out just about somehow. And barbers are already upgrading themselves to hair stylists. Though the Rashtrapati Bhavan has the distinction of housing every possible department a saloon seemed missing so far, at least.

VVIP Security

As a bungalow on Prithvi Raj Road is reportedly getting readied for outgoing President K.R. Narayanan, residents staying in the multi-storeyed buildings/ complexes on the other side of the road are almost fuming. They say, the particular stretch has the bungalows of the Union Home Minister, the Cabinet Secretary and now with the former President also moving in, the security bandobasts would reach frightful limits.

Incidentally, this particular road also houses a former Cabinet secretary- Zafar Saifullah. But he leads a quiet life. The same is said of the present Cabinet Secretary T.S.R. Prashad. It's a complete contrast to his predecessor Prabhat Kumar's glamorous set up.

"It's all about leadership and we are trained for that"

In a telephonic interview from Chennai, A.P.J. Abdul Kalam spoke to Executive Editor Raj Chengappa on how he felt about being the ruling coalition's nominee for India's highest office. Excerpts:

Q. What is your reaction to your selection as NDA nominee for President?

A. I am overwhelmed by the gesture. Being the President of India is an onerous task.

Q. Many say you are being made president because of your religion.

A. Really? To be honest I never thought of it that way at all. I have always regarded my self as an Indian.

Q. What sort of a role would you like to play?

A . For any president the major task is thinking of the best way to integrate the nation. While speaking to 3,000 children in Porbandar recently a young girl asked me what my message was to them. I told her that our minds should be embedded with thoughts of the nation and that the nation is always bigger than the individual. I think that message is relevant here too.

Q. Does being a scientist equip you in any way to perform your new duties?

A. No doubt. This will be a new type of mission. But essenntially it is all about leadership and that is something we were trained for, even if the missions may have been different. We had a systems approach of careful analysis, design and integration that is relevant for any type of task. Also, we were not confined to conducting scientific research. We looked at the overall development of the nation.

Q. But you have never handled the intricacies of politics.

A. My own definition of politics is that it is all about creating leaders to evolve policies that will take the country to higher levels. It is multi- dimensional leadership that focuses on the nation's economic, social and political development. If you look at politics through this perspective then everything falls into place.

Q. How do you view the current tensions between India and Pakistan?

A. I have not had time to study this thoroughly. All I would like to say at this moment is that India is a strong nation. That its strength doesn't come just from its weapons, but from its economic development and maturity in politics.

Q. As president you would have to do things you never really enjoyed doing—like dressing formally and hosting formal dinners. Are you ready to change?

A. (Laughs) Let us say it will be a new experience. Besides, You can achieve a lot of work even while having dinner.

Deserving Muslim like Kalam. When the People's Front met again later in the day., the lines remained unaltered. Surjeet, who had kept unusually silent, said. "To phir kya hoga (so what will happen)? A

Left leader provided thereply: The People's Front is over.

Sonia was still not convinced that Kalam was the NDA's final choice. "There might push Alexander's name at the last minute." She told Amar Singh. Her suspicions were rooted in Kant's name being circulated. Then Alexander popping up again and then Kalam being named as NDA presidential nominee.

During People's Front meeting, the communists raged against Mulayam for backing Kalam. He behaves like a fascist. CPI(M) Politburo member Sitaram Yechury said. Mulayam recalled that he had proposed Kalam's name and had also recommended him for a Bharat Ratna, said Amar Singh. Let us face it. People are happy with Kalam.

Within the Congress, vociferous opposition came from senior leaders Manmohan Singh and Natwar Singh while career politicians in the CWC warned against dovetailing the party's interests with the Left.

When Vajpayee turned in for the night on June 10, the day the NDA endorsed Kalam's candidature, he may have recalled standing shoulder to shoulder with the scientist at the Pokaran pit. This time too. He had exploded another bomb , as politically seismic as the one designed by India's next President.

Simply Profound

Boatman's son, rocket builder, Kalam is a man with an uncomplicated worldview

Greatness comes in the cloak of humility, Samuel Butler once wrote. He may well have been describing Avul Pakir Jainulabdeen Abdul Kalam. As Principal Scientific Adviser to the Prime Minister, a cabinet-rank post he retired from in November last year. He was entitled to a palatial bungalow in Lutyens Delhi. Yet he chose to occupy two rooms in a Defence Ministry guest house that had been his home even when he headed the DRDO between 1992 and 1999.

But such is the irony of fate that if all goes according to the NDA's plan, by July Dr. Kalam, a bachelor, will move into the country's most coveted piece of real estate—Rashtrapati Bhavan.

"Kalam, who prefers bush shirts to suits and chappals to shoes, will have to get used to other prerequisites of power: formal wear for state dinners. Back in 1980, when the late Prime Minister Indira Gandhi called him to Delhi to personally felicitate him for putting the country on the world's space map. Kalam was in a panic as he owned neither a suit nor shoes. Satish Dhawan, the then head of the ISRO, told him, "You are already wearing the suit of success. So just be there."Kalam's suit has been well-earned. Not only was he responsible for building India's first satellite launcher, the SLV 3, but in the 1980's he also made the country a missile power by developing the *Agni* and *Prithvi*. His role in 1998s Pokhran blast came in a decade devoted to weaponising nuclear capability.

If the Bharat Ratna in 1997 was a token of the nation's appreciation, the presidential nomination is the real thing. For those who ask why Kalam, the question really should be why not. For who can be a better candidate than a poor boat owner's son, whose sister had to pawn her jewellery to send him to the Madras Institute of Technology for a diploma in engineering?

It must irk Kalam that there are many who say he has been nominated entirely because of the religion he was born into. He prays twice a day but religion to him has always been an intensely individual quest. He refers to the *Bhagvad Gita* as he does to the *Quran*. It was the Gita he quoted when he met reporters in Chennai after his nomination was announced. His spartan study has books on several religious philosophies.

He was there discussing the doctoral thesis of a student when Prime Minister A.B. Vajpayee called to inform him of the NDA's decision. All he said then was that he was "overwhelmed" by the decision.

In Kalam's worldview there is no room for complexities. India lost its greatness, he believes, because in the past she became technologically inferior. So to regain it, India must be self-suffcient in science. If that sounds distinctly Nehruvian, Kalam's view on the atom bomb, which he helped build, is vastly different. He believes that such arms deter other nations from attacking or subjugating India and are therefore , "weapons of peace".

His hobbies are calming: playing the rudra veena and writing poetry. It is this innate pacifism which stood him in good stead when he could not take up an assignment at the Indian Institute of Science, Bangalore, after conservative academics raised questions about his lack of a doctorate degree.

There are no such questions in his native Rameswaram, where his house on Thittakudi's Pallivasal Street is a testament to what Arun Tiwari, the co-author of his biography *Wings of Fire*, calls, "the best example of the meek inheriting the earth:"

Shooting into a New Orbit

His trajectory from Rameswaram to Raisina Hill

Young S.M. Abhishek recalls a proud moment he shared with India's most famous scientist. The higher Secondary student at Padma Seshadri Bala Bhavan in Chennai was hosting a science quiz at school when chief guest A.P.J. Abdul Kalam decided to fire a salvo himself. "We know the revolution of the earth is one year. How old is a person if he is on his 15th orbit round the sun?" He asked.

Abhishek took a while before giving the answer—14, since the sun is in its 15th orbit. "It was simple, but he made it sound tricky," he says.

The wizard of India's missile technology may be a media recluse, but he is a great hit with children. "His humility is shocking," chorus J.Darshana and S.Priya, who interacted with him in a science project.

Least interested in a presidential nomination until it happened , Kalam, after quitting as principal scientific adviser to the Prime Minister, was back to school last year with a mission to ignite at least one lakh young minds with a scientific vision. His advice to the 45,000 students he met so far has been to "dream, dream and dream and convert these into thoughts and later into actions."

"He does not pass a single chance to attend a school function or visit students during a break," says R.Radhakrishnan, personal secretary to the vice-chancellor of Anna University, where he is Professor Emeritus, Technology and Societal Transformation. The long queue outside his residential quarters on the campus was primarily of students and academicians, and he replied to every student query on the Internet.

The excitement that ran through the campus when the 71-year-old professor walked in six months ago had been experienced in the corridors of the Defence Research and Development Organisation (DRDO) a decade earlier. Entrusted with the integrated guided missile development programme, Kalam brought in scientific talent from defence laboratories, academic institutions and private industry to modernise the Indian defence juggernaut. The height of his achievement was Pokharan II nuclear tests in 1998.

He was conferred the nation's highest civilian honour, Bharat Ratna, in 1997. He had been honoured with the Padma Vibhushan in 1990 and the Padma Bhushan in 1981.

With the Congress backing Kalam's nomination by the National Democratic Alliance, his ascent to the top post is a foregone conclusion. Unmindful of the din his candidature created, Kalam quietly worked on his book *Ignited Mind: Unleashing the Power within India*.

The contrast, however, could not be sharper in Kalam's hometown of Rameswaram. His nondescript house on Pallivasal Street, Thittakudi, became a beehive of activity, with journalists arriving in droves to make a date with history. Bedtime stories to children and tea stall conversations revolve round A.P.Ambalam Jamaludeen Jainulabdeen Maraikayar's and Asia Amma's youngest of seven children (four brothers and three sisters). Maraikayar owned two boats which ferried people between Rameswaram and Dhanushkodi, and despite financial constraints, Kalam persevered in school.

He went to Rameswaram panchayat elementary school and moved to Schwartz School in Ramanathapuram town. None of his siblings finished school, and he became the first graduate in the family. After B.Sc. from St. Joseph's College, Tiruchirapalli, he took up aeronautical engineering at Madras Institute of Technology. Classmate and relative M.M.A. Noordeen mentions that Kalam took up aeronautics on the advice of Professor Fr. Sequeira while he was at St. Joseph's.

In 1958, Kalam joined the Directorate of Technical Development and production in the ministry of defence but fame and adulation came with SLV-3 project at the Indian Space Research Organisation. R.V.Perumal, associate director at the Vikram Sarabhai Space Centre, Thiruvananthapuram, hails Kalam for his fiery determination to make India a strong and rich nation.

Kalam sees four milestone in his career. The years at ISRO; when *Agni* met its mission requirements in 1994; the nuclear tests "which made me feel proud as an Indian" and when he made lightweight callipers for children at the orthopaedic centre at the Nizam Institute of Medical Sciences in Hyderabad. The man who led the nuclear weaponisation programme and believed only strength respects strength, is now involved in a brain research centre for mentally-challenged children, a project to digitally format knowledge preserved on palm leaves, and a cochlea implant for deaf children.

Kalam is strict vegetarian (nicknamed Kalam Iyer), teetotaller and remains a bachelor. He plays the veena, writes poetry in Tamil and admires poet Subrahmanya Bharati. He prays twice a day, and can quote with equal ease from the *Quran* and *Gita*.

India's problem, says Kalam, is not with its youth, but with its national vision. "The nation should have a vision", he writes, That vision should echo in Parliament and the nation should decide. The vision should further echo in family and among children. It is this vision that students like C. Srivatsan and A. Eshaam hope Kalam will hold up as President.

The Role of Atomic Energy, Space and Defence

Atomic Energy

The main mandate of the Department of Atomic Energy is the production of safe and economical nuclear power. The department has successfully developed the capability to build pressurized heavy water reactors based on indigenous resources. While a series standardized 220 M We reactors are operating and are under construction, the design of the 500 M We nuclear reactor is also ready for implementation. The effort in the development of this technology has been of multidisciplinary nature since nuclear technology is not just one technology. The component technologies include mechanical engineering, fuel and structural materials, manufacturing, control systems, fuel reprocessing, nuclear waste management and numerous other disciplines related to physics design, water chemistry, chemical engineering, robotics, backed up by the concept of quality assurance in every area.

The professional capability in the nuclear fuel cycle developed in the country is unique and is available only with a few countries in the world. To maintain this position we must ensure on continuous upgradation of this technology, integrating the latest developments in safety and advanced engineering concepts. The advanced heavy water reactor, which is evolutionary related to the existing proven PHWR design, is being studied. Fast breeder reactors, which will enable India to produce an order of magnitude more power from the existing uranium resources are important for India and a fast breeder test reactor has been built. The next step will be to use our vast thorium resources. Some initial steps have already been taken in this to enable us to move into the thorium-uranium 233 cycle.

While pursuing the above programmes, capabilities have been developed in numerous areas of advanced technology, particularly related to mechanical and chemical engineering, electronics and computer engineering, control systems, advanced instrumentation such as mass speedometers, information technology and materials technology which can be made use of by Indian industry to achieve other social and economic goals.

In addition to nuclear power reactors, efforts have also been put in by the R and D organizations of the Department of Atomic Energy to indigenously build a variety of research reactor. Skills have also been developed to build accelerators including the synchrotron radiation sources, lasers and other advanced systems. Research reactors and accelerators also require capability in a variety of technologies like magnet design, R.F.Systems, control systems, cryogenics, high precision mechanical engineering, etc., which can again provide spin-off support to Indian industry.

Scientists of the Department of Atomic Energy have also been pursuing basic research in various frontier areas, particularly in nuclear sciences, solid state physics, spectroscopy, nuclear chemistry, radiochemistry, biology, etc. In addition , multidisciplinary basic research capabilities also exist in the Department of Atomic energy and DAE scientists have interacted successfully with the Indian university system. These interactions must be strengthened both with a view to make synergistic advances as well as to provide major facilities of the department like research reactors and accelerators to the university system. In this context, an inter-university consortium for making use of the DAE facilities has been set up. The department has also set up national facilities like Joanki for preparation and supply of labelled biomolecules. This is located in CCMB campus. The Centre for Compositional Characterization of Materials has been set up adjoining the NFC campus.

The safety of reactor and environmental protection against radiation has been the prime concern of the DAE. Capabilities in the areas of biology, health and environmental sciences, which exist here, can again provide avenues of collaboration with university system as well as suitable inputs to industries in these areas.

A major R and D effort in the laboratories of the Department feeds the industrial units within the department. However, in addition, there are many spin-off technologies which can be made available to Indian industry. As an example, DAE has contributed to industrial radiography, health care through supply of isotopes and associated equipment, agriculture through improved seed varieties, railways, space and so on . Specific technologies have also been passed on to industries for their commercial exploitation. This process must also be strengthened further.

Space

Direct Benefits

Telecommunication. (Already available): Satellite telecommunication including business networks, rural telegraphy, communication for disaster warning and management, search and rescue, facsimile, etc.

(Future): Personal communication through low earth orbiting satellites, radio determination satellite service, computer interconnection, inter-library network, integrated data network, etc.

Television and education. (Already available): National coverage reaching even the remotest and inaccessible areas of the country, education through UGC programme, regional network, etc.

(Future): Dedicated satellites for eradication of rural illiteracy using one-way video two-way audio, continuing education for industrial workers and special social groups, video conferencing interconnecting business houses from different places, university education, single-video multiple-audio TV system benefiting people all over the country to see the programmes in their own languages, etc. High power direct broadcast transponders for reception with small dish antennas.

Meteorology. (Already available): Half-hourly VHRR imagery, meteorological data collection from unattended platforms, cyclone warning systems, etc.

(Future): Improved short-term and long-term weather prediction through better sensors on-board meteorological satellites.

Remote sensing. (Already available): Agricultural crop acreage and yield estimation, soil mapping, land use/land cover mapping, urban sprawl mapping, ground water resources mapping, detection of erosionprone areas, generation of flood mapping in near real time, groung water potential maps, coastal environmental monitoring, forest survey, mineral prospecting, identification of prospective zones for fishing, detection of forest fires, environmental impact assessment, snowmelt run-off estimates, monitoring of water levels in major reservoirs, etc.

Combining space data with socio-economic data, Integrated Mission for Sustainable Development (IMSD) at each village level already initiated.

(Future): Better monitoring of the agricultural crops, especially

crop stress and pest detection, incorporation of camera payloads with better spatial and spectral resolutions, on-board recording, stereo viewing and more frequent revisits to help in enhancement of scope in resources management and monitoring. New types of remote sensing payload such as synthetic aperture radar for imaging during day and night for a number of possibilities of using remote sensing in many areas of development.

Indirect Benefits

Technological upgradation of industrial infrastructure in the country through participation in the space programme. New materials development such as magnesium alloy, managing steel, beryllium, a variety of composite elements, chemicals, etc., which find applications in many areas, (e.g. composite materials used in textile industry, artificial limbs (Jaipur foot), prosthodontics, chemical intermediates for use in fertilizers for oil seeds, etc.).

-New products such as batteries, solar cells, optical instruments, telemetry systems for aircraft flight tests, etc., which have direct applications in many other fields.

-New technologies such as EBW, CADCAM, a variety of software (FEAST and ISROVISION).

-Development of scope for a number of industries manufacturing satellite communication equipment, remote sensing data interpretation equipment, etc., which have a very large and ever-expanding market both within and outside the country.

Infra-structure utilization and commercial exploitation of space technology.

-Sophisticated and elaborate infrastructure built under the space programme such as major precision fabrication facilities, test facilities, computer facilities, can be allowed to be used by industries depending upon the spare capacity.

-Major R and D facilities including computers, electronics test facilities, various chemical laboratories, etc., can be utilized by R and D institution and industries.

-ANTRIX Corporation already set up to exploit the immense potential of country's space capability by marketing space hardware and software in the international market. Export of up to one billion dollars per year is expected in five years. ANTRIX will coordinate with industries and the space establishments to exploit infrastructure and manpower base for commercial purposes. Export of many materials, components and propulsion system has already begun.

Future Thrusts

-Advanced propulsion systems, high strength/light weight materials , fault tolerant avionics systems.

-Serviceable satellites, space platforms, planetary missions, microgravity applications and life support systems for generating the necessary technologies.

Technology of source generation and management, energy storage system, long life control systems, thermal management systems and the means of communications to and from the space platforms.

R and D laboratories may be involved in the development of indigenous technologies in the above areas to meet the demands of the space programmes of the future. However, R and D laboratories need a reorientation in the management of their programmes. They need to work in a target and goal-oriented environment. R and D efforts are to be pursued with the same vigour as projects and should keep in view commercialization aspects of such efforts from the very beginning. Also, the R&D laboratories should concentrate on a few areas, which are need based rather than thinly spreading their scarce resources research. They should work in close liaison with industries and academic institutions to maximally utilize the existing infrastructure.

Defence

DRDO's major technology projects are based on the requirements of Armed Services. These requirements are essentially for state-of-the-art high-tech. Products and systems. This means DRDO essentially performs user-driven technology tasks. The technologies developed and accepted by the Armed Services are then transferred to different production centres like HAL, BEL and Ordnance Factories. Quality Assurance Organizations are entrusted with the task of acceptance of the products on behalf of Armed Services. Regular weekly reviews at high levels ensures timeliness of delivery of results with consequent production for Armed Forces. There is a continuous technology transfer from R and D laboratories to production units. In 1992 this resulted in a substantial technology transfer from defence laboratories to production units the value of production being about Rs. 1000 crores. Mission-oriented projects and programmes have also resulted in scientific and technological breakthrough in the areas of millimetric wage components, speciality ferrite phase shifters, guidance control technology and advanced composites. DRDO's experience in mission management and technology transfer could be very valuable for our scientific technological community.

Joint Advanced Technology Programmes have been started with five academic institutions, resulting in state-of-the -art science and technology partnerships between the Academia and DRDO. Through its research and training programmes, DRDO is also promoting aeronautical and electronic and materials research in twenty universities, several IITs and IISc. DRDO would like to share with scientific communities the results obtained.

Recently DRDO's technology on advanced composites has resulted in a joint sector company formation with COMPROC-DRDO and private company. Also through DST-DRDO collaboration and agency consortium for development of composites has been formed. A society for Non-ferrous Materials Technology Development Centre (NFDTC), a consortium of four public sector companies (HCL, NALCO, HZL and BALCO) of Department of Mines and DMRL of DRDO, is a successful venture already. There are other scientific/technical areas that have been opened out to industries recently.

17

His Vision : Developed India

President-in-Waiting A.P.J. Abdul Kalam, who is fond of saying "science seeks truth", is likely to hold the truth back in his latest book.

Ignited Minds: Unleashing the Power within India was to be an "honest" expression of what is right and what is wrong with India. It was completed well before Kalam was a contender for president. But now, the 178- page book's launch, originally scheduled for this month, has been postponed because Kalam wants to make "changes".

Kalam arrives in the Capital on Monday and will file his nomination papers on Tuesday. The book will now be released next month around the time Kalam moves into Rashtrapati Bhawan.

Scientists close to Kalam in Chennai, Bangalore and Hyderabad say that Kalam is making the changes after being told by colleagues and friends that "some porfions" in the original text may not be "palatable" to "some people" now that he wil be President.

Kalam agreed with his advisers that the book may send the "wrong signals at this crucial juncture or may be misinterpreted by NDA's political opponents".

The book was to be a sequel to *India 2020: A Vision for New Millennium* which Kalam co-authored with Y.S. Ranjan in 1999. According to scientists and the publishers, it examines "while given all our skills, resources and talents, we (Indians), so obviously capable of being the best, settle so often for the worst". Early this month publisher Penguin put up the cover of the book and a synopsis of it in the 'coming soon' category on its website.

After Kalam decided to make the changes, Penguin dispatched four editors to Chennai where they spent a long time with him taking dictation of the changes.

Kalam planned the book after surviving a helicopter crash last year. He felt this was God's message that he should serve some useful purpose. Consequently, the book was meant to contain fearless "reflections and musings".

Kalam had retired from government service, and wanted to put his feelings down in print honestly even if that made some people unhappy. The presidential nomination appears to have made him revise his position.

Neither Penguin nor those close to Kalam are revealing exactly what changes Kalam wants to make. They only confirm that the book's launch has been postponed.

The good news for the next president is that the print run of the book has been doubled to 12,000.

Missile Man Asks for a Smile, Gets It

In his maiden press conference as Presidential nominee A.P.J. Abdul Kalam sought a smile from the serious-looking scribes. They did not let him down. The venue was all smiles as he took centre-stage. But the follow-up was sans smiles as Kalam rambled through his replies replete with technology, development and GDP. It appeared as if the professor in his persona had taken over. The pep talk was serious stuff. Missiles flew even in interpretations of issues loaded with political undertones.

The Hindustan Times recently revealed Kalam's plans to rework his book *Ignited Minds: Unleashing the Power Within India* originally set for launch later this month. In response to a question about the plan, Kalam said:" I am the author and I can make whatever changes I want".

Apparently at ease in talking about science and technology, Kalam made some opening remarks from a prepared text. The draft came handy as he responded to questions on some ticklish issues such as Gujarat. These replies were obviously put together by his election campaign managers—Parliamentary Affairs Minister Pramod Mahajan and Defence Minister George Fernandes. The duo is reported to have roped in several experts to brief the prospective President.

Known for his passion for Tamil poetry, Kalam commenced the proceedings with a reference to his *Song of Youth* and the Constitutional directives for citizens to imbibe a scientific temper. In his poetic ode to a developed India, Kalam recalled his youthful yearnings:

"As a young citizen of India, armed with technology, knowledge and love for my nation, I realize, small aim is a crime. I will work and sweat for a great vision, the vision of transforming India into a developed nation, powered by economic strength with value system.... I will keep the lamp of knowledge burning, to achieve the vision: Developed India. " The theme ran through his formulations during the media event.

Minutes after the formal media- interaction ended, Kalam looked upwards when asked who his political Guru was. It was his way of seeking Allah's approval to embark on an otherwise smooth run to nation's highest constitutional office. Someone asked him who would perform the duties of first lady, once he took up residence at the imposing Rashtrapati Bhavan? Kalam took little time in repeating just one word amid controlled laughter-"Brahamachari Brahamachari!"

I'll Learn on the Job: Kalam

A.P.J. Abdul Kalam, the Missile Man who would-be-president, said on Wednesday that it was India and Pakistan's nuclear capabilities that had averted a war.

Quite in control of proceedings at his first press conference on Wednesday, a day after filing the nomination papers for the country's highest office, he nimbly avoided stepping on dangerous ground when answering questions on Gujarat, India-Pakistan tensions, India's nuclear capabilities and the Ayodhya dispute.

At the end of the 45-minute interactive session, the presidential nominee left his largely sceptical audience reassured he would be no babe in the woods in Rashtrapati Bhavan.

He also rejected the view (aired recently by Left Front's presidential candidate Lakshmi Sehgal) that electing him President would send the"wrong signals because he was a missile technologist. He said he favoured the integration of technology with development of the nation.

Probably addressing concerns on his greenhorn status among politicians, Kalam made it a point to tell the media he has dealt with six Prime Ministers over the past decade. "Even if your job is to put a satellite into orbit or develop a missile, you have to work within the political system. Working with politicians wouldn't be for me a new experience," he said.

Agreeing the Gujarat events were painful, Kalam said, "We

should prevent it at all costs. One way of doing it at all costs. One way of doing it is by elevating religion to spiritualism."

Kalam, however, parried questions on the handling of the situation in Gujarat and the impostition of President's rule in the state. Justifying the nuclear programme in the land of Gandhi, he said, "When the invaders would come with guns, we used to defend ourselves with swords... When your neighbour has nuclear weapons you cannot be doing *tapasya* (meditation)."

On minimum deterrence, Kalam said it depended on what India's adversaries did. The government has already declared a moratorium on nuclear tests, he said.

However, Kalam seemed a trifle out of step with the government's claim of a India-Pakistan conflict being averted because Islamabad buckled under New Delhi's demands on infiltration. He said, "(The) nuclear deterrent on both sides has helped... (avert) a big war".

Asked to comment on the India- Pakistan tension, Kalam said it was a "very sensitive" issue. The PM had already said the government was in "full control " and "I would not like to discuss it further", he said.

On Ayodhya and the use of Article 356, Kalam said, "The question is, what (do) the people need and what a few others are looking for".

Head of State, Without the Trimmings

A.P.J. Abdul Kalam may make it to Rashtrapati Bhavan without a hair out of place. The scientist has shot down suggestions from friends that he lop off his rock star locks to look more, presidential. "People are used to seeing me this way", he told them.

Kalam is proud of his mane , said a scientist at the Defence Research Development Laboratory (DRDL). "He preens himself before the mirror before going out; and often, pulls out the comb he carries in his pocket. In the middle of work, he suddenly gets up saying he'd be back in an hour. he returns with his hair trimmed."

No one at either Chennai's Anna University or at DRDL knows where the scientist gets his hair pruned though. Nor has anyone the foggiest idea why or when Kalam began to grow his thatch. A former Hyderabad colleague hazarded a guess: "He might have been influenced by the *sadhus* he saw as a child at Rameswaram and during his visit to Rishikesh."

Sometimes, family elders would scold him for the mess he carried on his head, but Kalam simply laughed it off, said his nephew Jainulabuddin.

But the hair, parted down the middle with locks hanging on either side, had been a hit with young scientists at Vikram Sarabhai Space Centre where Kalam spent 20 years.

But the mane may not be the only part of his get-up to rock the audience at his swearing-in.

When colleagues told him that formal wear was a must for the occasion, Kalam happily informed them that he has two sets of Western suits, one of which he had worn while receiving the Bharat Ratna in 1997.

"Some of us thought of suggesting the *achkan*," a friend said. "But then he might then have wanted to wear the *dhoti* and *jubba*."

It could be worse, though. "I have seen him wearing sandals with a three-piece suit," recalls Parameswaran Nair, a lodge-keeper at Thiruvananthapuram.

At the sewearing-in that would indeed be a hair-raising experience.

Fresh Blood Need of the Hour: Kalam

Presidential candidate Dr. A.P.J. Abdul Kalam apparently think that the present generation of old leaders cannot lead the country into the league of developed nations. At the convocation of the Indian School of Business at Hyderabad, the missile scientist said India needed young leaders to transform the nation into a developed one in the next two decades.

Dr. Kalam said India had been endowed with natural resources and human resources in abundance, but what it needed was young leaders with vision who could transform India into a developed nation and a knowledge society.

"The vision particularly ignites the young minds. The ignited soul is the most powerful resource on the earth, above the earth and under the earth compared to any resource. It is essential to keep the lamp of knowledge burning to achieve the vision—Developed India," he said. Dr. Kalam said at the dawn of freedom, India had the best of leaders in education , science, technology, history, politics and industry but today there was all pervasive mediocrity.

"Quality leaders are like magnets who will attract the best of persons to build the team for the organisation and give the inspiring leadership even during failures of individual or organisation as they are not afraid of risks," he said.

He had a word of advice for the ISB graduates. "You remember that change is the progress and hence change is the challenge. I wish you all to take up the challenge of transforming India into a healthy, wealthy, happy and empowered nation by becoming invisible leaders."

He said having achieved the first vision of gaining independence, all should work for attaining the second vision: to develop India into a strong nation, economically strong , self- reliant, and its people globally respected.

Kalam Moots Citizen Card for Information Security

While hacking and spreading of the worm is becoming a matter of concern, Presidential nominee A.P.J. Abdul Kalam has suggested introduction of a multi-purpose smart card 'National Citizen Card' in the country to prevent the breach of information security.

"Our communication network and information generators have to be protected from electronic attacks through surveillance, monitoring and building technologies to handle such attacks," Dr. Kalam said while addresing a NASSCOM seminar on Information Security.

"The hard earned wealth and the transformed society, which are the two pillars on which the knowledge society is supported have to be protected in order to sustain the knowledge society," he added.

Stressing on dynamic leadership for steering the country to prosperity, Kalam said, "When the leader of any institution empowers his or her people, leaders are born who can change the nation in multiple areas. Indian history is witness to this." When the political leaders of the nation empower the people through visionary policies, the prosperity of the nation is certain, he added.

World competitiveness is decided by a triangular combination consisting of progressiveness of industry, technological push and status governmental deregulation, all working in unison. "The World Economic Forum in its report had ranked India 41st in the table of world competitiveness," he said. In this regard, Kalam suggested putting in place an innovation system for competitiveness of both the service and manufacturing sector.

Stating that 70 per cent of India's population is young, he said, "Only the vision of the nation can ignite the young minds. The ignited mind empowered with knowledge is the most powerful resource on the earth to bring about this transformation."

Queue for Raisina Hill

The fall in the standard fo politicians and of people in other walks of life is apparently beginning to affect the choices for the Rashtrapati Bhavan as well. Some of the names that have been mentioned for the post of the president (and vice-president) reflect the Hindutva camp's wish to keep the *bhagwa dhwaj* of the RSS flying even when the BJP is not in power at the Centre. But more of that later. For the present, it can be said that even the current incumbent was not really an ideal candidate. Nor is his likely successor, A.P.J. Abdul Kalam.

To start with K.R. Narayanan, if he was not a favourite of the present government, it was because of his supposed activism. For once, however, the BJP was right. When Narayanan assumed office, he made it clear that he wouldn't be a quiescent President. However, there is no provision for an active President in the Constitution. Under it, the President, like the British monarch, is no more than a figurehead.

He can have opinions of his own, of course, about, for instance, the undesirability of a superpower acting like the headman of a global village. He can express it in a private conversation. But he shouldn't say it at an official banquet if the government does not share this view. In other words, the president should only read out from a text prepared by the government.

There is little doubt that Narayanan did not abide by such restrictions, If some of his 'activist' speeches, as about tampering with the Constitution, were received with approval, it is because the government's motive was suspect and a presidential rap on the knuckles was thought to be well deserved. But it will obviously not be a happy situation if the president and the government are often seen to disagree on crucial issues.

There were, of course, far more serious disagreements between Rajendra Prasad and Nehru. But Indian democracy was in a formative stage then and the respective spheres of authority in a parliamentary systems had not yet been delineated or even understood by all. In fact, it took a threat of resignation from Nehru for Rajendra Prasad to pipe down. Fifty years later, a recurrence of such incidents will be extremely unfortunate. No less unfortunate are the sectarian considerations which still influence the choice of a president. In

Narayanan's case, his dalit background clinched his nomination five years ago although his other qualifications for the position are undeniable. But even today it is the dalit factor which was again mentioned in the context of giving him a second term.

Similarly, the name of Maharashtra Governor P.C. Alexander was floated primarily because he is a Christian. There might have been other, less wholesome, reasons as well, including the BJP's calculation that Sonia Gandhi, a Christian, might find it a little more difficult to become Prime Minister if there was a Christian President. Besides, the BJP probably also believed that his nomination would partly erase its anti-minority image.

But the very fact that considerations based on caste and community can play such an important part in the choice of a President in the 21st century is not a matter of pride. If there was any reason to oppose Alexander's candidature, it could only be the suspicion that he was a closet saffronite, a surmise confirmed by the support extended to him by Bal Thackeray.

The name of another player to the BJP gallery—L.M. Singhvi—has also been mentioned. His claim to fame is that he teamed up with Murli Manohar Joshi's *kar sevaks* in the academic field to support the weird thesis of excluding all controversial references to well-known figures from history textbooks. According to Singhvi, hurting the feelings of any community was "unconstitutional" and therefore, he was in favour of deleting those portions from texbooks where "a deliberate attempt has been made to hurt the feelings of others".

As a child, Avul Pakir Jainulabdeen Abdul Kalam remembers being fascinated by the flight of seagulls. He grew up on the island of Rameswaram in south India, where his father was a boat builder. Kalam's interest in flight led to a degree in aeronautical engineering, and eventually to his supervising the development of India's guided missiles. Along the way, he found time to write Tamil poetry and learned to play the veena, an instrument similar to the sitar.

Perhaps all frontiersmen are like that. Avul Pakir Jainulabdeen Abdul Kalam has spent all his life near the three water frontiers of India. The newspaper boy of Rameswaram coast on the Indian Ocean spent 20 years dreaming of space frontiers at Thumba space centre on the Arabian Sea. The dreams of the next 20 years were mostly conjured up on the shores of the Bay of Bengal at Chandipur where he test-launched missiles and checked on vehicles that re-enter the atmosphere from space.

The dreamer of these oceanic frontiers is also one of India's frontiersmen in technology. A technology that not only fired Agnis, ingnited Prithvis but also can green the barren lands, provide foods to the starving, and profit in world commerce. A first world dream for a third world nation.

It is a dream he shares with Yagnaswami Sundara Rajan, another technologist who had his stints in the Indian Space Research Organisation, the department of space contributing significantly to the communication satellite programme, the remote sensing programme and satellite metorology and mapping systems.

From the sea frontiers and space frontiers, the duo are now dreaming frontiers of technology-driven prosperity for one billion people. In this they are inspired as much by the grain-rich fields of the green revolution as by the successes of remote-sensing satellites and reentry vehicles. They see infinite energy that can be released not only from thermonuclear explosions but also from the human resource latent in the ordinary people of India.

Dr Kalam and Rajan believe that as a nation India should aim to reach at least the fourth position by 2020. And nobody is going to help us reach there, except ourselves. As the globe is shrinking into a village, there is also simultaneous denial of technologies.

But the same sense of purpose that made Pokharans and Prithvis possible can propel whole populations into prosperity. In the book *India 2020, A Vision for the New Millennium,* published by Viking-Penguin India, they identify exactly the bricks of technology that could build the dream. (Incidentally, Dr. Kalam even otherwise seems to have the perfect 20-20 vision.

Some significant aspects of Dr. Kalam's life. That Dr. Abdul Kalam is a bachelor and teetotaller? That he recites the Holy *Quran* and the *Bhagvad Gita* daily and is equally at home with both Holy Scriptures?

That Dr. Abdul Kalam has gone abroad for studies only once in 1963-64 to the National Aeronautics and Space Administration (NASA) in the United States?That as a young boy, he sold newspapers to enhance his family's income?

That he is so modest about his achievements that at every felicitation ceremony he gives full credit for India's success to his colleagues?

Teacher

The Presidential candidate Dr. A.P.J. Abdul Kalam teaches at the Anna University in Chennai. While Dr. Kalam is not speaking to the media just yet, his colleagues and students are thrilled—saying there couldn't have been a better man for the post. While working on technology and societal transformation from his simple office at the Anna University, Professor APJ Abdul Kalam used to take inspiration from the life of Mahatma Gandhi, his role model, to stimulate young minds in their research work and encourage them to dream big. Dr. Kalam's only student, Fr George, has been working on implanting a computer chip in mentally challenged children. George says the Presidential nominee has promised to continue to assist and monitor his project even if he assumes the highest political office.

"During this crisis period I feel that he knows the strength and weakness of both India and Pakistan. So he should be at the helm of affairs now. He is such an incorruptible man that nobody can object. You will never feel that this is that great scientist who has been working with misiles and other things. He is 100 per cent human," says George. Even his old classmates and colleagues at work are overjoyed at Kalam's nomination. They remember fondly his simplicity, humane nature and his zeal to inspire young minds.

"He has got that basic humility and humaneness to interact with everybody in all walks of life. He always enthuses people to build," says R Balakrishnan, Kalam's classmate. There is a sense of jubilation and elation at Prof Kalam's nomination for the post of President. Students here believe that he will continue to ignite young minds not only in Anna University but throughout the country, to make his dream of a self-reliant India come true.

On November 2, 2001

Amrita Institute of Computer Technology at Amritapuri played host today to the Principal Scientific Advisor to the Government of India, Dr. A.P.J. Abdul Kalam. He has been honoured with numerous national awards including the Bharat Ratna in1998, which is the highest civilian award given in India. A great humanitarian, he extended his knowledge of space technology and mechanisms to help disabled children, replacing their 3-kg metal support braces with very light braces made of carbon, weighing just 300 grams. Dr. Abdul Kalam was on campus to seak to the AICT faculty and students.

Seated on stage were Dr. Abdul Kalam, as well as Dr. Balakrishnan of the Indian Institute of Science , and Dr. Madhava Nair of Vikram Sarabhai Space Centre, and Dr. Abhayamrita

Chaitanya.

The evening was inaugurated by Br. Abhayamrita, who lit an oil lamp and performed *arati* to Amma's picture. He was aided by Dr. Abdul Kalam, who gave the keynote speech, entitled 'How to Transform India into an Integrated Knowledge Society." Dr. Kalam opened his remarks by sending all best wishes to the members of the audience. He then said that upon entering the AICT building, seeing Amma's picture, he was reminded of a poem he had composed in Tamil years ago:

"Divine beauty enters into me and blossoms happiness into my body and soul."

Mindful of the youth of much of his audience, he related a formative story from his own youth. Dr. Abdul Kalam said that on the day after India achieved her independence, he opened the newpaper and found two photographs, side by side. The first was of India's flag flying high, surrounded by jubilant citizens celebrating their new-found freedom. The second was of Mahatma Gandhi, taken the very day of India's independence. As Father of the nation, all expected him to hoist the flag high. But rather than celebrating or resting on his laurels, he was found moving among the poor, sick and injured in East Bengal, new Bangladesh, working to alleviate their suffering amid inter-religious strife between Hindus and Muslims. From this image, Dr. Abdul Kalam said, he learned the real meaning of nobility in leadership: in success or failure, one should go on giving. The body of Dr. Abdul Kalam's speech explored the meaning of a knowledge society vs. an agricultural society, an industrial society and the curently developing information technology society. He reflected that in tomorrow's world knowledge will be the primary production resource, rather than capital and labour. The keys to developing a knowledge society, the doctor said, are the ability to create and maintain the knowledge infrastructure, develop knowledge workers and enhance their productivity through creation, growth, and exploitation of new knowledge. Dr Abdul Kalam stresses that this will lead to comprehensive wealth for the nation and to improved quality of life in terms of better health, education, infrastructure and other social indicators.

Dr. Abdul Kalam also placed a special emphasis on the tapping into the unique power and resources of the young, reminding the audience that 70 per cent of India's population is under thirty- five. He also related a story of having recently toured a steel mill and seen thousands of workers extracting and refining steel. What struck him the most, he said, was the sweat of the worker's. Sweat, he said, creates Agni (the Hindu god of fire). This Agni gives power to the nation. He told the youths gathered in the audience to think that they themselves are that Agni-- to be willing to work hard for the nation so that India will grow strong. Dr. Abdul Kalam: "Thinking is growth. Non-thinking is the destruction of the society. Only the vision of the nation can ignite the young minds. The ignited mind is the most powerful resource on the earth."

He closed his remarks with a quote from Patanjali's Yoga Sutras: 'When you are inspired by some great purpose , some extraordinary project, all your thoughts break their bounds: Your mind transcends limitations, your consciousness expands in every direction, and you find yourself in a new, great and wonderful world. Dormant forces, faculties, and talents become alive, and you discover youself to be a greater person by far than you ever dreamed yourself to be." The stiring lecture from one of India's greatest intellectual luminaries was followed by a question and answer session. One questioner asked: "Sir, you must have faced so many difficulties and challenges in becoming a scientist of your order. Where did you find the strength to overcome these obstacles?"

Dr. Abdul Kalam answerd by again referencing Mahatma Gandhi as a major inspiration, and concluded by relating a story from his time working on the Indian Space Research Organization. The doctor said that in 1979, after ten years of planning a dreaming to launch an Indian satellite from Indian soil, despite the computer's warnings of a serious error, Dr. Abdul Kalam proceeded to launch the satellite, which went into orbit "in the Bay of Bengal." After this devastating disappointment, the scientific team 's director (Dr. Abdul Kalam's superior) went before the press and took all the responsibility for the failure on himself. One year later, when a similar rocket launched successfully, the team's director asked his team to meet the press and receive credit for the success. From this, the doctor said, he learned that one should always absorb the failures in life, and share the fruits of success with all.On his way out of the building, Dr. Abdul Kalam was approached by a group of awed students, one of who said "Dr. Kalam, I want to become a scientist." The doctor answered with a question of his own. "Do you have a piece of paper?" The student eargerly retrieved paper and pen, ready to record the advice of this esteemed scientist. Dr. Abdul Kalam continued, "write down. Dream, dream, dream. Think, think, think—And then put that thought into action, action, action. OK?

Later the same evening he came to Amritapuri Ashram, where he met with Amma. He discussed spiritual matters as well as various national problems with Her, and received her guidance and blessings.

I have three Visions for India. In 3000 years of our history, people from all over the world have come and invaded us, captured our lands, conquered our minds. From Alexander onwards. The Greeks, the Portuguese, the British, the French, the Dutch, all of them came and looted us, took over what was ours. Yet we have not done this to any other nation. We have not conquered anyone. We have not grabbed their land, their culture, their history, nor have tried to enforce our way of life on them. Why?Because we respect the freedom of others.

That is Why My First Vision is that of Freedom

I believe that India got its first visions of this in 1857, when we started the war of independence. It is this freedom that we must protect and nurture and built on. If you are not free, no one will respect us.

My Second Vision for India is Development

For fifty years we have been a developing nation. It is time we see ourselves as a developed nation. We are among top nation of the world in terms of GDP. We have 10 per cent growth rate in most areas. Our poverty levels are falling, our achievements are being globally recognized today. Yet we lack the self-confidence to see ourselves as a developed nation, self-reliant and self assured. Isn't this right? I have a third vision. The India must stand up to the world. Because I believe that unless India stands up to the world. no one will respect us. Only strength respects strength. We must be strong not only as a military power but also as an economic power. Both must go hand-in-hand.

My good fortune was to have work with three great minds. Dr Vikram Sarabhai of the Department of Space, Professor Satish Dhawan, who succeeded him, and Dr. Brahm Prakash.

Kalam happy at being chosen for Prez post; to decide stand on Dr kalam's candidature NDTV Correspondent Tuesday, June 11, 2002: The Peoples Front comprising the left, the Samajwadi party and the Rashtriya Janta Dal, is meeting today to decide whether they will back the NDA government's candidate, Dr APJ Abdul kalam, as the next president of the country. Though the ruling coatition has the numbers, the government is still keen on evolving a consensus on the issue with the opposition. Meanwhile, TDP Chief and Andhra Pradesh Chief minister, Chandrababu Naidu has reiteratedt that Abdul Kalam is the best choice as president and a consensus has to be built for his candidature. "I can say the nation itself. It is not just politiccal parties, but it is a consensus for the whole nation itself. He is the best choice. Also we are giving the right signals to he whole country and outside the country." The National Democratic Front proposed Dr Kalam as its nominee for the post of president yesterday. "Dreams : Kalam" Dr Kalam spearheaded the country's missile programme. The high point of his career was no doubt the 1998 Pokhran nuclear tests, but there are many milestones that Avul Pakir Jainulabdeen Abdul Kalam passed since his birth on 15 October 1931 in Rameshwaram, Tamil Nadu. Dr. Kalam was the first graduate in his family. He did aeronautical engineering at he Madras Institute of Technology in 1957 and joined the Defence Research and Development Organisation (DRDO). He left DRDO in 1963 and joined the Indian Space Research Organisation (ISRO) where he was instrumental in the launch of the Rohini-I satellite using indigenously designed Space launch vehicles (SLVs). A completely indigenous product, his only foreign exposure was during 1963-64 when NASA invited him to spend four months at the wallops Island rocketry Centre and Langley Research Centre. After staying in ISRO for 19 years, he returned to DRDO in 1982 to head its Integrated Missile Development Program (IMDP), which produced the Agni, Trishul, Akash, Nag and Prithvi missiles. In recongnition, Dr Kalam was appointed the Scientific Advisor to the Defence Minister in 1992 and in 1999 was elevated to the post of Chief Scientific Advisor to the Vajpayee government , his last official post from which he retired in November 2001. His mission, he says , is to teach others. Educated in India, it is Dr Kalam's dream to make the country self-reliant in every way. Dr Kalam's motto in life is to dream and he claims that people should be allowed to dream. "Allow them to dream. Don't curtail their dreams, dream, dream, transform into thoughts and thoughts result in action, he says.

18

The Missile Man in Scientific Research

To uphold our secular values and constitutional tenets, we do not necessarily need a constitutional expert or a politician but a person who is proud of our secular fabric and has firm faith in our constitution, qualities which the NDA Presidential candidate, Abdul Kalam, possesses in abundance.

The choice of Dr. Kalam is a matter of pride and rejoicing for the country. We have selected a scholar of international fame in the field of nuclear and space sciences. It is a matter of regret that people bring in religion as a factor for his selection and seek a secular label for the BJP on that account. It is derogatory to say that such an eminent person like Dr. Kalam was selected because of his religion.

That Dr. Kalam made nuclear deterrence a point in favour of averting a conflict between India and Pakistan is disturbing (June 20). Being associated with nuclear energy and missile development, the scientist in him was apparent the question arises whether a President should involve himself in formulating policies when an elected Prime Minister, answerable to Parliament, is charged with such responsibility. In fact, a President under our Constitution talks less and listens more.

Kalam is happiest at the drawing board, in discussion with his scientists on how their dreams for the next millennium can be fulfilled. The projects envisaged include an air breathing hyperplane spacecraft that draws oxygen from the atmosphere rather than carry it all the way from the ground, reusable missiles and stealth technology. Kalam has shown that with adequate funding, freedom from procedural holdups and a people-oriented management, India can make products or internationally acceptable technical standards in a demanding arena like defence. Science, according to Kalam , is a global phenomenon. He feels there are a few areas where India can develop its core competence. These areas are software engineering, computer products and design, agriculture and food, aviation, defence research and space technology and chemical engineering. "This will lead to a highly beneficial economic and social progress for the nation". Kalam's advice to the youngsters of the nation is to "dream, dream and dream and convert these into thoughts and later into actions." Also to "think big" "We are a nation of a billion people and we must think like a nation of a billion people. Only then we can become big." On 25th November 1999, Dr A.P.J. Abdul Kalam was appointed Principal Scientific Adviser to the Government of India and accorded the rank of a Cabinet Minister. His role was to advise overall scientific development in the country on issues relating to scientific and technical policy in different sectors. Kalam also advised on matters relating to achieving technological self-reliance and foreign collaboration.

On December 8, 2000, the Deputy Chairman of Planning Commission, Shri K.C. Pant conferred the "Life-time Contribution Award in Engineering 2000" on Dr A.P.J. Abdul Kalam at the annual function of the Indian National Academy of Engineering in New Delhi. Speaking on the occasion, Kalam said that Engineering and technology should be used for the upliftment of the people living below the poverty line.

Kalam (left) with the Award

On November 10, 2001, Dr. A.P.J. Abdul Kalam quit as Principal Scientific Adviser to the government. Sources close to Kalam , said he quit because of "lack of executive authority". However, Kalam had been for quite some time keen on pursuing academic interests and helping scientists across the country in developing their research capabilities. That's why after quitting he took over the job as ISRO's distinguished Professor.

Dr. Kalam has spent the past few years developing the concept of "India Millennium Missions 2020"—a blueprint for transforming India into a developed nation. He calls it "the second vision of the nation" and says he wants to focus on the children of India to ignite in their minds a love for science and the nation's mission: a developed India.

A.P.J. Abdul Kalam could be an unusual President in more ways than one. While the Left parties objects because of his lack of political experience, Kalam's informal style could give the uptight members of our protocol department some anxious moments.

When Kalam was Scientific Adviser to the Defence Minister his habit of turning up in rubber chappals for meetings was frowned upon by bureaucrats, but he was excused on the grounds that he was after all an absent-minded scientist. Kalam's casual dress code of rubber chappals, shirts and bushshirt is not the only point of concern; the length of his white locks may seem a trifle too hip for a head of state. The Students Council felicitated Dr. APJ Abdul Kalam, Scientific Adviser to the Defence Ministry on 21st February 1998 at the fully packed J N Tata Auditorium. Dr. Kalam was accorded a traditional welcome. He was offered a garland shawl, flowers, a lemon, a fruit basket and a citation. The Students Council also presented him a Freedom run T-Shirt and the campus magazine, its proud production. Offering salutations to the eminent people who had assembled, Dr. Kalam spoke on "Vision and the Young". In his message to the younysters he said, the lesson is never to be beaten and never to let the problems become your master. He recounted that in 1986 he and Dr Arunachalam went to the US to negotiate for the CRAY XMP. He said there were nice lunches, dinners, lots of smiles, and finally no computer. They then decided to make a super computer indigenously. He quoted a couplet of Tiruvalluvar, a Tamil poet who lived during 200 BC "Just as the level of water lilies is determined by the flood, the greatness of people is determined by their attitude". They searched for a person who could develop super computers in India and finally found Dr. S.R. Venkataraman. Dr Venkataraman's team built a computer whose power was 7 times the power of CRAY XMP. Now it can deliver 6 Gflops and 30 Gflops in a year's time. Dr. Kalam further said that the young ignited own minds and that the ignited mind is the most powerful resource, more powerful than any resource on over or below the earth.

In his talk Dr. Kalam dealt with dynamics of vision, technological assessment of the country and how research in multiple areas is required for excellence. He said our strengths are manpower, high intellectual capacity, hi-tech institutions, industrial infrastructure, natural resources and the value system. Our accomplishments are the green revolution, operation flood, launching vehicles, nuclear capability, missile technology, super computers and microprocessors, materials science, software engineering. The problems he said are low productivity, weak economy, low R&D investment, and lack of leadership. Illustrating the various strengths that India has in his lecture, Dr Kalam concluded with his dream of a 21st century India which has economic prosperity, national security and a rightful place in the world and said that we should hold such a dream since dreams lead to thoughts which lead to actions. He said this could be achieved only through sustained effort and technological leadership by the young and scientifically competent.

Kalam was something of a curiosity at Thumba. A bachelor, his spartan lifestyle as a vegetarian and teetotaller who lived in a single room in a lodge in Thiruvananthapuram earned him the nickname Kalam Iyer. Kalam then moved back into the Defence Research Complex at Kanchanbagh, on the periphery of Hyderabad's Old City, as Director of DRDL. He came to Hyderabad at a time when morale was low at the laboratory as a result of the foreclosure of its ambitious missile project, code name 'Devil'. He brought a whiff of ISRO informality to a laboratory that was used to an Army atmosphere. He refused to move into the bungalow allotted to the Director, preferring to stay in one of the eight suites in the Defence Labs Mess. The suite, with a small study and a tiny bedroom, was his home for the next decade.

Kalam was instrumental in the re-emergence of the DRDL. This was made possible, as Kalam and the then Scientific Adviser to the Defence Minister, Dr. V.S. Arunachalam (who brought him back to defence research), have always acknowledged, by the crucial role played by R. Venkataraman, who was Defence Minister, Kalam was asked to prepare a blueprint to make India a missile nation. After working with DRDL veterans for over six months, followed by consultations with Arunachalam, Kalam gave a proposal to Venkataraman. It was a staggered scheme under which five missile development programs were to be taken up one after the other. "Take it back! said Venkataraman who, though unfamiliar with the technical nitty gritty, had an instinctive feel for larger strategic issues. The Minister suggested that Kalam and Arunachalam recast the plan in such a way as to develop all five missile types under one programme. They did it, as they now admit, by adding "zeroes all over the place."

Kalam's immediate concern was that he would have to tell his colleagues back in Hyderabad that he had committed to five formidable tasks instead of one. And the time-frame was 10 years. Out of this audacious initiative was born the guided missile programme. India's most successful military research task to date. Kalam's code-names for the programme's five components were: *Prithvi*, a surface- to-surface battlefield missile; *Nag*, anti-tank missile (ATM); *Akash*, a swift, medium- range surface- to- air missile (SAM); *Trishul*; a quick-reaction SAB with a shorter range; and *Agni*, an intermediate range ballistic missile, the mightiest of them all. *Trishul* has the unique distinction of being capable of serving all three services.

From his SLV-3 experience, Kalam had learned the advantages of team work and of sharing the tasks with partners in private and public sector industries. In the new management structure of the Missile Programme, Kalam, gave almost all executive and financial powers to five carefully selected Project Directors and kept himself free to address the core technology issues. His task was to inspire and monitor over 20 institutions and partners outside—ranging from large public and private sector suppliers to small specialist firms that needed seed money to take up the precision tasks. Kalam's contribution in this scheme has been acknowledged by all who worked with him. He set for himself a gruelling schedule. The first half hour of the day was reserved, for heads met him to take decisions on routine functions. During this period any employee could walk in and discuss administrative problems, which were usually sorted out the same day. The rest of the day was devoted to hand some interaction with project teams working on a campus spread over 40 hectares.

The missiles went up more or less on schedule: Trishul in 1985, Prithvi in 1988, Agni in 1989 and the others in 1990. And the Kalam legend had grown. He is well-versed in Tamil and has written poetry. Seventeen of his poems were translated into English by Manidarshi, and published as a book titled *My Journey* in 1994.

The establishment of the Research Centre Imarat (RCI), a campus 8 km from DRDL, in 1988 was perhaps the most satisfying achievement for Kalam during the missile years. He received generous funding from the government to build the futuristic centre, which is totally geared for work in advanced missile technologies. Its state- of-art facilities are set unique ambience and the level of comfort accorded to the individual worker is matched by few R&D institutions. And Kalam's interest in the environment saw Imarat emerge as an oasis in a rocky wasteland. It has a small orchard and a farm that meets the food requirements of those who stay in the

RCI quarters. Kalam was awarded the Padma Vibhushan in 1990. After 10 years in DRDL, he went to Delhi to take over from Arunachalam as Scientific Adviser to the Defence Minister reluctantly, many in DRDL felt. But the system created by Kalam had taken a firm hold in that decade and the missile programme passed on smoothly into its final phase of production and induction. In Delhi, Kalam as head of the DRDO had to "deliver other prestigious projects, such as the Main Battle Tank (MBT) Arjun and the Light Combat Aircraft (LCA) projects. While management practices he adopted for the missile programme have inevitably rubbed off on these projects, there are no miracles to be had in strategic development areas. There have been technical problems. Even within the missile programme, work on the SAMs and the ATM is slower than anticipated. But the recent multiple flights of Trishul demostrate that the system Kalam put in place his inherent strengths. As Arunachlam put it, "We are now mature; we learn from mistakes and push on ahead,"

"Strength respects strength." This is Kalam's usual response to the question why India needs its own missile or a battle tank or a combat aircraft. But Kalam is a technocrat. Although there are suggestions that he should use his status, which has been enhanced by the award of Bhara Ratna in 1997, to push for his active induction of Agni, it would be uncharacteristic of him to press his view too much in geopolitical matters.

Kalam is no miracle man. As the head of a vast network of laboratories—whose products include avalance- controlling structures in Kashmir, water desalination, kits for the Thar desert; a world class "Sonar" submarine finder for the new warship INS Delhi, and infra-red night vision goggles for the Army—Kalam's attention is necessarily a bit diffused. His self-effaacing persona cloaks a formidable catalyst who can make people work.

Hectic Programme

Anand Parthasarathy is a scientist who worked with Dr. Kalam on the Integrated Guided Missile Development Programme.

The call usually came late in the evening. "Kalam here," it always began, followed by the standard question, "What's happening?" One never knew how to respond, for a day's work at the missile- test bed, on the periphery of Hyderabad, meant a hectic 10 hours with everything seeming to go wrong. After preliminary queries came the real business, a key report had to be sent to to government the next day. "Eat your dinner in peace and come after you have finished", Kalam always hastened to add. He himself had not yet left the laboratory for the day.

This was how Kalam rounded up the usual suspects; an informal group of scientists and engineers, when some crucial work was at hand. It might be a no-holds-barred session to thrash out some issues to navigation and guidance before a Cabinet Committee on Political Affairs paper emerged, or to solve a problem dogging the elaborate quality assurance testing cycle to which a key missile component was being subjected.

The sessions were always held at a small round table—a table without a head, for protocol-free discussion. Sometimes the sessions would last till the next morning. For discussions during earthly hours, there was a bigger room across the corridor. But here too, failure to reach a decision was not a recognised option. Kalam attracted fierce loyalties from all those who came into contact with him. He was able to instil a sense of participation at every level, from the shop floor to the high-tech laboratory. His admirers include some children to whose lives he added a special touch. For nine-year-old Swarna, a polio victim from birth, the Composites Production Centre of the Defence Research and Development Laboratory (DRDL) had desiged an ultra lightweight, prosthetic foot support. Another child, a primary school student whose model of the Prithvi missile won the first prize in a contest in Secunderabad was taken to DRDL in Kalam's staff car so that he could see the real.

Kalam was asked to prepare a blueprint to make India into a missile nation. After working with DRDL veterans for over six months, followed by consultations with Arunachalam, Kalam gave a proposal to Venkataraman. It was a staggered scheme under which five missile development programmes were to be taken up one after the other. "Take it back !" said Venkataraman who, though unfamiliar with the technical nitty-gritty, had an instinctive feel for larger strategic issues. Venkataraman suggested that Kalam and Arunachalam recast the plan in such a way as to develop all five missile types under one programme. They did it, as they now admit , by adding zeroes all over the place. Kalam's immediate concern was that he would have to tell his colleagues back in Hyderabad that he had committed them to five formidable tasks instead of one with a time frame of 10 years. Out of this audacious initiative was bom the Integted Guided

Missile Development Program (IGMDP), India's most successful military research task to date.

Kalam's code-names for the program's five components were;

- Nag, an anti-tank guided Missile
- Prithvi, a surfce-to-surface battlefield Missile
- Akash, a swift, medium- range surface-to-air missile
- Trishul, a quick-reaction surface-to-air missile with a shorter range
- Agni, an intermediate range ballistic missile, the mightiest of them all

The Trishul has the unique distinction of being capable of serving all three services.

From his SLV-3 experience, Kalam had learned the advantages of team work and of sharing the tasks with partners in private and public sector industries. In the new management structure of the missile programme, Kalam, as the Chairman of the Programme Management Board, delegated almost all executive and financial powers to five carefully selected Project Directors and kept himself free to address the core technology issues. His task was to inspire and monitor over 20 institutions and partners outside—ranging from large public and private sector suppliers to small specialist firms that needed seed money to take up the precision tasks.

Kalam's contribution in this scheme has been acknowledged by all who worked with him. He set for himself a gruelling schedule. The first half hour of the day was reserved for what was called the morning meeting , where administrative heads met him to take decisions on routine functions. During this period any employee could walk in and discuss administrative problems, which were usually sorted out the same day. Rest of the day was devoted to hands-ou interaction with project teams working on a campus spread over 40 hectares.

The missiles went up more or less on time—Trishul in 1985, Prithvi in 1988, Agni in 1989 and the others in 1990. And the Kalam legend had grown. He is well-versed in Tamil and has written poetry. Seventeen of his poems were translated into English by Manidarshi, and published as a book titled *My Journey* in 1994. The establishment of the Research Centre Imarat (RCI), a campus 8 km from DRDL, in 1988 was perhaps the most satisfying achievement for Kalam during the missile years. He received generous funding from the government to build the futuristic centre, which is totally geared for work in advanced missile technologies. Its state-of- the-art facilities are set in unique ambience and the level of comfort accorded to the individual worker is matched by few R&D institutions. And Kalam's interest in the environment saw RCI emerge as an oasis in a rocky wasteland. It has a small farm that meets the food requirements of those who stay in the RCI quarters. Kalam was awarded the Padma Vibhushan in 1990. After 10 years in DRDL, he went to New Delhi to take over from Arunachalam as Scientific Adviser to the Defence Minister—reluctantly, many in DRDL felt. But the system created by Kalam had taken a firm hold in that decade and the missile programme passed on smoothly into its final phase of production and induction. In Delhi, Kalam's head of the DRDO had to deliver other prestigious projects, such as the Arjun MBT and the Light Combat Aircraft (LCA) projects. While management practices, he adopted for the missile programme have inevitably rubbed of on these projects, there are no miracles to be had in strategic development areas. There have been technical problems. Even in the missile programme, work on the SAMS and the ATM is slower than anticipated. But Trishul's recent multiple test flights have demostrated that the system Kalam put in place has inherent strengths. As Dr. V.S. Arunachalam put it, "We are now mature, we learn from mistakes and push on ahead." "Strength respects strength." This is Kalam's usual response to the question why India needs its own missiles or a battle tank or a combat aircraft. But Kalam is a technocrat. Although there are suggestions that he should use his status, which has been enhanced by the award of Bharat Ratna, to push for the active induction of Agni, it would be incharacteristic of him to press his view too much in geopolitical matters. He is the happiest at the drawing board, in discussion with his scientists on how their dreams for the next millennium can be fulfilled. The projects envisaged include an air breathing hyper-plane spacecraft that draws oxygen from the atmosphere rather than carry it all the way from the ground, reusable missiles and stealth technology. Kalam has shown that with adequate funding, freedom from procedural hold-ups and a people-oriented management, India can make products of internationally acceptable technical standards in a demanding arena like defence. Kalam is by no means a miracle man. As the head of a vast network of laboratories—whose products include avalanche-controlling structures in Kashmir, water desalination kits for the Thar desert , a world class sonar submarine finder for the latest warship— INS Delhi, and infra-red night vision goggles for the Indian army—Kalam's attention is necessarily bit diffused. His self-effacing persona cloaks a formidable catalyst who can make people work.

(Excerpts from an interview by Pritish Nandy, 31/10/98)

"Unless India stands up to the world, no one will respect us. In this world, fear has no place. Only strength respects strength". As a devout Muslim, he prays twice a day. But he is also a Ram bhakt, plays the veena, loves the Shri raga, writes poetry in Tamil and, like every proud Indian, swears by Pokhran II and self-sufficiency in science and technology. At 67, Dr A.P.J. Abdul Kalam, is not just another Dr Strangelove having a torried affair with the bomb. He is clever, sensitive, amazingly creative and, above all, a soft spoken patriot. India's answer to Western technological arrogance. What is your vision of India in the next millennnium? I have three. Three visions for India. But before that I speak about them, I have one question to ask of you, Mr Nandy. Can you tell me why, in 3000 years of our history, people from all over the world have come and invaded us, captured our land, conquered our minds? From Alexander onwards. The Greeks, the Portuguese, the British, the French, the Dutch all of them came and looted us, took over what was ours. Yet we have not done this to any other nation. We have not invaded aynone. We have not conquered anyone. We have not grabbed their land, their culture, their history and tried to enforce our way of life on them. Why? Because, I guess, we respected the freedom of others. Absolutely right. That is why my first vision is that of freedom. I believe that India got its first vision of this in 1857, when we started the war of independence. It is this freedom that we must protect and nurture and build upon. If we are not free, no one will respect us.

My second vision for India is development. For fifty years we have been a developing nation. It is time we saw our selves as a developed nation. We are among the top five nations of the world in terms of GDP. We have a 10 per cent growth rate in most areas. Our poverty levels are falling. Our achievements are being globally recognised today. Yet we lack the self-confidence to see ourselves as a developed nation, self reliant and self assured. Tell me, Sir, is this right? Read the last chapter of my book, *India 2020, A Vision for the Next Millennium* and you will get what I mean. I have a third vision. That India must stand up to the world. I have written 12 chapters on that. Because I believe that unless India stands up to the world, one one will respect us. In this world, fear has no place. Only strength respects strength. We must be strong not only as a military power but also as an economic power. Both must go hand in hand. These are visions. What about the reality? What do you see as the most significant achievements of your rather distinguished career culminating in a Bharat Ratna in your lifetime? My good fortune was to have worked with three great minds. Dr. Vikaram Sarabhai of the Department of Space. Professor Satish Dhawan, who succeeded him. And Dr Brahm Prakash, father of nuclear material. I was lucky to have worked with all three of them closely and consider this the greatest opportunity of my life.

I see four milestones in my career. One: the twenty years I spent in Indian Space Research Organisation. I was given the opportunity to be the project director for India's first satellite launch vehicle, SLV-3. The one that launched Rohini. These years played a very important role in my life as a scientist. Two : After my ISRO years, I joined the Defence Research and Development Organisation and got a chance to be part of India's guided missile programme. It was, you could call, my second bliss when Agni met its mission requirements in 1994. Three : The department of atomic energy and the DRDO had this tremendous partnership in the recent nuclear tests, on May 11 and 13. This was my third bliss. The joy of participating with my team in these nuclear tests and proving to the world that India can make it. That we are no longer a developing nation but now among them. It made me feel very proud as an Indian. And, finally, four : The fact that we have now developed for Agni a re-entry structure, for which we have developed this new material. A very light material called carbon-carbon. One day an orthopaedic surgeon from the Nizam Institute of Medical Sciences (in Hyderabad) visited my laboratory. He lifted the material and found it so light that he took me to his hospital and showed me his patients. There were these little girls and boys with heavy metallic callipers weighing over 3 kg each, dragging their feet around. He said to me: Please remove the pain of my patients. In three weeks, we made these Floor Reaction Orthosis 300 gram callipers and took them to the orthopaedic centre. The children could not believe their eyes! From dragging around a 3 kg load on their legs, they could now move on ground freely with these 300 gram callipers. They began running around! Their parents had tears in their eyes. That was my fourth bliss.

Apart from science and technology, what else interests you? Poetry and music. I have this big library at home and my favourity poets are Milton, Wait Whitman and Rabindranath Tagore. I write poetry too. My book of poems, Yenudays Prayana, has now been translated into English. It is called *My Journey*. You must read it. I will send you a copy. Who are your favourite poets in Tamil, the language you write in? Bharatidasana, who died in 1965. And Subramaniya Bharathiar, who died in 1939 at the age of 35, killed by an elephant while giving it a coconut. I also enjoy Carnatic music and play the veena. What is your favourite raga? The shri raga. You know my favourite kirtan? It is the one that Swami Thyagaraja, a Ram Bhakt like me, recited in the shri raga when he was called by this powerful Tanjore king to sing a poem in his sabha. He sang: "IN this gathering whoever are great in front of God, I salute them." He never said: I salute the king. That is strength of conviction. That is courage.

You have asked me so many questions, Mr Nandy, may I ask you two? By all means. Tell me, why is the media here so negative? Why are we in India so embarrassed to recognise our own strengths, our achievements? We are such a great nation. We have so many amazing success stories but we refuse to acknowledge them. Why? We are the second largest producer of wheat in the world. We are the second largest producer of rice. We are the first in milk production. We are number one in remote sensing satellites. Look at Dr Sudarshan. He has transformed the tribal village into a self sustaining, self driving unit. There are millions of such achievements but our media is only obsessed with bad news and failures and disasters. I was in Tel Aviv once and I was reading this Israeli newspaper. It was the day after a lot of attacks and bombardments and deaths had taken place. The Hamas had struck. But the front page of the newspaper had this picture of a Jawish gentleman who in five years had transformed his desert land into an orchard and a granary.

It was this inspiring picture that everyone woke up to. The gory details of killings, bombardments, deaths, were inside the newspaper, buried among other news. In India we only read about death, sickness, terrorism, crime. Why are we so negative? I guess we grew up with the maxim that good news is no news. The right to publish bad news has become synonymous with freedom. That is why our press is so strong, so fiercely independent if not always encouraging of success stories. Another question : why are we, as a nation so obsessed with foreign things? Is it a legacy of our colonial years? We want foreign television sets. We want foreign shirts. We want foreign technology. Why this obsession with everything imported? Do we not realise that self respect comes with self reliance I guess that comes from repression. When you lock in your economy for years and leave it in the hands of local pirates and cheating banias, you are bound to get a backlash. Foreign things have indeed come in but they have also brought down prices, taught us quality, stopped us from cheating consumers with shoddy, overpriced local products. Like in cars, consumer electronics, fabrics, processed food. Nationalism for too long has been a convenient cover for looting. Let us not forget that. But yes, I agree with you, it is time we started giving value to ourselves as a people, a nation. I was in Hyderabad giving this lecture, when a 14-year-old girl came up and asked me for my autograph. I asked her what her goal in life was. She replied: I want to asked her what developed India. For her, you and I will have to build this developed India. You must proclaim this through your writings, through your speeches in Parliament. Our achievements. Dream—Convert the dreams into thought, action. Mr Kalam, 66, has never hidden the passion for a powerful India that has driven him since he was growing up in a poor family on the coast of Tamil Nadu. Among colleagues a new word "Kalamitous" was corined to capture the outspokenness with which Mr Kalam greeted each new delay in the tests, or in getting the money to develop the missile to deliver nuclear bombs. When he returned to New Delhi from the test site in Rajasthan, Mr. Kalam found himself a national hero, applauded and besieged for autographs, though the tests drew widespread condemnation in the rest of the world. "We must think and act like a nation of a billion people and not like that of a million people," he said. "Dream, dream, dream! Convert these dreams into thought and then transform them into action." Only a few years ago, Mr Kalam became so frustrated with a reluctance of successive governments to approve nuclear tests that he came close to quitting as the government 'scientific adviser to become Vice-Chancellor of the University of Madras. When he appeared with other members of India's nuclear team at a news conference , nobody was surprised when Mr Kalam stole the shows with his readiness to flirt with plolitical issues. In the middle of a baffling explosion on "subcritical fissionable materials" and "electronic arming and fusing subsystems," Mr Kalam tuysed to a favourite political topic: how a nuclear- armed India will be free of the fear of foreign invasions which have constantly remolded the ancient Hindu civilization as armies of Macedonians, Persians, Afghans and Britons swept in. "For 2,500 years India has never invaded anybody, " he said. "But others have come here, so many others have come." For many Indians, the references to invasions, many by Muslims, underscored an aspect about Mr Kalam that is almost as engaging as his unguarded remarks, a biographical fact that is rarely mentioned: Like the captain of the national cricket team, like some of India's top generals and newspaper editors and diplomats, like many of its top filmmakers and artists, Mr Kalam is one of the 120 million Muslims in a nation of 700 milion Hindus. As India celebrated its arrival as a nuclear arms power, some said Mr Kalam's role meant the world now has an "Islamic bomb" but one that belongs to India—an India ruled by Hindu nationalists. The term "Islamic bomb" describes the yearning among some of the world's one billion Muslims for the development of nuclear weapons by a Muslim country, most likely Pakistan, India's archrival, which is considering whether to respond to the Indian tests with one of its own. But though Mr Kalam is an observant Muslim, his attitudes and tastes speak of his immersion in the broader culture of India. He is an avid reader of ancient Hindu scriptures. He has published poems in Tamil, his first language. And one of his pastimes in his modest walk-up apartment in New Delhi is playing a *veena*, a stringed instrument with a curved musical box at each end. According to one Indian biography, Mr Kalam knows by heart sections of the best known Hindu sacred book, the *Bhagavad Gita*. If so, this would give him another link to Robert Oppenheimer, the physicist who led the team that tested the first American atomic bomb in New Mexico desert on July 16, 1945. According to some accounts, after the predawn flash signaled the birth of the atomic age, Mr Oppenheimer quoted a line from the *Bhagavad Gita*."Now I am become death, the destroyer of worlds".

Before becoming the chief scientific adviser and leader of the nuclear - weapons team, Mr Kalam was best known as a missile engineer, working on the programme that launched India's first space satellites,and later as the head of the team that developed and test fired missile designed to carry nuclear warheads. Boffiin named favourite to be next president. He is a popular icon among youths for his work with missile technology. And the man almost certain to be the next President of the world's biggest democracy has other attributes as well. A missile scientist is going to be the next president of the world 's largest democracy. This will be the first time in the history of independent India that a scientist has risen to become head of state. The nomination of A.P.J. Abdul Kalam for the top post by the ruling National Democratic Alliance has surprised many, but it never the less is widely welcomed. But not by all. Mr Kalam is not a politician, but his nomination has left a trail of political controversy. Mr Kalam is widely acknowledged as the father of India's missile and nuclear weapons programmes. He has served in india's space and defence research agencies for over 40 years. He retired as principal scientific adviser to the Indian government in November last year. He rose to prominence with the launch of the first surfce-to- surface missile, Agni, in 1994 and the Pokharan nuclear tests in 1998. He headed the team of defence research and nuclear scientists who conducted the tests. Much of his fame comes from the development of the surface-to-surface and surface-to-air missiles that include the nuclear-capable Agni and Prithvi missiles, with a maximum range of 3,500 km. Development of an Indian combat aircrat called LCA is yet another of his pet projects. He also conceived a hyperplane, but the idea remains on the drawing board. The 71 year-old Mr Kalam is the only scientist decorated with the highest civilian order of Bharat Ratna (the jewel of India). While nobody questions the sincerity, integrity and scientific achievements of Mr Kalam, what has given to a controversy during the timing of his nomination. Mr Kalam is a devout Muslim, and his nomination is being seen as a ploy by the ruling Bharatiya Janata Party (BJP) and its allies to divert attention from the anti-Muslim riots going on in Gujarat state. Leading political analysts and some political parties have accused the BJP of using Mr Kalam's religion for political gain. '"BJP's seemingly enthusiastic support for his candidature was a result of wholly extraneous factors underpinned as it was by an element of tokenism and a desire to deflect attention from the horrific and unpardohable communal carnage in Gujarat, said *The Hindu*, an independent newspaper published from Chennai in Tamil Nadu—Mr Kalam's home state—in an editorial. Mr Kalam also fits very well into BJP's definition of a reformed Muslim. He is equally conversant in the *Koran*, the Muslim holy book, and the *Bhagwad Gita*, the Hindu holy book. He is seen as a nationalist visionary who wants to make India a developed country through the use of cutting edge technologies in the defence and knowledge sectors. As the principal architect of the guided and ballistic missile programmes and a strong advocate of a militarily strong India, his selection identifies well with the BJP 's pursuit of a militaristic agenda. Through his selection, the BJP is trying to send a positive signal to the Muslim community, although Mr Kalam has denied that his being Muslim had nothing to do with his elevation to the top post. But contemporary Indian history shows that ruling parties have used this largely ceremonial post of President for short political gains. In the 1980s, then Prime Minister Indira Gandhi chose a relatively junior Sikh politician, Zail Singh to become President since she had to appease the minority Sikh community. Secondly, the missile scientist's selection is going to send strong signals to the Islamic neighbour of Pakistan. Mr Kalam is known for his strong views on making India a nuclear weapons state and a regional superpower. And herein lies some of the controversy surrounding his nomination. Being a missile and nuclear scientist will send the wrong signals to the world community, feels Ms Laxmi Sehgal, a veteran freedom fighter who has been fielded by communist parties for the presidential election. It is going to be two-way fight, but the electoral college is heavily tilted in favour of Dr. Kalam. Some analysts feel that there is no real need to read much into the scientist 's selection. The President, under Indian constitution, can hardly influence policy decisions. He is a mere approver of the decisions taken by the Parliament and the cabinet headed by the Prime Minister. A President's role becomes crucial when there is no clear majority to any political party in the Parliament—a hung Parliament. Under such circumstances, the President must act impartially and invite a party or a combination of parties that has a clear majority. Parliamentary elections in the recent past have shown that hung parliaments are a reality in India, forcing parties to form coalitions such as the present ruling National Democratic Alliance. Some amount of political knowledge and a thorough understanding of constitutional matters is required to handle such situations. Whether Dr. Kalam will be able to handle such situations remains a big question. In any case, Dr. Kalam's candidature has evoked a huge public response, since after the Pokharan blasts, he had come sort of a popular icon among youths and students. The scientific and academic community too is happy with his elevation. With Dr. Kalam expressing a desire to continue research and teaching activities even after assuming the new office, India may see a working president for the first time. There is another unique factor. For the first time both the head of state and the head of government will be bachelors, posing problems for protocol officers.

Kalam Stresses the Role of Energy in National Development

'Noble leadership, indomitable spirit and universal mind are the need of the hour, if we really want to achieve all the national missions, observed Bharat Ratna Dr. A.P.J. Abdul Kalam , Principal Scientific Adviser to the Government of India. Delivering the first endowment lecture instituted in the honour of Padmashri Dr. Narla Tata Rao, organised by the A P State Centre of the Institution, Dr. Kalam, the archtiect of missile technology in India, specified five mega missions to transform the nation into a developed country. He outlined these missions as agriculture and food processing; education and healthcare; information technology; strategic sectors of nuclear, space and defence technology; and reliable and quality electric power, where the country needed an integrated action. Energy is the elerctromotive force for nation-building but enegy shortfall poses a serious challenge ahead, said Dr Kalam. Referring to the draft paper on Energy for the Future: Options and Actions for India prepared recently by the Consultative Group of Eminent Senior Scientists (CGESS), constituted by he Government of India, Dr Kalam informed that India consumed about 3 per cent of world energy consumption despite having 17 per cent of global population. Driven by the rising population, expanding economy and quest for improved quality of life, energy usage in India is expected to double by 2010. Considering the limited reserves of petroleum and natural gas, eco-conservation restriction on hydel project and geopolitical perception of nuclear power, coal will continue to occupy centre- stage of India's energy scenario. Dr Kalam opined urging the young Indians to help build the country, Dr Kalam said the nation needs young leaders who can command the change for transformation of India into a developed nation embedded with knowledge. Later, Padmashri Dr Narla Tata Rao, former Chairman of th APSEB, said that there was nothing wrong with the power sector and the political leaders only were responsible for the crisis. The country had the best brains and vast resources which could be utilised to tackle the energy shortfall, Dr Rao opined. .

Speech at the Annual Function of the Indian National Academy of Engineering on 8th December, 2000

I am happy to be amongst you today at the Annual Function of the Indian National Academy of Engineering. I am particularly happy to learn that, among other awardees, Dr. A.P.J. Abdul Kalam, Principal Scientific Adviser to the Government, will be honoured with Life Time Contribution Award in Engineering 2000. Institutions like the Indian National Academy of Engineering help in the development of advanced technologies, which are necessay to survive in today's global society which is becoming increasingly competitive. Technology is the most powerful weapon for creating a competitive edge. The global economy of today carries the message 'Innovate or Evaporate'. To survive in this global economy, technological advancement has to be not only rapid, but also more wide-spread. India, therefore, needs to do much more in two key areas substantive corporate innovations and rapid diffusion of technology. We may be proud of our great scientific heritage and our contributions to the world of science, but we are still dependent on external technologies in many areas. Hence, new policy initiatives are needed for deepening and broadening India's technological base so as to meet the challenge of tehchno-globalism. I hope indeed, I am confident that the Indian National Academy of Engineering will continue on its path of excellence and contribute thereby to the technological advancement of India. Under pressure, India has given impressive proof of its inherent capability to find indigenous technological solutions, as is evident in the case of agriculture, atomic energy and space. There is a need to extend this capability even under normal circumstances, to the entire techno-economic spectrum of the country. This Academy must ensure that excellence in science leads to the blossoming of appropriate technologies to suit Indian conditions. The Academy is, I am sure, conscious of the importance of its role. My purpose here is only to emphasis the urgency and speed with which it has to perform.

A review of the development of the last fifty years indicates that there is inadequate linkage between Indian science and technology and Indian industry. Except for Atomic Energy, Space and defence this is generally true. The Indian heavy industry has been set up predominantly with foreign collaborations and has not felt any great pressure to carry out independent or in-house Research and Development. Indian industry must make greater efforts to upgrade its existing technological levels if it is to survive and thrive. In this respect, the Indian National Academy of Engineering can play an important role as an interface and facilitator of technological development and diffusion in the country.

In particular, I would like to draw your attention to the fact that it is infrastructure development which provides the backbone for the all-round growth of a nation. Inadequacy and imbalances in the infrastructure are today threatenig to become a major constraint on growth partly because there was inadequate investment in this area and partly because of technological inadequacy. The challenge before us is to provide infrastructure facilities of international standards, particularly in the Transport, Telecommunications and Power sectors, and at affordable cost. This will require a major effort in the form of technological upgradation of facilities in all these sectors. This is particularly essential since the projected growth rate of at least 7 to 8 per cent would make heavy demands on the infrastructure. Since infrastructure is non-tradable, the additional demand has to be met by expanding domestic supply.

A Task Force on Infrastructure has been set up by the Government. An important initiative that has been launched within the ambit of this Task Force is to develop the National Highways. This National Highway Development Project (NHDP) would enable the development of a transpot network. The Golden Quadrilateral will link Delhi-Mumbai-Chenni and Calcutta. The North South Corridor will connect Kashmir to Kanyakumari and the East . West Corridor will connect Silchar to Saurashtra. This project is being executed by the National Highway Authority of India. This will result in improving accessibility, enhancing mobility and adding to the existing capacity. The successful implementation of this project would address the important issue of capacity constraint experienced in the Transport Sector. This project is likely to be completed in ten years, at the end of which about 13,000 kms. of road length would have proper transport infrastructure.

There is, likewise, a need for upgradation and modernization of infrastructure in Railways, Ports, Power and Telecommunications. In the Power Sector, we need very large investment in the next ten years since an addition of approximately 10,000 Megawatt per annum is required. The government will obviously find it very diffficult to provide the required level of investment from its own funds. Therefore, the private sector has to play a very important role in the growth of the Power Sector. In addition, every effort will have to be made to improve our energy efficiency, which will require considerable technological upgradation of practically every sector of the economy. The Telecommunication sector too needs to expand, particularly in keeping with the prospect gradual convergence with the Power, IT and Entertainment sectors. The government has already taken initiatives regarding his Convergence, and the convergence Bill 2000 is under consideration. At the same time, there is a need to continue with acceleration in the pace of reforms in the power and Telecom Sectors in order to bring about the desired synergies. It will be the Planning Commission's endeavour during the Tenth Plan to promote realization of the potential synergies of greater convergence to maximize efficiencies. While the government recognizes the need for a well developed and efficient infrastructure, it will find it difficult to provide the required level of investment from its own funds. The scale of expansion required in infrastructure needs resources of an unprecedented magnitude. It is only by forging public-private partnerships in both technological know-how and financial resources that India can move faster towards achieving the requisite inf rastructure. Such interfaces are only in their nascent stage, and considerable efforts will have to be made to bring them about in a fairly short time-frame.

The Planning Commission recognizes the role of private initiative in nation building. Private initiative whether individual, collective or community based, forms the essence of the Ninth Plan development strategy. Events like this function organized today play an important role by bringing together the private and public sectors. The private sector must come forward in contributing further to the growth of infrastructure sectors through advancements in technology. One of the problems facing various sectors including infrastructure is that the productivity levels are substantially lower than international standards. The lower productivity is, inter alia, on account of inadequacy of training and research and development efforts. The Indian industry has not invested sufficiently in the creation of technological capability to enable it to compete globally. The Indian industry must increase its investments in Research and Development so that the supply side of technology improves.

Another reason for low productivity and lack of proper quality is our tendency to accept comparatively lower standards. Engineers, therefore, have an important role to play by not accepting any work below a particular standard. This would give the right message to all those who are engaged in provision of goods and services, including infrastructure. It may also be necessary to encourage those who contribute towards raising productivity and quality levels.

There is another area of concern which I would like to share with you. The Indian National Academy of Engineering is associated with the creation of a large supply of technical manpower. However, there is a trend for a significant number of technocrats educated and trained in India to work abroad. The task of nation building can move forward only with the help of indigenous human resources. Engineers and other technocrats must stay in India and contribute to its technological advancement. For this to happen, a conducive environment needs to be created not only in the conditions of living but also at the work-place. We must give our technical manpower the recognition and credit that they deserve.

I have great pleasure in inaugurating this Annual Function of the Indian National Academy of Engineering".

The National Democratic Alliance today despatched a Union Minister to Chennai to meet its presidential candidate, Dr. APJ Abdul Kalam. A Minister attached to the Pime Minister's Office. Vijay Goel was closted with Dr. Kalam for over half an hour at the latter's office in the Ramanujam Centre for Computing, Anna University. Though Mr. Goel said that it was only a "Courtesy call", he told newspersons that Dr. Kalam was likely to file his nomination papers on Monday.

However, the Union Minister declined to comment when asked if he was carrying some letter from the BJP Leadership or the Prime Minister. Dr. Kalam, however, chose to remain indoors and refused to meet the Press or be photographed with Mr. Goel.

Before meeting Dr. Kalam, the Union Minister visited Kancheepuram and had a meeting with the Sankaracharya of the Kanchi Sankara Math, Jayendra Saraswathi, who is performing a 'Yagna for economic prosperity and curbing evil.

So many phone calls, e-mails and media reports are pouring in continuously from Monday onwards, after the announcement of my candidature for the President of India. I am really overwhelmed. Everywhere both in internet and in other media, I have been asked for a message. I was thinking what message I can give to people of our country at this point of time. I would like to thank the leaders, political parties and the entire nation for the confidence and faith they have reposed on me. The post of President of India indeed reflects the integrated aspirations of the nation. When this process is going on, I recall a great Indian thought which is apt and reflects the mood of the nation.

"What ever happened has happened for the good"

Strive to achieve self-reliance: Dr. Kalam

India could become economically self-reliant only when poverty is wiped off the country, Dr. A.P.J. Abdul Kalam, former Principal Scientific Adviser to the Government of India, said here on Saturday.

Addressing a meeting on 'Technology and Society' as part of the National Technology Day celebrations at SVIMS here, Dr. Kalam stressed the importance of human genome project and biotechnology for the future. At present, over 40,000 genes and two million protein have been discovered with which a comprehensive genomic health care can be established in the country in the near future.

Dr. Kalam said the nobility of the leadership is the most important factor for a person to offer sincere services to the country. He enlightened the conclave, especially the students, with quotations of Maharishi Patanjali and Dr. C.V. Raman.

Andhra Pradesh Information and Technology Minister B.Gopala Krishna Reddy assured Dr. Kalam of proposing a biotechnology department on SVIMS campus and said the SVIMS would emerge as "a super-specially hospital" in the sate with a concept of serving the poorest of the poor as its prime goal.

SVIMS Director Dr. Subramanyam, Tirupati MLS Chandalawada Krishnamurthy, Puttur MLA Reddivari Rajasekhar Reddy, Dr. Mohan Vemuri and Deputy Registrar Bhaskar were present.

Fusion of Science and Spirituality

The father of India's first nuclear bomb, the architect of our sophisticated space and missile technology, and a rare scientist whose vision to develop society upon the foundation of values, the 70-year-old Bharat Ratna, Dr. APJ Abdul Kalam came calling upon HDH Pramukh Swami Maharaj, with his fellow scientist, Y.S. Rajan, Scientific Secretary to the Government of India and Executive Director of the Technology, Information, Forecasting and Assessment Council.

They sought blessings and guidance for Vision 2020. This special meeting on 30 June 2001 turned out to be a beautiful fusion of science and spirituality. Some illuminating sparks have been compiled from the hour-long session of questions and answers.

AK: Swamiji, India and the vision, since 1857, for independence. It took ninety years to get freedom. At that time the whole nation, the young and old, had united to get freedom. Our first goal was to acquire Independence. Swamiji we are thinking, what is or what can be such a vision now? Since the last 50 years, India is a developing country. It means economically it is not strong, socially it is not stable, security is not enough.... that is called a developing country. Five hundred members like me are thinking, what should be the next vision for India? How do we transform a developing country into a developed country in the next 30 years. We have identified five important areas to transform India: Education and Healthcare, Agriculture, Information and Communication, Infrastructure and Critical Technology.

Swamiji, our problem is that we may present this before the Government, but how do we create people with values to carry out such a big vision. What we need is a cadre of value-based citizens. For this you are an expert. We need your advice.

Swamiji: Along with these five, add a sixth-faith in God and developing people through spirituality. This is very important. We need to first generate a moral and spiritual atmosphere. Unlike the present system and climate of crime and corruption, we need to raise people who live by the laws of the scriptures and bear faith in God. For this we need to rekindle faith in our scriptures and God. This will make things easier. Questions will be solved and we shall be able to achieve what we dream.

AK: Swamiji, for carrying forward such a big vision of transforming India, should we first create a spiritual tradition, make people spiritual and then embark upon our vision, or focus on one of the important areas like education or health? Or should we integrate everything and begin simultaneously?

Swamiji: Simultaneously. Work in the five fields you have identified for the country's progress should be continued and together with it this should be parallely incorporated. Our culture teaches us to learn both *Para* (spiritual) and *Apara* (worldly) *Vidya* (knowledge). Therefore, together with knowledge of the *Apara*, one should learn the *Para* as well. If one learns this then *Apara*—worldly knowledge will become founded on *dharma* and spirituality. The goal behind God's creation of the universes is that every person, every soul attains bliss. For this, together with knowledge of His creation, He has given the knowledge of Himself. So, together with this worldly knowledge, knowledge given by God—spirituality is equally necessary.

AK Swamiji: To realise this great dream, three types of people are needed *punya atma* (virtuous people), *punya neta* (virtuous leaders) and *punya adhikari* (virtuous officers). If the population of all the three increase in our society, then India would become the *jagadguru* (world leader). How can their numbers be increased?

Swamiji: Together with your academic and scientific efforts, give spiritual training in our schools and colleges. Nowadays, spiritual education has been removed from schools and colleges. That which should be received from infancy is not being given and we continue to teach mere academic knowledge only. But from the beginning, right from birth, people should be taught values, only then will people become virtuous. From the cradle , such values should be inspired. In the education syllabus, knowledge of our scriptures and great sadhus and sages should be given. Such a system will help produce virtuous people. The virtuous social, spiritual and political leaders we see today have attained their values from the very beginning. In the past, such values were taught in our gurukul system of education. Whether a prince or a pauper, everyone studied together. Along with academics, lessons such as: *satyam vada* (speak the truth), *dharmam chara* (tread the path of righteousness), service towards others and faith in God, were taught. Swamiji, what a pity good citizens are not produced by the laws of the Government. They are created only by Swamijis like you. Can you preach to families that upto the age of 15, parents should take interest in their children and inspire values in them. Similarly, in all elementary schools, teachers should also teach values to their pupils. But if we miss this age of 15 of instilling values by father, mother and teacher, then the Government can not produce good honest citizens. Is my understanding correct? yes, It's true. It's definitely true. We Swamiji: have been saying this from the very beginning that values should be taught by parents at home, teachers at school and the guru in life.

AK: Swamiji, when I first launched a rocket it failed and I became very depressed and disheartened. At that time I thought about becoming a sannyasi, and give up every thing. (in this context, one sadhu added, "Dr. Kalam studies the Gita. Reads it every day, and has tremendous patriotism.). Because he Swamiji:posseses such noble thoughts , such patriotism is but natural. That's why we say, if spiritual knowledge is given from the begining, love and pride for one's society and dharma is a natural result. However , spiritual values should form the foundations. (The grand plans for the Akshardham complex in New Delhi were explained. While seeing them, Dr. Kalam was himself filled with pride).People should see this monument and realise that India is not weak, but is an extremely powerful and cultured country. (Then with the mention of Indian culture flourishing along the banks of river Saraswati, Abdul Kalam suddenly asked.)

AK: Do you feel the Saraswati river was existing?

Swamiji: It exists, it is written in our scriptures that it exists.

AK: India was a rich country. Economically it was rich, culturally it was rich. My mind always asks a question, for 3,000 years India has been invaded again and again, but not once has India invaded others. Why?

Swamiji: It is the virtue of God. A divine quality—not to take another's. And not to forcibly usurp. Not to hurt or harass others.

AK: Spiritual strength is important. And alongwith this, if we have financial strength, we will not remain poor. A combination of both is necessary. Seeing what you will present here (in Akshardham) should inspire the children of India to adore their culture and dedicate themselves to the country. They should contribute to bring our country forward. I have authored a book in which I have written about these two factors—that the progress of the country should be based on spiritual and financial strength. And to achieve both, there is only one answer—sweat! Hard work is a must. We often say, Swamiji: Human effort and God 's grace. Even failure of the first rocket which you faced was for your good, it prodded you to make things better. The way you have worked, for the invention of the rocket brought success. God has ultimately given you success.

AK: For India's development, I wish to establish a trust vision 2020. I seek your blessings for this. God's blessings are Swamiji: already upon you. I shall pray that your ideas are successfully realised. May India prosper both spiritually and economically. What I wish to say is that the stronger the spiritual wealth, the stronger will become all other forms of wealth. If you increase material wealth alone then man will be lost in luxury and worldly pleasures. Spirituality will guide him back, help him retract from mundane indulgences. In reality, we rarely provide what is really needed. We provide everything to man—clothes, food, drinks. . . economic needs—but with all this we should also provide spiritual wealth. Man should be given what is necessary. Clothes, food and other things be given what is necessities. But by surplus wealth, merely more and more of everything, man loses control. . . when man gains extra money and power, more than what is necessary, then he invites ruin, restlessness and destruction.

AK: I've visited 'Akshardham' in Gandhinagar and now seen the plans for another Akshardham in Delhi. All this has given me one single thought—that you, only you can produce one lakh (100,000) virtuous, cultured youths every year. Only you can do this.

Swamji: It is our guru Yogiji Maharaj's wish to produce such youths. Accordingly, we are channelising our efforts and training children, teenagers and youths all over the world.

At the end of the meeting, Swamiji said, "It's good that you've come here today. It's given us much joy. The rishis of the past have also given us science. You, too, are a rishi. In the past, rishis were householders. They used to keep long locks of hair on their head (pointing to Dr. Kalam's long hair). They lived simply, like you. You have achieved such a high post, yet your life is simple pure. Somebody else in your position wouldn't care to listen to others. The rishis also kept long beards (pointing to the Vedas and Upanishads—what we call *para* knowledge. You two are both rishis. Blend spirtiuality to your science and experiments you have discovered things, and our ancient rishis discovered things through the spriritual power of the soul and God. Your dedication lies in your field, and their devotion to God gave them spiritual powers. All this is amply described in our scriptures.

Swamishri remained seated in the meeting hall while Dr. Kalam and Y.S. Rajan were ushered into the next room for dinner. The sadhus gathered around Swamiji. When they described Dr. Kalam's simple lifestyle, Swamiji, spontaneously said, "He is not bothered about anything else. He is engrossed in his work. He has dived deep into science. Dr. Minochar Modi, who often treated Yogi ji Maharaj, would forget to eat or drink when engrossed in his reading. He said that one day, his wife came and told him, "Why are you just reading and reading? Don't you even care for eating?" Such people are not concerned about food and drink. They only pursue the work they want to achieve,. Similarly, we want to attain God, some should not deviate here and there and become attached to other things. Yogiji Maharaj has told us to be aware of this. Do everything, do a world of activities, but remain focussed on God. If you deviate from this, then you'll fall. And then you'll suffer misery and face difficulties. You'll become frustrated. We are out to attain God, so don't glance hither or thither, just fix your vision solely upon God."

Service to Society

Today's youth are tomorrow's nation builders. The youth power has to be property channelised for the welfare of the nation and its people. Hence it is no surprise when great scientist like Dr. Abdul Kalam has started meeting the youth to develop scientific temper and to make them vibrant and alive to the problems of nation and its society. Various fora, at both school and college levels, have opened up many avenues to channelize the raw youth power to optimal use for constructive purposes. National Cadet Corps (NCC) would save the country from enemies. Scouts and other outfits concentrate on character building. But NSS offers a different perspectives. The NSS students mingle with people and do village-oriented services. They lay roads and stress the importance of health to rural folk. The NSS students of Pallathur Seethalakshmi Atchi college are no exception to this. They resurrected the culturally rich Sri Kailasanathar Sivan temple of Kanadukathan from decay. The students were motivated by college Principal Ms.Kalpagam and teachers Malleswari,

We have H-Bomb, nukes safe; India possesses a hydrogen bomb and its nuclear weapons are "absolutely safe" says noted scientist Dr. APJ Abdul Kalam as reported in the *Times of India*. "Scientist and technicians who conducted the Pokhran II tests in 1998 are all satisfied with the results, and we have a thermonuclear device" Kalam, regarded as the father of India's missile systems, told PTI on Sunday-II-Nov. 2001.

Asked about the safety of nuclear assets, Kalam, who demits office on Monday as Principal Scientific Adviser to the government, said : "Safety standards are in-built in our country. We possibly have much better safety standards than many others".

On whether India should develop missiles with strike ranges longer than Agni II, which can reach a target at a distance of over 2,200 km, he said: "It depends on what kind of enemy the country faces and its strategy for the next 10 or more years. India is capable of manufacturing (a longer-range missile) if the necessity arises".

Kalam, who will be succeeded in the key post by R. Chidambaram, former chairman of the Atomic Energy Commission, said he is quitting his job as he wants to work with younger people and high school students to create a scientific culture and push India to a developed nation status.

Kalam skirted a question as to who had given the command for triggering the underground nuclear blasts in Pokhran in 1998, saying: These days computers are there (to do the job)".

Describing himself as a "sea guy" Kalam said he had worked all his life in sea coasts along the Arabian Sea and the Bay of Bengal." also found Pokhran challenging".

An Excellent Leader—His ex-associates speak to the *Times of India*

Dr. Kalam was known for his simplicity and leadership qualities—Dr. V.K. Aatre, Scientific Advisor to Defence Minister, who spoke to *The times of India* from Delhi. He termed Kalam as an excellent manager, who was always open to term Kalam an excellent to everyone". He respected difference of opinion and what better place than IISc can he find to fulfil his mission" Dr. V.K. Aatre said, Dr. Kota Harinarayana Programme Director (LCA), ADA, said that Kalam infected his experiences from SLV-3 and missile technologies to the LCA Project, which came in as an asset "His leadership qualities were excellent. He wanted technology spin-offs to reach the rural population", Dr. Kota said.

Prof Goverdhan Mehta, IISc Director said that he is yet to receive an official communication with regard to Kalam' plans to be associated with the institute. " I did receive a letter from Department of Space on the Professorship. We have lots of projects from DRDO and Kalam's association will help in our decision making", Mehta said.

Farewell to Dr. Kalam

In a rare gesture, the central government on Friday 30- Nov 2001 hosted a grand farewell for Dr. APJ Abdul Kalam, the doyen of Indian science, who recently resigned as Principal Scientific Adviser to the Government to spend the rest of his life for the cause of inspiring the youth to take up a career in science.

The distinguished gathering was led by the Prime Minister, Mr. Atal Behari Vajpayee and included the Deputy Chairman of the

Planning Commission, Mr.K.C. Pant. A highlight of the party held at the Union Science and Technology Minister , Dr. Murali Manohar Joshi's residence was a recital by the sarod maestro, Pt. Biswijit Roy Chowdhury. The function was attended among others by the Minister of State in the PMO , Mr. Vijay Goel, the minister of State for Science and Technology, Mr. Bachi Singh Rawat, Dr. Kalam, Prof . Goverdhan Mehta, President, Indian National Science Academy and other top scientists and senior government officials.

He said students could interact with him through his website. Recently, he posed a question to children on his website why India could not become a developed country even after 50 years of Independence and when did they think it would become one. "the best answer came from a boy in Atlanta. "He said India will be a developed country the day we have the power to put sanctions on any country in the world". India should concentrate on a mission to Mars rather than the moon as it would be more useful scientifically, feels A.P.J. Abdul Kalam, the man who launched India into the space age with the successful launch of the Satellite Launch Vehicle (SLV-3) on this day (July 18) 20 years ago. Mars has a good potential for space industrialisation, he told this newspaper on Sunday. The Indian Space Research Organisation has tentatively slated an unmanned lunar mission between 2005 and 2008 for carrying out scientific studies. The indigenously-made Polar Satellite Launch Vehicle (PSLV) or the Geo-synchronous Satellite Launch Vehicle (GSLV) are to be used for this flight. The cost of the project will be around Rs. 350 crores.

Describing the SLV-3 flight as a mission of great significance, Mr Kalam said in the last two decades space technology in India has developed a lot and globally become technology- competitive. said Mr Kalam: Space technology is going to play an important role in the future development of this country.

The architect of India's space programme said the 'vision put forth by Vikram Sarabhai and Satish Dhawan has been realised. Recalling the SLV-3 flight, Mr Kalam, who was the mission director, wrote his autobiography, "Wings of Fire:" I experienced mixed feelings. I was happy to achieve the success which had been evading me for the past two decades, but I was sad because the people who had inspired me were no longer there to share my joy. The responsibility for the successful SLV-3 flight lay first with the giants of the Indian Space Programme.

Nilambar Pant, a member of the space commission, who was the director of the Sriharikota space centre when the launch took place in July 1980, described the SLV-3 flight as an exhilarating moment because it was the first time India successfully gained entry into the exclusive space club. The Sriharikota complex was fully geared for this launch, he recalled.

According to Mr Pant, in the last two decades the country's space programme has more or less attained its target and fulfilled the different promises it made to the country." The primary mission of India's space projects is application—driven and aimed at benefitting the common man and I am happy this has been achieved. For example, the space programme is used for telecasting TV programmes, providing communication and helping in meteorlogical forecasts and studies, he said".

Regarding India's lunar Mission, Mr Pant was confident that the country had the technological capability for such a massive project. The scientific community has now to evolve a good programme to justify such a mission, he said.

According to Mr Pant, for a country like India spending Rs 350 crores for such a mission was not an exorbitant amount.

"Nobody raises any questions when India spends huge amounts on buying Boeings and Airbuses. So, I think we can easily afford to spend Rs 350 crores on the moon mission. This will be technologically complex mission, he added".

19

Dedicated and Disciplined Life

Dr. Kalam spent his long career of six decades with a keen sense of discipline and dedication. This was mainly on account of his best teachers who taught him, his society with good students and natural realization for hard work in order to achieve something unique in his career.

It is quite evident from his school days, MIT days and later on his service in the scientific departments.

Not caring for his dress and food—which were very often casual in contents—he was more careful for the work assigned to him by his seniors. He was a consistent learner and meticulous innovator. He always wished to invent something new so that the name of India should shine in the history of the world, and to achieve it, he spent sleepless nights along with numerous dedicated workers whose cooperation he sought at every step.

It has entered into me, the ignited mind. Compared with any resource, is the most profound resource on the earth, above the earth and under the earth.

I will keep the lamp of knowledge buming to achieve developed India.

Spruning the international non-proliferation regime, and the global norm against nuclear testing embodied in the Comprehensive Test Ban Treaty (CTBT), India announced two sets of nuclear tests on May 11 and 13, prompting Pakistan to announce its own tests on May 28 and 30. The first nuclear detonations since the CTBT opened for signature in September 1996, the Indian and Pakistani tests are feared to be the first steps toward a new and destabilizing arms race between the neighbour-states , which have gone to war three times in the past 50 years. As a result of the tests, both countries, already straining to develop their economies, face international economic sanctions that will drive up the cost, reduce their access to international development assistance. Indian Prime Minister Atal Bihari Vajpayee announced India's first tests and said they included a fission device, a thermonuclear device and a low-yield device. Two days later, New Delhi declared it had conducted two more tests, both alleged to have sub-kiloton yields. India's tests were conducted at the Pokhran test site near the Pakistani border. At a May 17 press conference, Rajgopala Chidambaram, Chairman of the Atomic Energy Commission, announced the yields of the first tests as 12, 43 and 0.2 kilotons, respectively. The second set of tests did not produce any secretary of India's Department of Atomic Energy and chairman of the Atomic Energy Commission, announced the yields of the first tests as 12, 43 and 0.2 kiloos, respectively. The second set of tests did not produce any seismic signal, and their yields cannot be confirmed beyond A.P.J. Abdul Kalam, noted at the May 17 press conference that the explosions had provided "critical data for the validation of our capability in the design of nuclear weapons of different yields for different applications and different delivery systems."

Abdul Kalam also said that data from the tests would be put to use in modelling nuclear explosions with supercomputers. Seventeen days after the first Indian test, Pakistani Prime Minister Nawaz Sharif announced that Pakistan had tested five nuclear devices. Two days later, Islamabad declared that it had conducted two more tests, although Foreign Secretary Shamshad Ahmed retracted that claim on May 30 saying only one subsequent test had occurred. The Pakistani tests took place in the Chagai Hills region, close to the Iranian border. A.Q. Khan, who heads Pakistan's nuclear programme, said on May 30 that one of the five devices tested on May 28 was in the 30 to 35-kiloton range, with the other four producing small yields suitable for tactical weapons. The test on May 30 yielded 15 to 18 kilotons, according to Samar Mobarik Mand, a Pakistan Atomic Energy Commission official.

Following their respective tests, India and Pakistan announced unilateral moratorioms on nuclear testing, and New Delhi declared itself a nuclear-weapon state—a classification rejected by the rest of the world. Under the nuclear Non-Proliferation Treaty (NPT), only states that conducted a nuclear test prior to January 1, 1967, are recognized as nuclear-weapons states. All other states-parties are non-nuclear-weapon states. India, a non-signatory of the NPT, has long been an outspoken opponent of the two-tier structure of the regime, denouncing it as "nuclear apartheid" because it does not require a time-bound framework for disarmament by the nuclear-weapon states. Pakistan has also remained outside of the treaty, but has in the past indicated that it would sign the NPT if India did. Both states, however, have refrained from proliferating the nuclear technology or materials they have acquired and have pledged to maintain their no-transfer policies. India has had a nuclear weapons capability since 1974 when it conducted a "peaceful nuclear explosion." It operates several natural uranium-fuelled reactors whose spent fuel can be reprocessed to extract plutonium for weapons use. India is believed to possess about 400 kilograms of weapons-grade plutonium, enough for 60 to 80 weapons

Pakistan is believed to have first acquired its nuclear weapons capability in the mid-1980s. In 1992, President Bush imposed sanctions on Pakistan under the so-called Pressler amendment because he could no longer report that Islamabad did not possess nuclear weapons . Pakistan's nuclear programme depends on highly-enriched uranium (HEU) produced by gas centrifuges in Kahuta. A shipment of ring mangnets from China to Pakistan for use in the centrifuge prompted the Clinton administration to threaten sanctions against Beijing in 1996. Pakistan is believed to have halted HEU production in 1991 after producing about 200 kilograms enough for 10 to 15 weapons.

The World Reacts

While the condemnation elcited by India's and Pakistan's nuclear tests has been nearly universal, only a few countries have translated their concern into consequences. The strongest response so far has come from the United States which has imposed a long list of sanctions. Canada. Denmark, Japan and Sweden have suspended millions of dollars of development aid and Germany has suspended planned aid talks with New Delhi. Australia and New Zealand withdrew their Ambassadors for consultations, while Britain, China, France and Russia have condemned the tests but have not imposed any sanctions.

In the United States, sanctions are mandated by the 1994 nuclear Proliferation Prevention Act. authored by Senator John Glenn (D-

OH). Under the so-called Glenn Amendment , the US government must prohibit the export of all sensitive technology (dual-use and munitions list items); end all forms of military and foreign aid; cease the provision of credit or credit guarantees through federal entities such as the Overseas Private Investment Corporation and the US Export- Import bank; and forbid lending to the Indian and Pakistani governments by US commercial banks.

Additionally, the law requires the administration to oppose the provision of credit to either country from international the provision of credit to either country from international financial institutions like the World Bank and the International Monetary Fund. Although the sanctions law provides several exceptions for humanitarian purposes, the administration estimats that US sanctions alone will cost India and Pakistan billions of dollars in lost assistance and trade.

Although US opposition alone would be insufficient to block lending from the international institutions, Washington's position will be suppported by the other seven members of the Group of Eight (G-8) industrial powers (Britain, Canada, France, Germany, Japan, Italy and Russia). Assembling this consensus however took several weeks. At a previously scheduled G-8 meeting May 16-17 in Birmingham, England , Washington was unable to persuade its allies to adopt any measure stronger than a joint statement condemning India's tests. Subsequently, following a June 4 meeting in Geneva of the five permanent members of the UN Security Council (which are also the five nuclear- weapon states under the NPT) and a June 12 being in London of the G-8 foreign ministers, the Clinton administration has managed to persuade the other G-8 nations to agree to block assistance to India and Pakistan from international financial institutions with he exception of humanitarian aid projects.

In a joint communique from Geneva, the G-8 also agreed upon a list of steps they have urged India and Pakistan to take in order to mitigate the consequences of the tests including their signature on the CTBT "immediately and unconditionally. India and Pakistan are among the 44 named countries whose ratification is necessary to bring the CTBT into force, although the treaty may be provisionally applied under certain conditions. Following India's first test, Brajesh Mishra, Principal Secretary to the Prime Minister, announced on May 11 that India "would be prepared to consider being an adherent to some of the undertakings" in the CTBT. So far, Pakistan's statements have downplayed the value of the treaty but have not ruled out accession, depending on what action New Delhi takes. The G-8 also called on both countries to participate in negotiations at the Geneva- based Conference on Disarmament (CD) of an internationally binding instrument the production of fissile materials for weapons purposes. Finally, the G-8 called on both India and Pakistan to renew their bilateral dialogue, including the issue of Kashmir, and to take steps to ensure their nuclear competition does not spil out of control. Both states were urged to refrain from further nuclear testing; producing more fissile materials for weapons purposes; testing ballistic missiles; and deploying nuclear weapons. While neither state is believed to have actually employed nuclear forces, the fact that such weapons could reach heir targets in a matter of minutes makes the danger of escalation especially acute. Reviving bilateral relations however, appears unlikely in the near term. On May 18, Indian Home Minister L.K. Advani, a hard-liner in the recently elected government led by the nationalist Bharatiya Janata Party (BJP), intimated that India's nuclear tests had strengthened New Delhi's position with regard to Kashmir and warned Islamabad to roll back its anti- India policy.' Advani's remarks were denounced by Sharif, who said Pakistan was prepared to respond to an Indian misadventure." Relations betwen the two states remain very tense, as the two sides have continued to exchange artillery and small weapons fire in Kashmir.

Vajpayee's Gambit

As part of his government's pre-test activities, Vajpayee prepared identical letters to the leaders of the G-8, justifying the nuclear tests. According to Vajpayee, the nuclear tests were prompted by a "deteriorating securtiy environment." In particular, the prime minister pointed to India's unresolved border dispute with a nuclear- armed China, Beijing's transfer of nuclear technology to Pakistan and Islamabad's continuing support for insurgent groups in Kashmir. Eight days prior to the first tests, India's Defence Minister, George Fernandes, also pointed to the threat to India from China, accusing Beijing of construction a helicopter landing pad near the Indo-Chinese border, stationing intelligence assets on Burmese territory in the Bay of Bengal and moving nuclear- tipped missiles directed at India into Tibet. Beijing has described both Vajpayee's and Fernandes threat accusations as groundless, and has asserted that New Delhi is using China as an excuse to develop nuclear weapons.

While a variety of explanations have emerged as to why India decided to challenge the international no-testing norm, some critics of U.S. South Asia policy have suggested that the rationale offered in Vajpayee's letter is correct; that is, much of the blame rests with President Clinton for not taking a harderline regarding Chinese proliferation practices. Other observers have claimed that India's motive was nationalistic; that the tests represent both a protest against the discriminatory nature of the NPT, and an assertion of India's status as an emerging power. A third explanation focuses on the nearly universal Indian domestic approval and the surge of nationalist sentiment that has strengthened the BJP's otherwise tenuous hold on power. US sanctions on both India and Pakistan are of indefinite duration, and can only be lifted by an act of Congress. Notably, the Glenn amendment contains no presidential waiver authority if sanctions are imposed on a country for testing a nuclear device. Without any substantial movement by New Delhi and Islamabad on the arms control and regional security issues listed by the G-8, sanctions are likely to remain a long term component of US policy toward South Asia.

Following is the message from APJ Abdul Kalam appeared in *Bombay Times*: 13-Oct issue, a chat with Pritish Nandy. I liked it so much that I wished to share it with you people. I have three visions for India. In 3000 years of our history, people from all over the world have come and invaded us, captured our lands, conquered our minds. From Alexander onwards. The Greeks, the Portuguese, the British the French, the Dutch , all of them came and looted us, took over what was ours. Yet we have not done this to any other nation. We have not conquered anyone. We have not grabbed their land, their culture, and their history and tried to enforce our way of life on them.

Why? Because we respect the freedom of others That is why my first vision is that of FREEDOM. I believe that India got its first vision of this in 1857, when we started the war of independence. It is this freedom that we must protect and nurture and build on. If we are not free, no one will respect us.

My second vision for India is DEVELOPMENT. For fifty years we have been developing nation. It is time we see ourselves as a developed nation. We are among top 5 nations of the world in terms of GDP. We have 10 per cent growth rate in most areas. Our poverty levels are falling, our achievements are being globally recognized today. Yet we lack the self reliance being globally recognized today.

Yet we lack the self—confidence to see ourselves—as a developed nation, self reliant and self assured. Isn't this right?

I have a third vision. India must stand up to the world because I believe that unless india stands up to the world, no one will respect us. Only strength respects strength. We must be strong not only as a military power but also as an economist power. Both must go hand- in- hand.

My good fortune was to have work with three great minds. Dr. Vikram Sarabhai of the Dept of Space Professor Satish Dhawan, who succeeded him, and Dr. Brahm Prakash, father of nuclear material. I was lucky to have worked with all three of them closely and consider this the great opportunity of my life. I see four milestones in my career:

ONE : Twenty yearsI spent in ISRO . I was given the opportunity to be the project director for India's first satellite launch vehicle, SLV3—the one that launched Rohini. These years played a very important role in my life of scientist.

TWO : After my ISRO years, I joined DRDO and got a chance to be the part of India's guided missile programme. It was my second bliss when Agni met its mission requirements in 1994.

THREE : The Dept. of Atomic Energy and DRDO had this tremendous partnership in the recent nuclear tests, on May 11 and 13. This was the third bliss. The joy of participating with my team in these nuclear tests and proving to the world that India can make it . That we are no longer a developing nation but one of them. It made me feel very proud to be an Indian. "Do things yourself. Do not indulge in short-cuts by importing equipment" thundered the great scientist after the famed Pokhran-2 neclear blasts in 1998. A strong advocate of this philosophy, he distributed newpapers at a young age to help with household expenses.

Thoroughly Indian, the only brief exposure that he got abroad was in 1963-64 when he was invited by NASA (National Aeronautics and Space Administration) to spend four months in the United States at the Wallops Island Rocketry Centre ISRO (Indian Space Research Organisation) where he succeeded in putting the 35 kg Rohini-I satellite on a low-earth orbit with the help of the SLV-II (Satellite Launch Vehicle). After spending 19 fruitful years in ISRO, he returned to DRDO to head the country's Integrated Missile Development Programme, which culminated in the successful launch of the Agni and Prithvi missiles.

A great humanitarian, he extended his knowledge of space technology and mechanisms to help disabled children, replacing their 3-kg metal supporters with very light braces made of carbon, which was just 300 grams.

A vegetarian and a tetotaller, Abdul Kalam recites the *Quran* and the *Bhagvad Gita* with equal ease. A confirmed bachelor, his modesty is evident from the fact that he gives all the credit to his colleagues. He burst into the limelight after the Pokhran nuclear explosions in 1998. Totally dedicated to the development of the nation, he has been felicitated with many national awards. He was awarded the Padmabhushan in 1981, the Padma Vibhushan in 1990 and the HK Firodia Award for Excellence in Science and Technology in 1996. More recently , he was honoured with the Bharat Ratna in 1998, the highest civilian award in India. Abdul Kalam is a dreamer. He dreamt of a strong India. "We must think and act like a nation of a billion people." His next goal is to produce a reusable missile which no country in the world has been able to produce. And judging by his earlier achievements, this invention does not seem a distant possibility for this genius.

One aspect, which is interesting, is how, whenever India achieves something that is commendable, the developed nations tend to trace it to some know-how, equipment or manpower that was provided by the West. For instance, in July 1980, when we launched our first satellite launch vehicle and put the Rohini satellite into orbit India became one of four nations to have a satellite launch facility. But within a week, a news item originated from the USA saying that I had a few months training at NASA and that is where I picked up the technology that was used for the launch. This was supported by the rest of the western press. In Germany they claimed that the wind tunnel test was carried out in their facility, and so they had indirectly enabled the launch. When we heard the news about the reactions of the western scientists, technologists and the press, the general response of my team of scientists and technologists at the Vikram Sarabhai Space Centre, Trivandrum, was one of great amusement. We knew that thousands of scientists, engineers and staff had worked on the project from the drawing board to the development stage and right through till the launch. The technology was completely indigenous.

The SLV used proportional control for its first stage control systems with a sharing logic software. This was a first in the world.

Similarly, we had made other innovations in comparison to any launch vehicle at that point of time. As for the Scout, the American Satellite Lauch Vehicle from which our technology was alleged to be lifted, only the fifth launch of the Scout had proved successful. In comparison, our second, third and fourth launches were all successful. This is a pointer to the technological strength of our nation. Again, when I was involved in the Guided Missile Programme and we successfully launched the Prithvi Missile several times, the Western press including some of our own analysts insisted that we were using Russian technology. In fact, Prithvi had a distinctive design, using a particular gyrosystem with a uniquely configured software, which nobody in the world had tried; when the flight is in progress, the drift can be monitored through the on- board computer. It had other innovations too: the type of thrust termination is so innovatively configured that for a multiple payload, multiple ranges can be achieved. Today, Prithvi is comparable to any world class missile system, and probably is the best of its class in payload capability. Let us come now to a third, very important milestone, namely Agni. We launched Agni in 1989 and it was successful. We have so far done three launches. Surprisingly, again, there were two claimants who wanted to take credit for the success. Germany said that their guided system which was used for scientific experiments in India had gone into the making of Agni. And the USA claimed again that my NASA training was responsible for Agni. Actually, in Agni, there were innovations made in the guidance technology. We can manoeuver the payload and the complete re-entry hypersonic flow was simulated in the Computational Fluid Dynamics in one of the best computers that we ourselves had designed. The re-entry structure, in fact, has used a specially designed material to withstand the 3500 ^{0}C heat generated upon re-intering the atmosphere. It is really amusing that the Americans think that it is only with their technology that India can succeed.

Recently two departments, the Department of Atomic Energy and the DRDO, working in an excellent partnership, tested several nuclear devices in Pokhran. Three tests were carried out simultaneously; there were two more tests subsequently. We had excellent results, well reported universally by nearly 125 seismic stations. This indicates that India had reached the stage of nuclear weaponisation. We were extremely happy with our achievement. But the next day we found the Western press alleging that Israeli technology had gone into the triggering system of the nuclear device. There was also the familiar accusation that the scientists and technicians who had visited the USA had helped India achieve this breakthrough. This was puzzling because nobody in the world has used the type of triggering mechanism we have developed. Multiple innovations have gone into the nuclear technology and nuclear device testing area. In all four of these cases, I was fortunate to be continuously involved directly or indirectly in various teams of ISRO, DAE and DRDO.

I find myself asking why in spite of innovative and excellent design capabilities in India, an impression is created by the West that no one other than the developed nations can achieve such technological excellence. Just as there has been a racial element in human history, it would appear that this element is entering into technological arena too. Developed nations feel that only they are capable nuclear technology. But we should ignore this and go ahead with our technology development. Dr. Kalam is of the opinion that India can give missile technology to friendly nations subject to government approval.

"Some unique solutions in guidance and rocket propulsion systems and system engineering" could be given to friendly nations with government approval, Kalam said in an interview to Doordarshan.

With a range of 2,000 km, Agni-II the Intermediate Range Ballistic Missile (IRBM) test fired on Aprill 11, is "uniquely configured for special types of warheads", but deployment of the Agni class of missiles is subject to "Government decision depending on world condition, various situations", he said in the interview telecast to night.India with its Integrated Guided Missile Programme (IGMP), is the only country in the world which can develop different types of missiles simultaneously, he said. Asked whether Pakistan's competitive testing of missiles bothered India, Kalam said, We can build any type of missile depending on mission requirements." The missile system was designed and configured at a new missile test centre "Somewhere in the east coast of Orissa in a beautiful island", he said.

India is not dependent on any country for any of the components, sub-systems or software used in Agni-II, Kalam said. Describing Agni-II as "Agni plus', he said it was highly mobile and could be moved to any region on rail or road. A computer on board the missile monitors all its components during flight and sends data on 600 parameters required for effective control of the missile, to the ground.

The "ruggedised" Agni-II can be to the ground, minutes with limited facilities and man power, he said, adding the missile trajectory could be quickly shaped and the payload manoeuvred to reach the target. "It has been operationalised irrespective of what payloads or warheads will be integrated with the system, " he said. Advanced Instrumentation and Computer Simulation has helped reduce the number of test flights of missiles from 30-40 in the 1960's to less than ten now. The number of flight parameters has also increased from 100 in the 1980 's to 600-1,000 now, Kalam said.

Out of this audacious initiative was born the guided missile programme, India's most successful military research task to date. Kalam's code names for the programme's live components were: Prithvi, a surace-to-surface battlefield missiles; Nag, an anti-tank missile (ATM); Akash, a swift medium range surface-to-air missile (SAM); Trishul, a quick reaction SAM with a shorter range; and Agni,,an intermediate range ballistic missile, the mightiest of them all. Trishul has the unique distinction of being capable of serving all three services.

From his SLV-3 experience, Kalam had learned the advantages of team work and of sharing the tasks with partners in private and public sector industries. In the new management structure of the missile programme, Kalam, as the Chairman, executive and financial powers carefully selected Project Directors and kept himself free to address the core technology issues. His task was to inspire and monitor over 20 institutions and parters outside ranging from large public and private sector suppliers to small specialist firms that needed seed money to take up the precision tasks. Kalam's contribution in this scheme has been acnowledged by all who worked with him. He set for himself a gruelling schedule. The first half hour of the day was reserved for what was called the morning meeting, where administrative heads met him to take decisions on routine functions. During this period any employee could walk in and discuss administrative problems, which were usually sorted out the same day. The rest of the day was devoted to hands-on interaction with project teams working on a campus spread over 40 hectares.

The missiles went up more or less on schedule: Trishul in 1985, Prithvi in 1988, Agni in 1989 and the others in 1990. And the Kalam legend had grown. He is well-versed in Tamil and has written poetry. Seventeen of his poems were translated into English by Manidrshi, and published as a book titled *My Journey* in 1994.

The establishment of the research Centre Imarat (RCI), a campus 8 km from DRDL, in 1988 was perhaps the most satisfying achievement for Kalam during the missile years. He received generous funding from the Government to build the futuristic centre, which is totally geared for work in advanced missile technologies. Its state-of-the-art facilities are set in a unique ambience and the level of comfort accorded to the individual worker is matched by few R&D institutions. And Kalam's interest in the environment saw Imarat emerge as an oasis in a rocky wateland. It has a small orchard and a farm that meets the food requirements of those who stay in the RCI quarters.

Scientists greet Abdul Kalam after the successful launch of Agni on May 22, 1989.

Kalam was awarded the Padma Vibhushan in 1990. After 10 years in DRDL, he went to Delhi to take over from Arunachalam as Scientific Adviser to the Defence Minister—reluctantly, in DRDL felt. But the system created by Kalam had taken a firm hold in that decade and the missile programme passed on smoothly into its final phase of production and induction. In Delhi, Kalam as head of the DRDO had to "deliver " other prestigious projects, such as the Main Battle Tank (MBT) Arjun and the Light Combat Aircraft (LCA) projects. While management practices he adopted or the missile programme have inevitably rubbed off on these projects, there are no miracles to be had in strategic development areas. There have been technical problems. Even within the missile programme, work on the SAMs and the ATM is slower than anticipated. But the recent multiple flights of Trishul demonstrate that the system Kalam put in place has inherent strengths. As Arunachalam put it, " We are now mature: we learn from mistakes and push on ahead ."

"Strength respects strength." This is Kalam's usual response to the question why India needs its own missiles or a battle tank or a combat aircraft. But Kalam is a technocrat. Although there are suggestions that he should use his status, which has been enhanced by the award of Bharat Ratna, to push for the active induction of Agni, it would be uncharacteristic of him to press his view too much in geopolitical matters. He is the happiest at the drawing board, in discussion with his scientists on how their dreams for the next millennium can be fulfilled. The projects envisaged include: a terminal guidance system for Agni so that it can be precision-targeted; an " air breathing" hyperplane spacecraft that draws oxygen from the ground; "reusable atmosphere rather than carry it all the way from the missiles; and stealth technology. Kalam has shown that with adequate funding, freedom from proceduaral holdups and a people-oriented management, India can make products of internationally acceptable technical standards in a demanding arena like defence. Kalam is no miracle man. As the head of a vast network of laboratories, whose products include avalanche-controlling structures in Kashmir, water desalination kits for the Thar desert; a world class "Sonar" submarine finder for the new warship INS Delhi, and infraed night vision goggles for the Army—Kalam's attention is necessarily a bit diffused. His self-effacing persona cloaks a formidable catalyst who can make people work.

Importance of being Abdul Kalam

Kalam quotes the *Bhagvad Gita* and other Hindu scriptures, too, on all conceivable occasions. *Daily Times (Lahore) Sunday*, June 16, 2002, Importance of being Abdul Kalam SRI RAMAN Kalam quotes the *Bhagvad Gita* and other Hindu scriptures, too, on all conceivable occasions. That makes him even more of a model Muslim. On a visit to Bhuj in Gujarat in the wake of the terrible earthquake, he compared the power of compassion behind the relief efforts to "the energy of thousands of nuclear bombs in the *virat swarup* (cosmic form) of God" as revealed in the Gita. What would have been the reaction in India, if Dr Abdul Qadir Khan had been nominated for the post of Pakistan's President?" asked an anti-nuclear- weapons scientist, who serves a government-funded establishment and so cannot be named. He was rewording the main question about the nomination of A. P. J. Abdul Kalam as the candidate of India's ruling coalition for the post of the country's President. A question that few, even among opponents of the coalition's choice , ask for fear of being tagged " anti-national". The question is: is not Kalam's candidature a calculated provocation in the current regional context? What signals does it send out amidst tensions created by the threat of a full-scale war between the nuke-rattling neighbours? A rhetorical question, if there was one. He is the coalition's choice for India's highest constitutional office because he (like Qadir Khan in Pakistan) is a symbol of India's nuclear might and militarism. Whether Kalam is the Bomb Man or the Missile Man is not the question as some media sophists make it out to be. The point is that he was not the eminent scientist" he is extolled as now before the Pokharan nuclear-weapon tests of 1998. And since then every Indian missile (with a potential nuclear tip) that has been test-fired has enhanced his stature further. He has been picked up and promoted as a symbol of the ruling militarism, particularly because he is a Muslim. He has not been a mere scientist carrying out his masters' orders. Participating in Pokharan under the code name of General Prithvi Raj, he attempted an Oppenheimer- like greeting of the explosion that " shook the earth". Speaking at numerous Rotary Club meetings since then Kalam has recalled his pride of the hour—that "we could do it" and that India could now " stand up to the world". And, in a very unbureaucratic manner, the then Adviser to the Prime Minister asked the anti-bomb activists to go agitate in London and Washingtion. He has been not just any bomb man, but one of the Bharatiya Janta Party- variety. With his militarism goes a world outlook that the worst morons of the Sangh Parivar, the extended family of India's far Right, can identify with. He has repeatedly gone on record that India has "never invaded.... (or) conquered anyone" that it has "never grabbed their land, their culture." Just the kind of history that the BJP would like school kids to be taught. The kind, for example, that would rewrite the history of Sri Lanka and South-East Asia (repeatedly invaded by Indian rulers), besides inventing an ancient and medieval India where kings did not conquer each other's land. The Bomb Man quotes the *Bhagvad Gita* and other Hindu scriptures, too, on all conceivable occasions. That makes him even more of a model Muslim. Sample speech on a visit to Bhuj in Gujarat in the wake of the terrible earthquake last year. Here, he compared the power of compassion behind the relief efforts there to " the energy of thousands of nuclear bombs in the *virat swarup* (cosmic form) of God" as revealed in the *Gita*. Likely, there's trouble with his 'Hindutva hosts' translation, but you get the general idea. It may be notable that Kalam has not deemed it necessary to visit Gujarat during or after the recent communal riots. Little wonder, Tarun Vijay in the RSS mouthpiece *Panchajanya*, says: "Indianism is Hindutva. This does mean that Muslims should convert to Hinduism. What it does mean is that you can be what you like but must share the vision of Dr Abdul Kalam." Little wonder, Praveen Togadia of the Vishwa Hindu Parishad says the BJP's choice shows that the party is not against "a Muslim who is a diehard nationalist". Kalam is a model Muslim not only in relation to internal issues but in his international outlook as well. An illustrative quote that also puts mediapersons like this columnist in their place: "I was in Tel Aviv once and I was reading an Israeli newspaper. It was the day after a lot of attacks, bombardments and deaths. The Hamas had struck. But the front page of the newspaper had the picture of a jewish gentleman who in five years had transformed this desert land into an orchard and a granary. It was this inspiring picture that everyone woke up to. The gory details of killings were inside the newspaper. In India, we only read about deaths, sickness, terrorism, crimes." I shudder to think of Kalam's reaction to the predictable front page of any of our newspapers on the morning after a nuclear war in South Asia. The writer is a journalist based in Chennai, India. A peace activist, he has contributed the main essay to " The Media Bomb", a study of Indian media responses to India's nuclear-weapon tests of 1998. He is also the author of a sheaf of poems under the title . *At Gunpoint.*

Dr APJ Abdul Kalam

By Zafarul-Islam Khan

Dr. APJ Abdul Kalam suddenly resigned his office as the Principal Scientific Advisor to the Government of India on 10 November. He has said that he will devote himself to research, teaching and interaction with the youth in order to motivate them work for a strong India. A world-renowned scientist, Dr Kalam has won many awards including India's highest, Bharat Ratna as well as many honorary doctorates. Born in 1931 at Rameswaram in Tamil Nadu, Dr Kalam is an eminent aeronautical engineer. He was mainly responsible for propelling India into new frontiers of aerospace and missile technologies before moving to supervising the modernisation of defence know-how. India's first indigenous Satellite Launch Vehicle (SLV-3) to launch Rohini Satellite in the near earth orbit and development of advanced technology guided missiles for the country's defence were made possible essentially because of his inspiring leadership. Today India possesses five such missiles namely Prithvi, Trishul, Akash, Nag and Agni which introduced India to the exclusive club of a few countries who possess this advanced technology.

To him also goes the credit of developing composite product technology at Vikram Sarabhai Space Centre (VSSC) and at Defence Research and Development Laboratory (DRDL) and establishing production centres for reinforced plastics. He has also established an advanced research centre for missile technology at Hyderabad. Dr Kalam was project director, SLV-3, at Indian Space Research Organisation (ISRO), chief executive of Intregrated Guided Missile Development Programme at DRDL and from 1992 scientific adviser to the Defence Minister and Secretary, Department of Defence Research and Development, director general, Defence Research and Dvelopment Organisation (DRDO). Dr Kalam is also the founder chairman of Society for Bio-medical Technology (SBMT) which promotes cost-effective medical systems as spin-off from Defence Technology. He is chairman of Technology Information, Forecasting and Assessment Council (TIFAC) that has brought out the national technological plan technology Vision: 2020, Western technology cartels, such as the Missile Technology Control Regime (MTCR), often used for political arm-twisting, spurred Dr Kalam and his team at the DRDO to work out a durable way out of external dependence. He believes that in the highly competitive world today, a nation is judged and respected for its indigenous technological strengths. As regards the Vision 2020 programme he said that it envisages the growth of the country in all directions—from farming to missile technology, field of life sciences to industry—and the goal set before the scientific community is to achieve 70 per cent self-reliance in indigenous systems from the present 30 per cent by 2005CE. Besides being an outstanding scientist, Dr Kalam possesses exemplary qualities of leadership. His capacity to inspire team work has been well acknowledged and has contributed greatly to a highly successful career. He is an individual who can bridge the spectrum from frontline technology development to production. Dr. Kalam is often referred to as 'father of Indian rockets'. Incidentally, it was an Indian Muslim, Tipu Sultan, the tiger of Mysore, who invented the first rockets in the world during his wars against the British colonialists. Some of those rockets are still preserved in a museum in Greenwich.

Wings of Fire

Recently I had the opportunity to read the autobiography of my idol—APJ Abdul Kalam. It's called "Wings of Fire" and contains a few golden moments of Indian Pride through Abdul Kalam . His life, knowledge and humbleness are inspiring. He is indeed one of the greatest scientists of our time. If you don't know who is behind our indigenous satellites, you will know now. His experiments with Nandi, SLV-3 and Agni are interesting to read (incl. the scientific notes which are easy to understand).

I definitely think the book is worth buying.

Chennai. June 10. Involving herself in the efforts to create a consensus on the Presidential candidate, the Tamil Nadu Chief Minister, Jayalalitha, today assured the Prime Minister, Atal Behari Vajpayee, of support to the candidate of the National Democratic Alliance.

Mr. Vajpayee spoke to Ms. Jayalalitha in the morning and the two leaders reached an agreement on the candidate. The Andhra Pradesh Chief Minister, N. Chandrababu Naidu, had talked to her seeking support for the same candidate. Now, she along with Mr. Naidu would join efforts to build a consensus.

The defence family of Bangalore reacted with joy to the news of Abdul Kalam being nominated on Monday as NDA's candidate for the country's top job". He is a great man. He is a great leader. He is an outstanding human being," said Kota Harinarayana, father of LCA project. Kota who reveres Kalam as his guru, said if Kalam becomes the President then it will be India's highest recognition to him for putting the country on the road to technology and growth.

Dr. P.S. Goel, Director, ISRO, Satallite Centre, said he felt elated. "It's hearty to note that a technologist is being tipped for this job. I have spent a lot of time with him and am confident that he will give his best." Terming Kalam as the Bhishmapita of Indian aerospace, Prof. Suryanarayana of Aerospace Engineering Department, IIT, Mumbai, said: "What more do we scientists need if Kalam gets to Rashtrapati Bhavan? It 'll be a great human being," he said . Having worked with Kalam during the SLV-3 project, NAL former Director T.S. Prahlad said: "I know him for so many years and he'll shine with vigour. It's a gift to the scientific community, if he accepts the post." If Kalam makes it to Rashtrapati Bhavan, he will be taking along with him sweet memories of Bangalore. " I love this city and I have very fond memories," Kalam had told this a few months back. Kalam, who started his career as a senior scientific assistant at aeronautical Development Establishment in 1957, loves Carnatic music, Maddur vada, idli- sambar, rasam and a morning walk in C.V. Raman Nagar. From Ramanathapurm to Rashtrapati Bhavan. If he makes it, it will go down in the history books as a unique journey of a great man, who always said: "We are all born with a divine fire in us. Our efforts should be to give wings to this fire and fill the world with the glow of its goodness".

Naidu played vital role in Kalam's candidature. From cobbling up a United Front government to extending a friendly hand to NDA coalition at any moment of crisis, TDP supremo Chandrababu Naidu played his part with precision, the candidature of A.P.J Abdul Kalam for President's post being no exception. The trajectory of several phone calls across the country besides the missiles of differences fired within the NDA and finally the consensus launcher vehicle which announced the name of "missile man" Abdul Kalam had all been part of the efforts of Naidu to push through his consensus mantra. Sources close to Chief Minister here say Naidu had hectic parleys after the NDA meeting was postponed, and was in touch with Prime Minister and other top leaders. He called up Kalam and took his consent before calling up the Prime Minister again to propose his name. Vajpayee told him he would get back atfer consulting the allies. The initiative of Naidu in suggesting the name of Abdul Kalam comes at a time when tense situation prevails at the borders and Gujarat is limping back to normal. The final call came at 6.30 am and the Prime Minister invited Naidu to Delhi as a consensus on Kalam's name could be reached soon. PM proposes Kalam for President. Prime Minister Atal Bihari Vajpayee on June 10, 2002 met Congress chief Sonia Gandhi and proposed the name of noted scientist A.P.J. Abdul Kalam for the post of the President. During the 15-minute meeting, Vajpayee said the government has made up its mind to field Kalam for the country's top post, senior Congress leader Manmohan Singh, who was also present, told reporters. Singh said Sonia told Vajpayee that she would hold consultations with her senior colleagues and others on the issue. The Prime Minister replied in the affirmative when the Congress President enquired whether Kalam's name for the post was final as the govemment had earlier proposed the candidatures of Vice-President Krishna Kant and Maharashtra Governor P.C. Alexander, he said. Sonia told Vajpayee that he had given a new name and "we will let the Government know our views after consulting senior party leaders". Asked about the Congress choice for the top post, Singh said "We have so far said President K.R. Narayanan is our preferred candidate but now we have been given a new name and we have to reflect on that."To a question whether Congress would" dump "Narayanan, she said" there is no question of dumping him". Besides Sonia Gandhi and

Manmohan Singh, Home Minister L.K. Advani was also present at the meeting.

The National Democratic Alliance on June 10, 2002 changed its mind on its preferred presidential candidate. The Maharashtra Governor, P.C. Alexander, is no longer " a front-runner " and, instead, the noted scientist,A.P.J. Abdul Kalam, has emerged as the man around whom a consensus between the NDA and the Opposition seemed very much on the cards.

Dr. Kalam's candidature was announced at a joint press conference addressed by the NDA convener, George Fernandes, the Parliamentary Affairs Minister, Pramod Mahajan, the Andhra Pradesh Chief Minister Chandrababu Naidu, and the Uttar Pradesh Chief Minister Mayawati. Mr Naidu described Dr. Kalam "as the best choice". In a day of dramatic developments, the NDA leadership found itself constrained to jettison Mr. Alexander, who was the combine's choice earlier. The NDA leaders woke up this morning to a realisation that they could no longer afford to risk the displeasure of the Andhra Pradesh Chief Minister, Chandrababu Naidu who had left no one in doubt about his preference for the vice-President, Krishna Kant. More than Mr. Naidu's displeasure, the NDA bosses understood that if the Andhra Pradesh Chief Minister, with his crucial votes, was not on board on the Alexander choice, then two other key potential "outside" partners—the AIADMK and the BSP could also become a doubtful proposition. The NDA bosses, after agonising consultations, reached a decision that the combine must find ways of cutting its losses. And since Mr. Naidu was not to be given the satisfaction of imposing his candidate just as the opposition was not to be allowed to calibrate a second term for the president , K.R. Narayanan, the "dark horse" Dr. Kalam made his appearance. Consequently, Dr. Alexander's most vocal Mr. Mahajan, was advised to appease Mr. Naidu. The two met in Hyderabad and Mr. Mahajan signed the surrender document on behalf of the NDA. With complete brazenness, Mr. Mahajan told newsmen in Hyderabad that the NDA had not taken any decision on any name. Later, he was instructed to covey to the Maharashtra Governor that he would no longer be the ruling combine's presidential candidate. Back in the capital, the Prime Minister set in motion a process of consultation with the allies and the opposition. Among those who met or talked to Mr. Vajpayee included the Congress President, Sonia Gandhi (who was accompanied by the Leader of the Opposition in the Rajya Sabha,

Manmohan Singh), the Samajwadi leader, Mulayam Singh Yadav, the Tamil Nadu Chief Minister, Jayalalitha, the Left leaders, Harkishen Singh Surjeet and A.B. Bardhan, and the NCP leader, P.A. Sangma. Indications were that the Opposition parties had no problem with Dr. Kalam. There is all- round satisfaction in the Opposition camp that the candidature of the Maharashta Governor had been spiked. "We deem it as an outstanding positive achievement to get Alexander out", asserted the Congress spokesperson, Jaipal Reddy. On its part, the People's Front asserted, in a statement: "The display of Opposition unity on the issue of presidential election after the BJP's efforts to unilaterally impose a candidate has compelled the BJP to beat a retreat". On the fate of Mr. Narayanan, Mr. Reddy said: "We won't say yes to anybody without consulting him since we have used his name to keep Alexander out". On what transpired at the meeting in 7 RCR, Mr Reddy said Sonia Gandhi and Manmohan Singh called on the Prime Minister and the Home Minister. They were told that "our candidate now is Abdul Kalam". When Dr. Singh asked whether he was "yourfinal candidate now we to ensure that you won't change your mind again, Mr. Advani intervened and said, "he is our final candidate. Further, Mr. Advani said: "We are going to have a meeting today and this is our final candidate". On the issue of Vice-President, the Congress was told that he two were different issues and would be dealt with separately. Mrs. Gandhi informed the Prime Minister and the Home Minister that "we need to consult our party and other parties before we take a view" upon which the Prime Minister told her that he would be contacting Mulayam Singh Yadav and Harkishen Surjeet. However, late night indications were that the Left was not at all excited about the idea of Dr. Kalam making it to the Rashtrapati Bhavan. Its final views, nonetheless, would depend on the stand Mr. Mulayam Singh takes. His votes have the same centrality to the Opposition calculations as do Mr. Naidu's for the NDA.

Kalam is NDA Candidate

Former Scientific Adviser to the government, A.P. J. Abdul Kalam, is the ruling NDA's official candidate for presidency. Following the support pledged by the Telugu Desam Party (TDP) and the Bahujan Samaj Party (BSP) which are not part of the motley alliance, the iconic figure of Kalam appears headed for Rashtrapati Bhavan as its next occupant. The Congress has indicated it has no major reservations about Kalam, while the People's Front constituents, the Left parties and the Samajwadi Party, have exulted at the announcement of his nomination by Prime Minister A.B. Vajpayee. That makes it certain that the man who played a key role in the country's missile and nuclear programme would be elevated to the highest post of the Republic.

20
Entry into Rashtrapati Bhavan

It has been well opined that some are born great, others achieve greatness and some have greatness thrust upon them". In case of Dr. A.P.J. Abdul Kalam marvellous, success in the field of science was achieved by him. For this grand success he did not seek petty recommendation of any colleague.

Undoubtedly he was a self-made person. Born in a humble family, he had to struggle hard to build up his career. Although he had to face the initial failure, he did not lose heart, but made up his mind to achieve something great in his life. He did succeed and succeeded with much honour in the estimate of his department as well as public as a whole.

His long-drawn scientific career did not touch upon anything having bearing on the politics of the Indian sub-continent. His politics was his work, consistent work, dedication, simple and disciplined life. See the missile man, either from a distance or from close quarters, how simple he looks. He wears ordinary clothes and a rubber chappal. Once he was called by Shrimati Indira Gandhi, the Prime Minister, to Delhi,in a meeting along with other prominent scientists of India. Simple as he was, Dr.Kalam told his boss that he did not have dress and shoes to attend such a high powered meeting. His boss laughed and told him that he should not worry at all because his great work would speak for itself.

In a democratic set up, it becomes essential for a candidate to seek the support and goodwill of his electorate through personal contacts or conveniently through correspondence. This kind of method has been adopted by Dr. A.P.J. Abdul Kalam in a respectable way. His candidature is fairly strong in every respect. This indeed is a fact which is known to him and everybody.

Kalam seeks support of all in electoral college

Presidential nominee A.P.J. Abdul Kalam has sought the support of all in the electoral college to his candidature declaring his "unflinching commitment" to secularism and asserting that Pakistan- backed cross- border terrorism aimed at destabilising India" is doomed".

He also said the basic structure of the Constitution was "Unalterable".

In a seven-page appeal to his voters—all MPs and MLAs cuttong across party lives, Mr. Kalam, the father of India's missile programme, who had played a key role in the 1998 Pokharan nuclear tests, emphasised that national security had to be recognised by everyone as a "national priority" along with speedy development aimed at elimination of poverty and unemploymemt.

Sharing the concern and outrage of the entire nation on cross-border terrorism, he said lamabad's policy aimed at destabelisation and dismemberment of India is doomed .

"Jammu and Kashmir was, is and shall always remain an inseparable part of India" Mr Kalam said in the letter despatched to members of the electoral college over a fortnight ahead of the July 15 presidential election in which he is pitted against Left party nominee—Lakshmi Sehgal.

Like millions of Indians and foreigners, Muchkund Dubey, the eminent former Foreign Secretary, Government of India, greatly eulogised the services of Dr Kalam. He called him a great achiever. "His achievements have been duly recognised by the award of Bharat Ratna. Dr. Kalam will be the role model for millions of young men and women in the country fired by the ambition of achieving greater things in life. Apart from this, his humility, simplicity and honesty have impressed us....

Some people have stated that Dr. Kalam has no experience in politics and may find somewhat difficult in dealing with several difficult problems which may seek solution at his level. But in proper assessment of his career, it does not appeal. In fact he had to deal with bureaucrats and politicians in high office to seek to their proper support in several scientific projects which he happened to start in his long career. He has the convincing power and some well-known Defence Ministers like R. Venkataraman and George Fernandes felt much happiness and satisfaction in his work and did not hesitate to give him liberal support including the financial help

On account of his consistent useful work, disciplined life and humility par excellence, he was conferred with numerous academic, scientific and civil awards from time to time. This missile and rocket man was made Bharat Ratna and in a few years, his name was recommended for the President of India. He accepted these unique honours with the highest sense of humility. When he joined service as a Senior Scientific Assistant in a lower scale of pay, who could say that a young boy from Rameswaram would, one day, achieve international stature. He himself mentioned about his restless hours late at night to give the finishing touch to a scientific problem. Time and again, he mentioned about the great lesson which he happened to learn from Prof Vikram Sarabhai and several others at ISRO, Thumba, and DRDO. He always realised that his was the endless work and his realisation did produce results with numerous achievements like Prithvi, Agni, Akash, Nag and Pokharan II which brought India on the map of the scientific world. His initial visit to NASA did pay him rich scientific dividends. He caught hold of the basic threads of research which he strengthened by his consistent efforts.

Where as he leads a simple life, with the minimum possible requirements, he is very humble and shows much interest in the growth and development of the younger generation. A 'well developed India' is the main aim of the missile man. He also wishes that India should be strong in every respect. This is the ardent desire and main slogan in his heart and mind.

While he helped the highest position of the Principal Scientific Adviser under Government of India, he maintained a few dozens of scientific laboratories in various regions of India. He was keen to see that dedicated and disciplined personel should receive due reward in terms of promotion and recognition. Indeed the personnel were happy with his 'open' behaviour in the sense that any employee could see him and discuss with him his personal problems as well as departmental problems. He always tried to gain new knowledge or experience gathered by young scientists in a few years. Therefore he encouraged them and placed them in high positions. They, on their part, showed much respect and love for Dr. Kalam. Indeed in his long career he did not find any difficulty with his colleagues; instead it was all cooperation, for further scientific development.

The Election Process

The NDA's candidate for the post of President A.P.J. Abdul Kalam addressed the media for the first time since his nomination for the highest constitutional office in the country.

Refusing to answer questions on the Indo-Pak standoff, Kalam quoted Prime Minister Vajpayee's statement that the situation on the border was under control. He however reiterated India's nuclear doctrine of 'no first use'. Kalam said that if India and Pakistan did not have nuclear weapons there would have been a war.

"Even the recent warfare would have seen that. Why it did not take place? It did not have nuclear weapons it would have taken place. Do you understand that? This nuclear deterrent on both sides has helped not to engage in a big war and to avoid the nuclear war," said Kalam.

Kalam on Gujarat

Talking about the situation in Gujarat, Kalam told members of the press, " What has happened in Gujarat is very painful. We should prevent it at all cost. I can only say whether religion can graduate into spiritualism. Can the political leaders turn in to political leaders with compassion? Can our education system work for 100 per cent literacy?"

On a question concerning, Gujarat Chief Minister Narendra Modi, Kalam said," I have given my views clearly, you can highlight.

The nuclear deterrence between India and Pakistan ensured that there was no war.

- India's nuclear doctrine was based on maintaining a minimal deterrent.
- Dual use technologies and new management structures from India's weapons programmes can be used in national development.
- The situation on the borders was under control.
- What has happened in Gujarat is very painful.

Electoral College

The President of India is elected indirectly by an Electoral College comprising elected members of the Rajya Sabha, Lok Sabha and the elected members of the state Legislative Assemblies.

Electoral College

Lok Sabha—543 MPs

Rajya Sabha—233 MPs

State Legislatures—4120 MLAs

Total number of voters—4896

Kalam Thanks President, PM, Sonia for Support

In the Capital to file his nomination for the Presidential polls, missile man A.P.J. Abdul Kalam was all about town on Monday but said little for public consumption. In a whirlwind of meetings, Kalam met President K.R. Narayanan, Prime Minister Atal Bihari Vajpayee, Defence Minister George Fernandes, and also Samajwadi Party leader Mulayam Singh Yadav and Congress President Sonia Gandhi, whom he thanked for their support. He will file his nomination papers to be endorsed by the PM, Sonia and Mulayam among a host of political leaders on Tuesday morning before addressing the press at 12.30 p.m. On Monday, accompanied by Pramod Mahajan from Chennai, Kalam arrived to a grand reception at the Delhi airport with Defence Minister George Fernandes, driving with him for a meeting with Vajpayee.

The one-to-one meeting with Vajpayee, described by oficials as a courtesy call lasted over an hour was followed by lunch. Among those who joined in for the afternoon repast included Congress leader Manmohan Singh, Union Minister L K Advani and Murli Manohar Joshi, apart from Mahajan and Fernandes .

Mahajan, briefing newspersons after the lunch said that Kalam would speak on Tuesday after filing his nomination in the morning. He brought with him a cheque of Rs 15,000 required to file the nomination, said Mahajan. Kalam drove off from Race Course with Fernandes to his residence for further " talks" followed by the meetings with the Samajwadi Party and the Congress later in the evening. A taciturn Kalam said little, nimbly skipping the waiting media at most ports of call. Where he could not avoid speaking, he limited the interaction. Asked what his main focus would be as President, he said: "The idea is to integrate the system with Parliament and how to integrate the minds of the people. The missile man dismissed the political controversies surrounding his candidature, saying he was a candidate of all parties. He also dissociated his role in the nation's missile programme with the one he was set to assume assuring that once he took over, he would only concentrate on his role as President.

Kalam hedged on the delicate Gujarat issue merely stating: "One has to have a vision for the nation that will reduce all tension in society".

I am an Indian first: Kalam Dr. A.P.J. Abdul Kalam has dismissed suggestions that he had been chosen for the top post because of his religion, saying he always regarded himself as an Indian. "Really to be honest, I never thought of it that way at all. I have always regarded myself as an Indian," he said in an interview to *India Today.* Sporting long hair and normally seen casually attired, Dr. Kalam seems not to be "Let us say, it will be a new experience. Besides, you can achieve a lot of work even while having dinner," he said. Dr. Kalam said he was overwhelmed by the gesture of the NDA in making him its nominee for the highest office." Being the President is an onerous task".On the role he would like to play in his new assignment,he said for any President the major task was thinking of the best way to integrate the nation. He said while he was speaking to children in Porbandar recently, a young girl asked him what message he would like to give them. " I told her that our minds should be embedded with thoughts of the nation and that the nation is always bigger than the individual. I think that massage is relevant here too", he said. Asked whether being a scientist equipped him in any doubt that this would be a new type of mission". But essentially, it is all about leadership and that is something we were trained for, even if the mission may have been different. We had a systems approach of careful analysis, design and integration that is relevant for any type of task," he said. Dr. Kalam contended that his work was not confined to conducting scientific research. "We looked at the overall development of the nation". On having no experience in handling the intricacies of politics, he said his own definition of politics was that "it is all about creating leaders to evolve policies that will take the country to higher levels". "It is a multi-dimensional leadership that focuses on the nation's economic, social and political development. If you look at politics through this perspective, then everything falls into place," he said.

Who's the Hostess?

History of sorts will be created with the two top positions in the country being held by bachelors—Dr. APJ Abdul Kalams, the presiential nominee of the BJP-led NDA and Prime Minister Atal Behari Vajpayee. However, in Mr Vajpayee's case his foster daughter Namita is always at hand and plays the hostess. This is where

Dr. Kalam might be handicapped given his status of a confirmed bachelor once be occupies Rashtrapati Bhavan next month.

The B.J.P. set up Dr. Kalam not just as an "eminent scientist", but as a symbol of nuclear militarism. Whether he is the Bomb Man or the Missile Man may be a subject of some sophistry. The significant point is that as a larger than life scientist, he is the product of Pokhran II. His is not the image of professional scientist who has merely carried out his master's orders. As millions have been made to see it, the *Bhagwad Gita* had inspired his Bomb and missile embodied. In fact, during all these days, in numerous Rotatry Club meetings around the country since Pokharan II had heard his own kind of rhetoric hailing the explosions as assertions of national self-esteem.

It is indeed a unique phenomenon in the thinking of the Bomb Man who very often quotes the *Bhagvad Gita* and other Hindu scriptures. It is significant proof of the fact that makes him more of a model Muslim, worthy of emulation by others of our largest minority community. A delightful example was his speech on a visit to Bhuj in Gujarat in the wake of the devastating earthquake last year. Here, he compared the power of compassion behind the relief efforts to the energy of thousands of nuclear bombs in the *Virat Swarup* (cosmic form) of god as revealed in the *Gita*.

Soon after his nomination as a Presidential candidate, by the NDA, the RSS called him a true Bharatiya.' The VHP leader Praveen Togadiya also spoke in the same tone. Tarun Vijay, the Editor of *Panchjanya* opined in Dr. Kalam's favour. He stated, Indianism is Hindutva. This does not mean that Muslims should convert to Hinduism. What it does mean is that you can be what you like but must share the vision of Dr Abdul Kalam.

The entry in Rashtrapati Bhavan indeed personifies the greatest achievement of any individual in our sub-continent. A massive structure with 350 rooms, beautiful grassy lawns, tennis courts, polo ground, and guarded by a Battalion strength of the army, came into existence after the decision of the transfer of the capital of India was made in 1911. After a dozen of viceroys lived here as the chief executive head of the British administration. The decorum of the office was well maintained by the highest standard in this building. Several national and international decisions are made here.

For a humble and very simple person like Dr. Kalam who always lived in one or two rooms, this massive structure would look something like beyond his way of life." Throughout his career, he avoided pomp and show which may have bearing on touch of mediocrity or it should give out a picture of vanity or pride. In matters of food, including style of service and ingredients, it would be something unusual in the new environments. But he has the capability and capacity to adjust himself well in the new ornamental environments in the Rashtrapati Bhavan.

In Rashtrapati Bhavan , the President has a powerful machinery of bureancrats who are picked up an account of their sterling merits. The President may seek their advice or advise them on various problems which would come on the way. He would he in touch with the office of the Prime Minister and any oficial statement would have the stamp of that office. As mentioned earlier the, nomination of Dr. Abdul Kalam was well-received at various levels and the opposition to him is quite marginal. Such category of people are well known politcians, scientists, social scientists, lawyers, teachers, scholars, bureaucrats and last but not the least the students having interest in his scientific temper of the highest degree. In this regard, I may mention the name of Dr. S.R. Bakshi, eminent social scientist who have greatly appreciated time and again, Dr. Kalam's humility, simplicity, disciplined life, consistency, sense of secularism and his qualities of head and heart. It is quite evident, he added, from his successful scientific career that he spent numerous sleepless nights in order to see a proper solution of the ticklish problem that proved a hurdle in his way. And unless he could achieve satisfactory and hundred per cent result, he would never breathe a sigh of relief. Dreams float on an impatient wind. A wind that wants to create a new order. An order of strength and thundering of fire—from a poem written by Dr A.P.J. Abdul Kalam. He is the undisputed father of India's missile programme. He has breathed life into ballistic missiles like the Agni and Prithvi, which put China and Pakistan well under India's missile range. It is too exhausting to track Dr. Abdul Kalam's achievements to date. In the 60s and 70s he was a trail blazer in the space department. In the 80s he transformed the moribund Defence Research and Development Laboratory in Hyderabad into a highly motivated team. By the 90s Kalam emerged as the Czar of Indian science and technology and was awarded the Bharat Ratna. His life and mission is a vindication of what a determined person can achieve against extraordinary odds. Even at 68, he is indefatigable and dreams of making India into a technological superpower. More importantly, he is still capable of acting on it.

Stepping in of Dr. Kalam in the Rashtrapati Bhavan, almost a month from now. appears a certainty. Guess what would be his first message to the nation? It may be on these lines; We must work together to transform our developing India into a developed India and the revolution required for this effort must start in our minds. His vision relates to a prosperous India without poverty; an India strong in trade and commerce; an India strong in many fields of science ad technology and an India with health and education to all. His space technology vision has come true and reaching out to the people. The achievements include communication through networks in remote areas; disaster warning system quick resource surveys to target ground water and save forest cover campaign.

The man, who has spent all his life learning rocketry and will now occupy the highest office of the land. Knows well how to manage men, matters and materials. Dr. Kalam is now well known in India and abroad but there are still little known facets of his life. His full name is Avil Pakir Jalaluddin Abdul Kalam and he hails from the southern most tip of India.

When Abdul Kalam addressed the alumni association of the Madras Institute of Technology, Chennai some years ago, he said: "It was a joy to study the structure of the aircraft." His interest in aeronautical engineering led him to a career in the Indian Space Research Organisation. He was the Project Director of the first successful SLV-3 flight from Defence Research and Development Laboratory, Hyderabad, and, Development Programme. He led the teams that developed the Agni, Prithvi, Trishul, Akash and Nag missiles. He is considered a good team leader and his gift for scouting talent. Still later, he was apppointed Scientific Adviser to the Defence Minister. He is the only scientist to have received the Bharat Ratna, India's highest civilian honour.

This world, fear has no place, only as a military power but strength. We must be strong not only as a military power but also as an economic power. Both must go hand in hand . These are visions. What about the reality? What do yoy see as the most significant achievement of your rather distinguished career culminating in a Bharat Ratna in your lifetime? My good fortune was to have worked with three great minds. Dr Vikram Sarabhai of the Department of Space. Professor Satish Dhawan, who succeeded him and Dr Brahm Prakash, father of nuclear material. I was lucky to have worked with all three of them closely and consider this the greatest opportunity of my life. I see four milestones in my career. One: the twenty years I spent in Indian Space Research Organisaion. I was given the opportunity to be the project director for launching Rohini. These years played a very important role in the Defence Research and Development Organisation and got a chance to be part of India's guided missile programme. It was, you could call, my second bliss when Agni met its atomic energy and the DRDO had this tremendous partnership third bliss. The joy of participating with my team in these nuclear tests and proving to the world that India can make nuclear tests and proving to the world that India can make it. That we are no longer a developing nation but one among them. It made me feel very proud as an Indian. And finally, four: The fact that we have now developed for Agni a re-entry structure, for which we have developed this new material. A very light material called carbon-carbon. One day an orthopaedic surgeon from the Nizam Institute of lifted the material and found it so light that he took me to his hospital and showed me his patients. There were these little girls and boys with heavy metallic callipers weighing over 3 kg each, dragging their feet around. He got: made these Floor Reaction Orthosis 300 gram callipers and took them to the orthopaedic centre. The children could not believe their eyes! From dragging around a 3 kg load on their legs, they could now move around freely with these 300 gram callipers. They began running around! Their parent had tears in their eyes. That was my fourth bliss. Apart from science and technology, what else interest you? Poetry and music. I have this big library at home and my favourite poets are Milton, Walt Whitman and Rabindranath Tagore. I write poetry too. My book of poems is : *Yenudaya Prayana.* You must read it. I will send you a copy. Who are your favourite poets in Tamil, the language you write in? Bharatidasana, who died in 1965. And Subramanita Bharathiar, who died in 1939 at the age of 35, killed by an elephant while giving it a coconut. I also enjoy Carnatic music and play the veena. What is your favourite raga? The Shri Raga. You know my favourite kirtan? It is the one that Swami Thyagaraja, a Ram Bhakt like me, recited in the Shri Raga poem in his sabha. He sang: " In this gathering whoever are great in front of God, I salute them. " He never said: I satute the king. That is strength of conviction. That is courage. You have asked me so many questions, Mr Nandy, may I ask you too? by all means. Tell me, why is the media here so negative ? Why are we in India so embarrassed to recognise our own strengths, our achievements? We are such a great nation. We have so many amazing success stories but we refuse to acknowledge them. Why ? We are the second largest producer of wheat in the world. We are the second largest producer of rice. We are the first in milk production. We are number one in remote sensing satellites. Look at Dr Sudarshan. He has transformed the tribal village into a self-sustaining, self-driving unit. There are millions of such achievements but disasters. I was in Tel Aviv once and I was reading this Israeli newspaper. It was the day after a lot of attacks and bombardments and deaths had taken place. The Hamas had struck, but the front page of the newspaper had this picture of a Jewish gentleman who in five years had transformed his desert land into an orchard and a granary. It was this inspiring picture that everyone woke up to. The gory details of killings, bombardments, deaths were inside the newspaper, buried among other news. In India we only read about death, sickness, terrorism, crime. Why are we so negative? I guess we grew up with the maxim that good news synonymous with freedom. That is why our press is so strong, so fiercely independent if not always encouraging of success stories. Another question: Why are we, as a nation, so obsessed with foreign things? Is it a legacy of our colonial years? We want foreign television sets. We want foreign shirts. We want foreign technology. Why this obsession with everything imported? Do we not realise that self-respect comes with self-reliance? I guess that comes from repression. When you look in your economy for years and leave it in the hands of local pirates and cheating banias, you are bound to get a backlash. Foreign things have indeed come in but they have also brought down prices, taught us quality, stopped us from cheat in consumers with shoddy, overpriced local products. Like in cars, consumer electronics, fabrics, processed foods. Nationalism far too long has been a convenient cover for looting. Let us not forget that. But yes, I agree with you, it is time we started giving value to ourselves as a people, as a nation. I was in Hyderabad giving this lecture, when a 14- year-old girl came up and asked me for my autograph. I asked her what her goal in life was. She replied: I want to live in a developed India. For her, you and I will have to build this writings, through your speeches in Parliament. As the day of election of the President of India is approaching, different types of comments are available on the lips of the people . Mrinalini Sarabhai wife of Professor Vikram Sarabhai, has given a novel solution of the Presidenal election. She wants that Dr. A.P.J. Abdul Kalam may be made the President of India and Captain Lakshmi Sahgal as the Vice-President. She made it clear that while one is her sister, the other is his late husband's favourite discipline.

It was a mere coincidence that two Presidential candidates arrived here for two differen functions. While Sahgal was on the campaign tail, Kalam was the chief guest at a function to unveil the statue of space scientist Prof. Vikram Sarabhai. He delivered the keynote address at theVikram Sarabhai Space Centre.

She did not agree that the President was a rubber stamp. "You know why Narayanan was not given a second term? He asserted his power and was not a silent spectator to all the doings of the NDA government," she said.

In his address, Kalam said young people should be given more opportunities. "We want youth with vision. Vision generates thinking. Vision never dies," he said. He recited a few lines from his poem 'Life Tree'.

"Mrinalini has agreed to dance to my lines. When it is enacted wherever I am, I will be there to watch her performance, " Kalam said. By giving vent to her feelings in favour of a very prominent freedom fighter under Subhas Chandra Bose, in Indian National Army, she has directly paid rich tribute to the womanhood of the Indian sub-continent. This kind of feeling has been greatly appreciated by Dr. Sangh Mittra an eminent social scientist of ICHR. She opines that it is high time that such a dedicated woman should find a proper place in Rajya Sabha of our country.Undoubtedly Dr. Kalam's rise in life was meteoric. In the long scientific journey of his career, he ardently believed in progress in day-to-day work and marked something for tomorrow. It was not his habit to look back. Evidently, he had faith in the dictum," Never say I shall do a thing, say, I have done it". He did not like the element of uncertainty in any kind of work he happened to undertake. He spent even odd hours at night brooding over problems and their solution, single-handed or in team work. He knew how to humour the members of his team in whom he always imbibed the spirit of discipline and dedication. In fact this was his way of life: this was also the secret of his grand success. One should greatly appreciate in fact that the son of an ordinary boat man with minimum financial assets for educational career, could attain national status and occupy the highest executive position in his own country. Jay Rana, a reputed author, has equated his qualities with Maulana Abul Kalam Azad. He has made a sensible analysis of his ways of life and scholarship.

A.P.J. however, is more of a communicator in the professorial mould. He lacks the gift of the gab. May be he makes up for this deficiency with 'veena vaadan'

From Rameswaram to Rashtrapati Bhavan, Kalam's flight to Presidency cannot be termed anything but meteoric. Has he been helped by the sheer conspiracy of circumstances or as a reward for being at the right place at the right time?

Despite Kalam's claims of being essentially a political his rise within the highly competitive and top heavy scientific institutions controlled by the government can be attributed to his uncanny sense of managing the system in a political manner. Any Indian scientist will feel the enormity of politics that plays a huge role in the functioning of most of our academic institutions.

Kalam has survived it all to take one leap after another. It may not be attributed to his genius' alone. It could have something to do with his political credo as applied to managing the system from within for optimum results.

Election

The election of the President is over. As it was quite evident Dr. Abdul Kalam, supported by BJP, Congress and a combination of NDA, would win with a thumping majority. He has got 41,52 votes and Capt. Lakshmi Sahgal 459 votes. To reach the top' in fact the main aim of life of the Missile Man came out to be true. It was a long drawn academic struggle for five decades. Indeed for the first time, an eminent scientist, with very humble origin, has stepped into the portals of Rastrapati Bhavan, with a tenure of five years. Constitutionally, he is the chief excutive head with numerous powers which he is to exercise with caution and restraint. Indeed he is required to abide by several constitutional norms which have been enshrined very vividly in the Constitution of India. This is what we expect from the scientist President.

Speech By Dr. A.P.J. Abdul Kalam on his Assumption of Office as President of India

New Delhi, 25 July, 2002, 3 Sravana, 1924

The Vision of India

Respected Shri Narayananji, Mr. Vice President, Mr. Prime

Minister, Mr. Deputy Prime Minister, Chief Justice of India, Speaker of Lok Sabha, Members of the Union Council of Ministers, Governors, Chief Ministers, Deputy Chairperson of Rajya Sabha, Deputy Speaker of Lok Sabha, Members of Parliament, Excellencies, friends and children - my greetings to all of you. When I see in front of me, the distinguished dignitaries including a number of senior diplomats representing their countries and other eminent personalities, a beautiful Thiagarajaswamigal's Keerthana in Sri Raga echoes from my heart - "Endaro Mahaanubhavalu andhariggi vandanamulu" which means, "I salute all the great noble hearted human beings".

I thank the Members of Parliament and State Legislatures for having elected me. The endorsement I have received from the nation, giving me the responsibility to realize our shared dream of India with prosperity, harmony and strength is really overwhelming. Ten illustrious personages have adorned this office of the President and contributed to the nation building with their outstanding personal qualities. I salute them all. While I assume the office of the President of Republic of India with humility and gratefully recognizing the immense trust, the people of the country and the political system have reposed in me, I promise to endeavour to fulfill the aspirations of our people.

Indian civilizational heritage is built on universal spirit. India always stood for friendship and extends warm hands to the whole world.

We have made significant achievements in the last fifty years in food production, health sector, higher education, media and mass communication, industrial infrastructure, information technology, science and technology and defence. Our nation is endowed with natural resources, vibrant people and traditional value system. In spite of these resources, a number of our people are below the poverty line, undernourished and lack primary education itself. Our aim is to empower them to be poverty free, healthy and literate. A country needs to have the characteristics as defined in Thirukkural, composed over 2000 years ago :

(Pini inmai Selvam Vilaivinbam Emam Aniyenba Nattirkiv vainthu)

That is, "the important elements that constitute a nation are: being disease free; wealth; high productivity; harmonious living and strong defence". All our efforts should be focused towards building these five elements at various levels in a coherent and in an integrated manner. I am convinced that our nation with a strong, vibrant and billion plus population can contribute to realize these elements.

Today our country is facing challenges such as cross border terrorism, certain internal conflicts and un-employment. To face these challenges, there must be a vision to ensure focused action of one billion citizens of this great country with varied capabilities. What can be that vision? It can be none other than transforming India into a 'Developed Nation'. Can government alone achieve this Vision? Now, we need a movement in the country. This is the time to ignite the minds of the people for this movement. We will work for it. We cannot emerge as a developed nation if we do not learn to transact with speed. I recall the saintly poet Kabir's wisdom to us:

'काल करे सो आज कर
आज करे सो अब'
'Kaal Kare So Aaj Kar
Aaj Kare So Ab'

that means, "What you want to do tomorrow do it today, and what you want to do today do it now".

This vision of developed nation needs to be achieved with Parliamentary democracy, which is the core of our governance system. The basic structure of our Constitution has stood the test of time. I am confident that it will continue to be responsive to the demands of changing situations. The first and foremost task is to respect and uphold the constitutional processes, in the best interest of our people and our nation, without fear or favour and with fairness and firmness. India is a Union of States based on the framework of co-operative federalism. Within the co-operative frame-work, there is also a requirement to develop competitive strengths for the States so that they can excel at the national level and the global level. Competitiveness helps in ensuring economic and managerial efficiency and to be creative to meet new challenges. These are essential to survive and prosper in a fast changing world of today. In addition, in order to strengthen democratic processes and institution, we should all truly strive for substantive decentralization.

I wish to emphasize my unflinching commitment to the principle of secularism, which is the corner stone of our nationhood and which is the key feature of our civilisational strength. During the last one year I met a number of spiritual leaders of all religions. They all echoed one message, that is, unity of minds and hearts of our people will happen and we will see the golden age of our country, very soon. I would like to endeavour to work for bringing about unity of minds among the divergent traditions of our country.

Along with speedy development aimed at elimination of poverty and un-employment, national security has to be recognized by every Indian as a national priority. Indeed, making India strong and self reliant - economically, socially and militarily - is our foremost duty to our motherland and to ourselves and to our future generations.

When the child is empowered by the parents, at various phases of growth, the child transforms into a responsible citizen. When the teacher is empowered with knowledge and experience, good young human beings with value systems take shape. When individual or a team is empowered with technology, transformation to higher potential for achievement is assured. When the leader of any institution empowers his or her people, leaders are born who can change the nation in multiple areas. When the women are empowered, society with stability gets assured. When the political leaders of the nation empower the people through visionary policies, the prosperity of the nation is certain. The medium for transformation to developed India is the empowerment at various levels with power of knowledge. A roadmap for realizing this vision of developed India is in front of us.

At this juncture, I recall a beautiful thought of Dr. G.G. Swell, an eminent leader from North East: "We must have a mental infrastructure. Mental infrastructure means sincerity of purpose, of vision, of purity of heart and mind".

When I travel across our nation, when I hear the sound of waves of the three seas around the shores of my country, when I experience the breeze of wind from the mighty Himalayas, when I see the bio-diversity of North-East and our islands and when I feel the warmth from the western desert, I hear the voice of the youth " When can I sing the song of India?". What can be the answer?. I have so far interacted with over 50,000 school children during the past one year. I would like to share with you my answer to the urge of these children. If youth have to sing the song of India, India should become a developed country which is free from poverty, illiteracy and un-employment and is buoyant with economic prosperity, national security and internal harmony. To create this transformation we all have to resolve ourselves to work and sweat for the national development. I would like to share the song of youth, which I normally recite with the school children, here at this juncture. I am very happy to see the children present here representing the future generation. Through them I would like to convey the song of youth to all children of our country and the people.

As a young citizen of India, armed with technology, knowledge and love for my nation, I realize, small aim is a crime.

I will work and sweat for a great vision, the vision of transforming India into a developed nation, powered by economic strength with value system

I am one of the citizens of the billion; Only the vision will ignite the billion souls.

It has entered into me ; The ignited soul compared to any resource is the most powerful resource on the earth, above the earth and under the earth.

I will keep the lamp of knowledge burning to achieve the vision - Developed India

If we work and sweat for the great vision with ignited minds, the transformation leading to the birth of vibrant developed India will happen. This song, when sung in our own beautiful languages will unite our minds for action.

I pray the Almighty: "May the divine peace with beauty enter into our people; Happiness and good health blossom in our bodies, minds and souls".

JAI HIND

Appendix I

Gandhian Missile Man Dr. A.P.J. Abdul Kalam * Achievements

Dr. Avul Pakir Jainulabhudin Adbul Kalam, was born on the 15th October, 1931, at Rameshwaram in TamilNadu. He did his B.Sc. at the St. Joseph's College, Tiruchi, and DMIT in Aeronautical Engineering at the MIT, Madras, during 1954-57. He joined the DRDO in 1958. During 1963-82, he served the ISRO in various capacities.

As Project Director, SLV-3, he was responsible for carrying out design, development, qualification and flight testing of 44 major sub systems. In 1982, as Director, DRDO, was entrusted with the Integrated Guided Missile Development Programme. He conceived the programme cnstituting 5 major projects for meeting the requirements of the defence services and for establishing re-entry technology.

The development and successful flight test of Prithvi, Trishul, Akash, Nag, and Agni established the indigeneous capability towards self reliance in defence preparedness. The successful launching of 'Agni' surface-to-surface missile is a unique achievement which made India a member of an exclusive club of highly developed countries. Thus, through SLV and Guided Missile Programme a solid foundation has been created in the indigeneous testing and development of high technology Aerospace Projects.

An Advanced Technology Research Centre, called Research Centre Imarat has also been established by Dr. A.P.J. Abdul Kalam as an extension of DRDL to undertake development in futuristic missile technology areas. He has also established a unique 3 tier management structure to integrate and commit technologists, academic institutions, Industries etc. As a crowing glory to all his achievements, he was appointed Scientific Advisor to Raksha Manthri and Secretary, Dept. of Defence Research and Development.

He is a member of Indian National Academy of Sciences, Astronautical Society of India and many other professional bodies. He has published two books.

Awards

- He has been Awarded with the India's Highest civilian Award "The Bharat Ratna" in 1997.
- Starting with Anna University's first D.Sc., Honoris Causa, he has received many such including the one given by IIT, Bombay, BHU and others.
- Other prestigious awards include Dr.Biren Roy Space Award, Om Prakash Basin Award for Science and Technology, National Nehru Award, Arya Bhatta Award.
- Dr. Abdul kalam, is praised as a welder of people and a Gandhian Missile Man by R.K. Laxman, in his cartoon in "Times of India."
- As a humanitarian and with his extreme simplicity, easy access, he has become a National Hero. He loves Tamil poetry and is interested in carnatic music. He has himself written poems in Tamil. He adores his Gurus of MIT and cherishes his education and training at MIT.

Return to Home Page

Dreams To Ignite Young Minds

India has to have vision to become a developed nation. A good dream for our young people is the vision. Can we ignite our young minds? These are the thoughts that frequently 'fire' the mind of India's missile man-- this year (1998) Bharat Ratna awardee Dr. A.P.J. Abdul Kalam.

In an interview to Science Express, the man who built biting molars and awesome muscles into India's missile programme outlined the vision he has of India of tomorrow. "Whenever there is a goal, the dynamics of performance changes, Technology is the economical strength of the nation", says soft-spoken Kalam. "India has people of high calibre and intelligence. The only thing required is more facilities in our labs, government funding and good leadership in scientific areas." After a pause, he fires another missile: "Most importantly, determined youngsters."

No wonder he advices the youth of the country to "dream, dream and dream and convert these into thoughts and later into actions."

Kalam's advice to the youngsters of the nation is to "think big". "We are a nation of a billion people and we must think like a nation of a billion people. Only then can we become big."

Dr. Kalam's, Scientific Advisor to the Defence Minister and Secretary, Defence Research and Development is the second scientist to receive the Bharat Ratna, the highest civilian award, after the late Dr. Homi Jehangir Baba.

This genius attributes his success to his parents and the team which worked relentlessly to achieve the goal.

Science, according to him, is a global phenomenon. He feels there are a few areas where India can develop its core competence. These areas are software engineering, computer products and design, agriculture and food, aviation, defence research and space technology and chemical engineering.

"This will lead to a highly beneficial economic and social progress for the nation," says Kalam.

The man who said, "Friends, you now have the fire to torch the Agni" turns out to be extremely shy. His love for the Bhagavad Geetha and the long mane almost gives the missile man the halo of a saint. In fact, his views on technology and life make him the copy book saint of science armed with Brahmastras and the power to heal wounds.

That is another passion of Kalam-using missiles that maime and kill to give a fresh hope to the disabled. In a U turn, Kalam has not shied in using the technology behind fire-spewing missiles to build artificial limbs and spring-like coils called stents to keep the heart vessels open.

He is one of those scientists who aims at putting technology created by him to multiple use. He used the light weight carbon-carbon material designed for Agni to make calipers for the polio affected. This carbon-carbon composite material reduced the weight of the calipers to 400 grams (from its original weight of 4kgs.) Nizam's Institute of Medical Sciences (NIMS, Hyderabad) was the birthplace for the defence technology spin offs from Kalam's labs via the DRDL (Defence Research and Development Laboratory), DMRL (Defence Metallurgical Research Lab) and the RCI (Research Centre Imarat). "It was a great experience to see, in the orthopaedic Department of NIMS, how the light weight caliper could bring happiness to the polio affected", remembers Kalam.

Another important event that took place in Hyderabad is the development of the Cardiac stent. Cardiac stents are used during a Balloon Angioplasty. The clogged arteries are opened up using a balloon and stents are inserted to prevent the vessels from collapse.

"The stent developed by us costed much less (he is modest not to say that the cost is less than half) than the ones imported," explains Kalam.

Kalam says there are many more avenues wherein defence technology can be used for a social cause. The technology used for defence imaging systems can be used for medical imagery which is yet another value product, he says. "We are also working on a cost-effective lighter substitute for the Jaipur foot," he adds.

He is of the opinion that a mission oriented programme should be chalked out where in medical equipments and their maintenance should grow out of indigenous technology, thus making us self reliant.

But personally, given a chance would he rather opt to use technology solely for social purposes or continue with his missile programmes? "If India has to become a developed nation it has to have overall development. That includes the field of medicine, defence technology and everything else," says Kalam in a matter-of-fact tone.

Having rolled out sophisticated missiles at regular intervals, Kalam is now striving to make the reusable missiles dream a reality. Like the space shuttles, the reusable missiles can carry war-heads to a pre-determined target, deliver the fire power and return for another run.

The reusable missile's close 'cousin' is Nishant - the Remotely Piloted Vehicle (RPV) or a one-time-use missile that can thumb its nose at even sophisticated radars.

Many of Kalam's pet projects like the Integrated Guided Missile Development Programme (IGMDP) and several other defence ventures under his command, are poised for a quantum leap next year.

According to a status report of major ongoing projects of the Defence Research and Development Organisation (DRDO) headed by Kalam, the development of the five indigenous missiles under the IGMDP is progressing as per schedule.

"Agni" missile, the crown of the IGMDP, is being given top priority and DRDO scientists have been able to indigenously produce carbon-

carbon composite material which could withstand temperatures upto 3500 degrees celsius during the flight of the missile.

UNI quoting Defence Minisry sources said production of 150-Km range "Prithvi" missile for the Army had already commenced and two flight trials of the 250-Km range, Indian Air Force (IAF) version, "Prithvi" had also been completed.

User trials of the other three missiles under the IGMDP - the 9 Km short range low level quick reaction Trishul for the three services, the 25Km medium range surface to air missile "Akash" with multiple target handling capability, the third generation 4Km range anti-tank "Nag" missile - were slated to commence next year.

In many ways, the "Akash" missile is emerging as a key weapon which is being developed by the DRDO as it employs ram rocket propulsion to facilitate carrying of bigger pay loads.

'Akash' is the key in the sense that ram rocket technology is also to be employed by India for the futuristic reusable missile systems.

As far as the current status of India's ambitious Light Combat Aircraft (LCA) was concerned, the second LCA was under integration along with the simultaneous development of technology demonstrator TD-1.

Several new technologies had been established with regard to the LCA. They included carbon fibre composite structure, control law for unstable aircraft, digital fly-by-wire control system and advanced computing system.

The Kaveri engine had been developed and was undergoing evaluation. Its integration with LCA was expected in early 1999.

No country can throttle India's missile programme despite technology denial regimes, believes Kalam.

An important aspect of "the integrated guided missile development programme was identification of critical technologies and their indigenisation as the missile technology control regime was primarily directed at India."

Elaborating on his future plans, the senior most serving defence scientist referred to the Technology Mission 2020 which proposes to change the national status from a developing one to a developed one and involve 500 people from academia, industry and govemment. He also spoke about working on a 10 year self-reliance programme in defence technologies.

Kalam was bom into a family of modest means in Rameshwaram,

a small town in TamilNadu. It was his father who wanted him to take up science in the college. After graduating from St.Joseph College, Tiruchirapalli, he joined the Madras Institute of Technology (MIT) to specialise in Aeronautical Engg. This was indeed his launching pad for this promising young man who was destined to become the father of Indian missile programme. After a brief stint in the Defence Research and Development Organisation (DRDO), he joined the Indian Space Research organisation (ISRO) in 1963. While at the Vikram Sarabhai Space Centre, he developed the Satellite Launch Vehicle (SLV-3) which put the Rohini Satellite into orbit.

He later re-entered DRDO at the Defence Research and Development Laboratory (DRDL), Hyderabad, as the director and this is where most of the research and development of his missile programmes were conceived and created. In his hour of glory, the missile man remembered his parents, co-workers especially at the Vikram Sarabhai Space Centre, Thiruvananthapuram and a Hyderabad-based defence research laboratory, besides teachers who collectively contributed in various ways towards this achievement.

Courtesy: The Indian Express/Science Express, 16th Dec. 1997.

Appendix II

Convocation Address at Delhi University

Vision Creates Great Leaders

I am indeed delighted to participate in the 70th Convocation of University of Delhi an illustrious university with a great tradition. My greetings to all the graduating students and professors and teachers who shaped them. It is a privilege and honour for me to deliver the 70th annual Convocation of University of Delhi. I was thinking what thoughts I can share with the graduating students on this important occasion when you will be entering into professional phase of life. I would like to tell the young. "low aim is the crime". In the knowledge era, successful people will always take untravelled roads rather than beaten path. This needs excellence in intellect that demands three unique traits or qualities, experienced during education phase and also career phase. They are noble leadership, indomitable spirit and universal mind. Time has come that we need to have a vision that can ignite the millions of young minds : Developed India. Friends, armed with these three qualities, let me take you on the journey of transforming India into a developed country.

Noble Leadership

In 1947, at the dawn of freedom, we had the best of leaders in science, in technology, in history, in politics and in industry and they are the results of first vision of the nation commenced in 1857. One incident I would like to narrate to you, which fascinated me when I was a young boy. On 15th August 1947, my high school teacher Rev. Iyadorai Solomon took me to hear the mid-night freedom speech of Pandit Jawaharlal Nehru. We were all thrilled when Panditji spoke that the mission was achieved. On the next day, that is on 16th August 1947, I had a great experience. An experience of best of education I can think of. In the Tamil newspaper, on the front page, two news items appeared. One item was India achieving freedom and Panditji's speech. The other news item and the most important one which has been embedded in my memory is about Mahatma Gandhiji walking barefoot in Naokhali, removing the pain of riot-affected families. Normally as Father of the Nation Mahatma Gandhi has to be the first to unfurl the national flag on August 15, 1947 in Red Fort. But he was not there at the Red Fort, instead he was at Naokhali. Mahatma Gandhi was an embodiment of nobility, elevated thinking and concern for human beings. What an everlasting positive impact in the mind of a schoolboy?

Indomitable Spirit

In this environment, I would like to quote Sir CV Raman, at the age of 82, while addressing young graduates. The Message is still reverberating in my mind: "I would like to tell the young men and women before me not to lose hope and courage. Success can only come to you by courageous devotion to the task lying in front of you. I can assert without fear of contradiction that the quality of the Indian mind is equal to the quality of any Teutonic, Nordic or Anglo-Saxon mind. What we lack is perhaps driving force which takes one anywhere. We have, I think, developed an inferiority complex. I think what is needed in India today is the destruction of that defeatist spirit. We need a spirit of victory, a spirit that will recognise that we, as inheritors of a proud civilization, are entitled to a rightful place on this planet. If that indomitable spirit were to arise, nothing can hold us from achieving our rightful destiny."

That was a great saying to the young. You would see the bridge of science and society. Friends, I request all who are responsible for the young, all who are creators of the young, for their children's growth, allow them to dream. Dream transforms into thoughts and thoughts result into actions.

Universal mind : Birth of space science and technology in a divine environment

I would like to recall an incident, which happened four decades ago. As you all know, Prof. Vikram Sarabhai is the visionary of space programme in the country. He is well-known for his cosmic ray research area that led to evolving the space research programme for the nation. Both Dr Homi J. Bhabha and Prof. Vikram Sarabhai were looking for a site to establish space research station in the equatorial region. These two great scientists visited a number of places. Thumba in Kerala was selected by the scientific community for space research as it was near the equatorial region and was ideally suited for ionospheric research in upper atmosphere apart from study of atmospheric structure. When Prof Vikram Sarabhai visited Thumba, the locality had series of villages and thousands of fishermen folk were living in that area. It also had a beautiful ancient church, St Mary Magdalene Church, Pallithura and a Bishop's House. Prof Vikram Sarabhai met many politicians and bureaucrats to get the place for the work of space science research. It did not move further because the nature of the place. He was asked to see the Bishop of Trivandrum, at that time in 1962—His Excellency Rct Rev Dr. Peter Bernard Pereira. It was a Saturday when Prof Virkram Sarabhai met the Bishop. The Bishop smiled and asked him to meet him the next day, i.e. Sunday. In the morning Service, the Bishop told the congregation, "my children, I have a famous scientist with me who wants our church and the place I live for the work of space science research. Dear children, science seeks truth by reasoning. In one way, science and spiritualism seek the same divine blessings for doing good for the people. My children, can we give the God's abode for a scientific mission?" There was a chorus of 'Amen' from the congregation and the whole church reverberated. Subsequently, the big event took place in 1962. His Excellency Rct Rev Dr Peter Bernard Pereira, the Bishop of Trivandrum, took the noble decision to dedicate the church in recognition of the national goal for the establishment of the Indian Space Research Organisation at Pallithura, Tumba. That was the church where we had our design centre, started rocket assembly, design of filament winning machine for FRP product and the Bishop's house was our scientists' place. Later, the Thumba Equatorial Rocket Launching Station (TERLS) led to the establishment of Vikram Sarabhai Space Centre (VSSC) and multiple space centres throughout the country.

When I think of this event I can see how enlightened spiritual and scientific leaders, all converge towards giving reverence to the human life. New church and new schools were established in record time. Of course, the birth of TERLS and the VSSC gave the country the capability of design, development and produce world class huge rocket system and subsequently, India has the capability of launching geo-synchronous, sun-synchronous and meteorology spacecraft, communication satellite, remote sensing satellite thereby provided fast communication, weather forecasting and also locate water resources for the country. Today, among us, Prof Vikram Sarabhai is not there, Rev Dr Peter Bernared Pereira is not there, but those who are responsible for creation and make the flower and blossom will themselves be different and set unique path for the nation. What a beautiful message for all generation of this nation, on integration of minds and universal sense. With the tradition of this experience of noble leadership, indomitable spirit and universal mind, young like you are armed with challenges of national development.

Evolution of knowledge society

India is a nation endowed with natural and competitive advantages as also certain distinctive competencies. But these are scattered in isolated pockets and the awareness on these is inadequate. During the last century the world has undergone a change from agriculture society, where natural labour was the critical factor, to industrial society where the management of technology, capital and labour provided the competitive advantage. In the 21st century, a new society is emerging where knowledge is the primary production resource instead of capital and labour. Efficient utilisation of this existing knowledge can create comprehensive wealth of the nation in the form of better health, education, infrastructure and other social indicators.

The two components of knowledge society

Such a knowledge society has two very important components driven by societal transformation and wealth generation. The societal transformation is built on education, healthcare, agriculture and governance. These will have to lead to employment generation, high productivity and rural prosperity. How do we do that?

The wealth generation is a very important task for the nation, which has to be woven around national competencies. The task team has identified core areas that will spearhead our march towards knowledge society. The areas are: Information and communication Technology, bio-technology, weather forecasting, disaster management, tele-medicine and tele-education, technologies to produce native knowledge products, service sector and Infotainment which is the emerging area resulting from convergence of Information and entertainment. These core technologies, fortunately, can be interwoven by IT. IT took off only due to enterprising spirit of the young. Thus there are multiple technologies and management structure that have to work together to generate knowledge society.

Indices of world competitiveness and we

Now more than fifty years have gone by and we are called as one of the hundreds of developing countries, in a distinct way a separation from G-8 countries. We have many challenges. Nearly 300 million people who are below the poverty line have to join the mainstream of a good life. 100% literacy, health for all, multiple industrial and agricultural productivity and life style with value system has to emerge.

One of the important needs is to understand, where we stand in the competitive world. The indices of world competitiveness are based on the global competitiveness report prepared by the World Economic Forum. The competitiveness is defined as, 'the ability of a national economy to achieve sustained high rates of economic growth'. In that order of ranking, USA is I, Singapore 2, Hong Kong, 3, Taiwan 4, Canada 5, UK 8, France 23, Germany 25, India 59. What decides world competitiveness? It is a combination triangle consisting of progressiveness of industry, technology push and governmental deregularisation status. All the three aspects have to work for achieving world competitiveness. With this background, let me present the second vision for the nation: developed India.

India Millennium Missions 2020

For several decades India has been addressed in every international forum as a developing country. It is the dream of every citizen of this country to see India transform itself into a developed nation in about 2 decades. The time has now come, when our thoughts and aspirations have to be converted into missions and thereafter into result-oriented actions.

A developed country, in my opinion, is one which has the capability and the capacity to comprehensively look at wealth generation and wealth protection and thereafter evolve integrated strategies, technologies and missions to meet these objectives. It is also a fact that technology is the established currency of geo-political power and in the Indian context, technology has to be the driving force for economical development and national security. Recognizing this and with the help of two different streams of national experts, one by TIFAC, an autonomous body under the Department of Science and Technology and another by Department of Defence Research & Development, involving few hundred man-years of combined efforts, two types of document emerged. These were Technology vision 2020 in 18 volumes and Integrated Strategies, Technologies and Missions for Comprehensive National Security. These two documents addressed the wealth generation and wealth protection aspects in a very comprehensive manner and identified technology as the linking factor. The fusion of these two documents has resulted in the India Millennium Missions 2020 (IMM 2020), which provides an excellent framework and road map for making a strong and developed India by the year 2020.

Concluding Remarks : Inspiring the great mission

When the child is empowered by the parents, at various phases of growth, the child transforms into a responsible citizen. When the teacher is empowered with knowledge and experience, good young human beings with value systems take a shape. When individual or a team is empowered with technology, transformation to higher potential for achievement is certain. When the leader of any institution empowers his or her people, leaders are born who can change the nation in multiple areas. The Indian history has witnessed this. When the political leaders of the nation is assured. Second vision for the nation is, transforming developing India into developed India. It should echo in the parliament, industrial houses, academic institutions and R&D labs and reach people of all the parts of India.

For building the developed India, what is needed? We have resources and we have human power. There are 700 million people below 35 years in the population of a billion people. The nation needs young leaders who can command the change for transformation of India into a developed nation embedded with knowledge society from now to twenty years. The leaders are the creators of new organizations of excellence. Quality leaders are like magnets that will attract the best of persons to build the team for the organization and give the inspiring leadership even during failures of individuals or organization as they are not afraid of risks. I have seen and worked with creators of vision and missions. The vision ignites particularly the young mind.

My best wishes.

79th Convocation Address
University of Delhi
Delhi, 22nd February 2002

Appendix III

Convocation Address

X L R I , J a m s h e d p u r

23 March 2002

VISION CREATES GREAT LEADERS

by Dr APJ Abdul Kalam
Professor, Technology & Societal Transformation
Anna University, Chennai

Untravelled Path

I am indeed delighted to participate in the 46th annual convocation of XLRI, Jamshedpur, My greetings to all the graduating students and professors and teachers who shaped them to have qualities of leadership to take up various missions and tasks of the nation. I was thinking what thoughts I can share with the graduating students on this important occasion when you will be entering into professional phase of life. I would like to tell the young, "low aim is the crime". In the knowledge era, successful people will always take untravelled roads rather than beaten path. This needs excellence in intellect that demands three unique traits or qualities, experienced during education phase and also career phase. They are noble leadership, indomitable spirit and universal mind. Friends, with foundation of these three qualities, let me take you on the journey of transforming India into a developed country.

Noble Leadership

In 1947, at the dawn of freedom, we had the best of leaders in science, in technology, in history, in politics and in industry and they are the results of first vision of the nation commenced in 1857. One incident I would like to narrate to you, which fascinated me when I was a young boy. On 15th August 1947, my high school teacher Rev. Iyyadorai Solomon took me to hear the mid-night freedom speech of Pandit Jawaharlal Nehru. We were all thrilled when Panditji spoke that the mission was achieved. On the next day, that is on 16th August 1947, I had a great experience. An experience of best of education I can think of. In the Tamil newspaper, on the front page, two news items appeared. One item was India achieving freedom and Panditji's speech. The other news item and the most important one which has been embedded in my memory is about Mahatma Gandhiji walking barefoot in Naokali, removing the pain of riot-affected families. Normally as Father of the Nation Mahatma Gandhi has to be the first to unfurl the national flag on August 15, 1947 in Red Fort. But he was not there at the Red Fort, instead he was at Naokali. Mahatma Gandhi was an embodiment of nobility, elevated thinking and concern for human beings. What an everlasting positive impact in the mind of a schoolboy?

Indomitable Spirit

In this environment, I would like to quote Sir CV Raman, at the age of 82, while addressing young graduates. The message is still reverberating in my mind: "I would like to tell the young men and women before me not to lose hope and courage. Success can only come to you by courageous devotion to the task lying in front of you. I can assert without fear of contradiction that the quality of the Indian mind is equal to the quality of any Teutonic, Nordic or Anglo-Saxon mind. What we lack is perhaps courage, what we lack is perhaps driving force which takes one anywhere. We have, I think, developed an inferiority complex. I think what is needed in India today is the destruction of that defeatist spirit. We need a spirit of victory, a spirit that will carry us to our rightful place under the sun, a spirit which will recognise that we, as inheritors of a proud civilization, are entitled to a rightful place on this planet. If that indomitable spirit were to arise, nothing can hold us from achieving our rightful destiny. "

That was a great saying to the young. You would see the bridge of science and society. Friends, I request all who are responsible for the young, all who are creators of the young, for their children's' growth, allow them to dream. Dream transforms into thoughts and thoughts result into actions.

Universal Mind birth of space science and technology in a divine environment

I would like to recall an incident, which happened four decades ago. As you all know, Prof Vikram Sarabhai is the visionary of space programme in the country. He is well known for his cosmic ray research area that led to evolving the space research programme for the nation. Both Dr Homi Bhabha and Prof Vikram Sarabhai were looking for a site to establish space research station in the equatorial region. These two great scientists visited a number of places. Thumba in Kerala was selected by the scientific community for space research as it was near the equatorial region and was ideally suited for ionospheric research in upper atmosphere apart from study of atmospheric structure. When Prof Vikram Sarabhai visited Thumba, the locality had series of villages and thousands of fishermen folk were living in that area. It also had a beautiful ancient church, St Mary Magdalene Church, Pallithura and a Bishop's House. Prof Vikram Sarabhai met many politicians and bureaucrats to get the place for the work of space science research. It did not move further because the nature of the place. He was asked to see the Bishop of Trivandrum, at that time in 1962,His Excellency Rct Rev Dr Peter Bernard Pereira. It was a Saturday when Prof Vikram Sarabhai met the Bishop. The Bishop smiled and asked him to meet him the next day, i.e. Sunday. In the morning Service, the Bishop told the congregation, "my children, I have a famous scientist with me who wants our church and the place I live for the work of space science research. Dear children, science seeks truth by reasoning. In one way, science and spiritualism seek the same divine blessings for doing good for the people. My children, can we give the God's abode for a scientific mission? "There was a chorus of 'Amen' from the congregation and the whole church reverberated. Subsequently, the big event took place in 1962. His Excellency Rct Rev Dr Peter Bernard Pereira, the Bishop of Trivandrum, took the noble decision to dedicate the church in recognition of the national goal for the establishment of the Indian Space Research Organisation at Pallithura, Thumba. That was the church where we had our design centre, started rocket assembly, design of filament winding machine for FRP product and the Bishop's house was our scientists' place. Later, the Thumba Equatorial Rocket Launching Station (TERLS) led to the establishment of Vikram Sarabhai Space Centre (VSSC) and multiple space centres throughout the country.

When I think of this event, I can see how enlightened spiritual and scientific leaders, all converge towards giving reverence to the human life. New church and new schools were established in record time. Of course the birth of TERLS and then VSSC gave the country the capability of design, development and produce world class huge rocket system and subsequently, India has the capability of launching geo-synchronous, sun-synchronous and meteorology spacecraft, communication satellite, remote sensing satellite thereby provided fast communication, weather forecasting and also locate water resources for the country. Today, among us, Prof Vikram Sarabhai is not there, Rev Dr Peter Bernard Pereira is not there, but those who are responsible for creation and make the flower and blossom will themselves be different and set unique path for the nation. What a beautiful message for all generation of this nation, on integration of minds and universal sense. With the tradition of this experience of noble leadership, indomitable spirit and universal mind, young like you are armed with challenges of national development.

First Vision for the Nation, Created the Leaders

The seeding for the national independence took place around 1857 or even before, I see the relationship between the urge for independence and the emergence of great minds. As the independence movement grew, it brought out the best of leaders like Lala Lajpat Rai, Lokmanya Tilak, Mahatma Gandhi, Pt Jawaharlal Nehru, Sardar Patel, Abul Kalam Azad, Bankim Chandra Chatterjee, Veer Savarkar. The list, if we take it from each part of the country, will be very big. This National movement had also brought simultaneously best of scientists and technologists. Though there was no full-fledged effort at the British ruled governmental level to bring up Indian science, industries and education, we have seen world class scientific, industrial and educational leaders generated during the pre-independent period.

Prof S. Chandrasekhar, the famous Astronomy scientist, in his biography "Chandra" by Shri Kameshwar Wali says, "I mean it is a remarkable thing that in the modern era before 1910, there were no (Indian) scientists of international reputation or standing. Between 1920 and 1925, we had suddenly five or six internationally well-known men. (He means, JC Bose, CV Raman, Meghanath Saha,

Srinivasan Ramanujam and Prof Chandrasekhar himself). I myself have associated this remarkable phenomenon with the need for self-expression, which became a dominant motive among the young during the national movement. It was a part of the national movement to assert oneself. India was a subject country, but in the sciences, in the arts, particularly in science, we could show the West in their own realm that we were equal to them. "

Coming now to the industrial field, Jamsetji Nusserwanji Tata brought the steel industry in India even though the British rulers were not favourably disposed to the idea. Acharya PC Ray brought up chemical and pharmaceutical industry. Likewise, in the pre-independent period we see the birth of many great institutions like Indian Institute of Science, Bangalore started by JN Tata, Benares Hindu University by Pandit Madan Mohan Malviya, and Aligarh Muslim University by Sir Syed Ahmad Khan. There were also some Indian Maharajas who started and nurtured universities like the one in Baroda. There are many examples in both industrial and educational fields. In all these cases the basic motivations have been to show the urge to build the Nation and demonstrate to the world that "India can do it".

Second vision for the nation

After 50 years of progress, the aspirations are mounting that India should become a developed country. This is the second vision for the nation. How we can prepare ourselves to this challenge? To become a developed India, the essential needs are:-

a. India has to be economically and commercially powerful, at least to be one of the six top nations in terms of size of the economy. Our target should be a GDP growth of 9-11% annually and that the people below poverty line to be reduced to 10%.

b. near self-reliance in defence needs of weapon, equipment with no umbilical attached to any outside world.

c. India should have a right place in world forums.

Technology Vision 2020 is a pathway to realise this cherished mission. The Technology Vision 2020 consisted of 17 technology packages in the core sectors such as agriculture and food, healthcare, infrastructure and strategic industries. The Task Teams formed by TIFAC with nearly 500 experts of our country worked for two years, deliberated national status of various branches of national development and generated 35 documents detailing the steps to be taken for creating wealth for the nation and the well being of our people. "Technology" is the most vital key for achieving the goals. The vision deals with agro food processing, food and agriculture, healthcare, electric power, civil aviation, waterways, engineering industries, life sciences and bio-technology, strategic industries and materials and processing. There is a tremendous link between each technology package.

Five mega projects to transform the nation to a developed country

We have identified five areas where India has a core competence for an integrated action:(1) Agriculture and food processing - we have to put a target of 360 million tons of food and agricultural production. Other areas of agriculture and agro food processing would being prosperity to rural people an speed up the economic growth. (2) Reliable and quality electric power for all parts of the country. (3) Education and Healthcare - we have seen, based on the experience, education and healthcare are inter related. For example, Kerala with education and better healthcare can bring down the population growth and provide improvements in quality of life of the people. Similarly, in Tamil Nadu also we have seen the downward growth of population resulting from a unique system of "mid-day meal" coupled with education. Studies about Andhra Pradesh also have different facets. These experiences, we feel, should be taken and spread in big states like Bihar and Uttar Pradesh. Beginning of agricultural prosperity through better yields in these States will help this process. (4)Information Technology - This is one of our core competence. We believe, this area can be used to promote education in remote areas and also to create national wealth. (5)Strategic sectors - This area, fortunately, witnessed the growth in nuclear technology, space technology and defence technology.

These five areas are closely inter-related and lead to national, food, economic and security. A strong partnership among the R&D, academy, industry and the community as a whole with the Government departments will be essential to accomplish the vision.

Concluding Remarks : Inspiring the great mission

For building the developed India, what are needed? We have resources and we have human power in abundance. Then nation needs young leaders who can command the change for transformation of India into a developed nation embedded with knowledge society from now to twenty years. The leaders are the creators of new organizations of excellence. Quality leaders are like magnets who will attract the best of persons to build the team for the organization and give the inspiring leadership even during failures of individuals or organization as they are not afraid of risks. I have seen and worked with creators of vision and missions. The vision ignites particularly the young mind.

I have worked with ISRO and DRDO for two decades each. Recently in multiple areas including industry. The vision leaders ignite multiple minds and mission takes shape. Then the mission takes over. For example, India should build its first satellite launch vehicle to orbit a satellite or the first IRBM has to be built and operationalised, are mission statements which have transformed into system products many a time. But, a few times failures have also become products. Technology and management were the driving forces. Also, one very important component for success is that the organisation creates capable people because the mission trigger capability. Organisation works and nation with a mission will advance towards prosperity.

Developed India 2020, second movement, second vision for the nation will definitely result, if our industry take the lead in multi fields. I can see a virtual image of India, the children by 2020 will not see the high illiteracy, poverty and social differentiation. They will see a new India. Our children will sing the song of prosperous India if we sweat in this decade. Today, the Indian mind has to get ignited by our second vision for the nation. The ignited human mind is the most powerful resource on the earth, under the earth and above the earth. My best wishes to you all for transforming industrial and commercial houses into establishments of substance and thereby the nation great.

Appendix-IV

Letter to Members of Parliament

Dear Honourable Member of Parliament,

My greetings to you, for your happiness and well-being.

As you are aware, I am contesting as a candidate for the election of the 12th President of India, with the support of many political parties, eminent leaders, and a broad cross-section of our people. I am truely overwhelmed at the wholehearted endorsement I have received from a wide spectrum of the country's political establishment, cutting across the divide between the ruling and most of the opposition parties. I take this to be a symbol of the essential unity of our political establishment, which transcends its proud diversity in matters of national importance. This is a good portent for our democracy.

I am, indeed, grateful to all those who have supported me for giving me this opportunity, which will enable me to work with you to realise our shared dream of transforming India into a strong, prosperous, peaceful, resurgent and humane nation playing its rightful role in the benign transformation of the affairs of the world. I also express my sincerest thanks to the people of this great nation, from whom I have received an enthusiastic outpouring of letters and e-mails in the past few weeks. In addition, the flood of messages sent to me by Indians residing abroad amplifies their sentiment. I am touched by the comments in the print and electronic media echoing the decision of the mainstream of India's political establishment to support my candidature. I have also been enriched by their different suggestions and ideas.

Friends, the people of India, as well as all of you in the Electoral College, know me to be a person with simple origins and who has served his country in his own humble way. It speaks for the power and vitality of India's democracy that a poor boy from a small island in Tamil Nadu can travel this far in the service of his motherland and now be considered for the responsibilities of Rashtrapati Bhavan. Legendary personalities like Dr. Rajendra Prasad, Dr. S. Radhakrishnan and Dr. Zakir Husain have occupied it in the past. If I have offered myself as a candidate for this highest Constitutional office in the country, it is entirely because of your trust and faith in me. Hence, the first pledge I would like to take is to remain true to your trust and, if elected, to always remain unwaveringly faithful to the latter and spirit of the Constitution in performing my duty.

Permit me to take this opportunity to briefly outline my vision for the Presidency.

Basic Structure of the Constitution Unalterable

We are truly blessed that the makers of our Constitution, under the farsighted and scholarly leadership of Dr. Babasaheb Ambedkar, have bequeathed to us one of the most enlightened statutes in the world. Parliamentary democracy is the core of our governance system, with the President as the Head of State and overall custodian of the Constitution. There is an excellent balance between the Legislature, Executive and Judiciary with proper checks and safeguards. The basic structure of our Constitution has stood the test of time and shown itself to be having the vigour, vitality and eternal freshness that make it capable of meeting any challenge that new circumstances might hurl at it. At the same time, our Constitution is also innately resilient so as to be responsive to the demands of changing situations. I am sure all of you will agree that we need to zealously preserve this principle of "change with continuity", which is indeed the signature tune of India's millennia-old civilisation. Thus, my first and foremost task is to respect and uphold the Constitutional processes, in the best interests of our people and the nation, as provided for in the Constitution without fear or favour and with fairness and firmness.

Harmonious Centre-State Relations

The second principle that I shall fervently uphold is the harmonious relations between the Centre and the States. India is a Union of States, based on the framework of cooperative federalism. I stand for a strong Centre and strong States. I also share the near consensual belief that the time has come to devolve more powers to the States, since decentralisation is the key to faster and more balanced development. At the same time, we should also move quickly to empower our Panchayati Raj institutions both financially and administratively, if necessary through relevant changes to the existing systems. Mahatma Gandhi's exhortation that India lives in her villages rings true even today and would be so in the future too.

Social and Economic Justice

An inescapable imperative of development in the Indian context is to ensure that the fruits of economic growth and social progress reach the deprived sections of our population. Scheduled Castes, Scheduled Tribes, OBCs, including those belonging to minority communities, constitute a large section of our society. India cannot become strong and developed if they continue to remain weak and underdeveloped. Therefore, our strategy for removal of poverty must be multi-dimensional with a strong focus on Social Justice. It should be centred around a sound programme for the removal of regional and social imbalances. One thrust area could be integrated rural development, with promotion of agriculture, agro-industries and cottage enterprises as its engine and multiple connectivities—physical, digital and marketing—as its propellant.

Women's Empowerment

Gender Justice, sadly, has still remained a neglected aspect of Social Justice. Indian women are the custodians of our cultural and family values. If properly empowered, they can contribute immensely to our nation's allround development much more effectively. I would, therefore, like to see that proper systems and mechanisms are in place to enable increased participation of women in our Parliament, State Legislatures and other political and public bodies. Simultaneously, both the Government and society should work together to expand the opportunities for women's education and for putting an end to all types of atrocities and injustices committed against them. I would like to see India to be a role model for the rest of the world in this crucial aspect.

Primacy of National Security

Along with speedy development aimed at elimination of

poverty and unemployment, national security has to be recognised by every Indian as a national priority. Indeed, making India strong and self-reliant—economically, socially and militarily—is our foremost duty towards our motherland. We owe it to ourselves and to the future generations. I have said this before, but it bears reiteration, that India, which has suffered invasions for many centuries in the past, must be in a position to defend herself against all and any odds. I am proud of my role in our country's space, nuclear and missile programmes, because I believe that these have greatly strengthened India's national security, enabled us to follow an independent foreign policy, and helped us to overcome challenges created by technology denial and economic sanctions by powerful countries. These S&T programmes, most of which also have numerous developmental spin-offs, have enhanced our national pride by putting India in the category of technologically advanced nations. Our national security strategy is guided purely by defensive considerations. It poses no threat to any country in the world.

Foreign Policy

India's foreign policy has always stood on a strong edifice of national consensus. Together with you, I wish to develop and further strengthen our ties of friendship and mutually beneficial cooperation with all countries in the world.

Jammu & Kashmir, an Inalienable Part of India

I share the entire nation's concern and outrage at cross-border terrorism, which our neighbour has pursued as a matter of state policy. This policy, aimed at destabilization and dismemberment of India, is doomed. Jammu & Kashmir was, is, and shall always remain an inseparable part of India. From Kashmir to Kanyakumari, from Kutch to Kohima, and from Lakshadweep to Andaman Nicobar Islands, we are one indivisible people and one outbreakable nation, united by the golden thread of our culture and civilisation and our common vision of a peaceful, democratic and modern India.

Secularism, the Essence of Indianness

Here I also wish to reiterate my unflinching commitment to the principle of secularism, which is the cornerstone of our nationhood. Intolerance and violence in the name of religion is the worst form of irreligion. True religion is that Ocean of Spiritualism into which all faiths shine in brilliance. To people in politics and government, it teaches the message of leadership with compassion and fairness. A unique source of my pride in being an Indian, since my school days, is that our country is home to all the world's religions and has always propounded and practiced the truth of *Sarva Dharma Samabhav* (equal respect for all religions). India is a plural society, with equal rights and responsibilities for citizens belonging to people of all religions, regions, castes, classes and linguistic communities. The broad and enthusiastic support I have received from all corners and communities of India is itself a resounding reminder that our secular ethos is alive and vibrant.

Unity of Minds

We are a country with rich diversity. We have developed a democratic polity under the framework of our Republican Constitution. These are our strengths. It is but natural that there are, and there will be, differences in viewpoints and perceptions on certain issues. Opportunity to express differing opinions and finding solutions through dialogue and due processes of the rule of law, are important elements of the functioning of democratic systems. It is also a fact that there are a few unresolved issues that trouble us occasionally and a few additional problems, sometimes painful, get added to our system. I would like to sincerely endeavour to work for bringing about unity of minds while fully respecting and maintaining the rich pluralistic traditions of our country.

Natural Resources and the Environment

Economic development and related actions are important and crucial. But it is also necessary to protect the nature's endowments available to our country. Conserving, sustaining and enriching our natural resources, including the environment, are extremely important for the well-being of not only the present but also our future generations. In fact, it is our ethical responsibility towards the whole globe.

Finer Aspects of Human Life—Arts, Literature, Sports, etc.

While economic, political, international, legal, scientific, technological and many other professional tasks, including national security, are vital for the nation, its soul also expresses itself through literature, music and arts, culture, crafts, religious and spiritual philosophies, sports, as well as other finer aspects of human life. The diversity of languages, traditions and religions in our country adds a unique dimension to this precious national heritage. Throughout my life, I have enjoyed many facets of this heritage and been a connoisseur of some. I would like to actively encourage the growth of aesthetics in all areas of our national life. I would like to explore possibilities of using modern technologies and systems to make our people, as also the peoples of the world, more aware of the richness and diversity of India's heritage. I would also like to emphasise probity and commitment to values in public life, including in polity.

Young People, Our Unique Strength

Although we are an ancient nation, India is a young country, demographically speaking. We have a large, and growing, percentage of young people in our society. It is a great strength today and is going to be so for decades to come. Therefore, we all need to cherish and encourage our young people, irrespective of where they are born and what they are doing. We all should dedicate ourselves to provide our young people all the opportunities: first of all good nourishment, good healthcare, sanitation and sound education that combines development of knowledge, skills and values and thus enables them to become useful citizens and prosper in a competitive world. We should pay greater attention to promote sports, the spirit of adventure, exploration and innovation, and their natural aptitude for idealism and voluntary social work. We should rekindle a strong sense of nationalism in them, manifesting itself in better work culture and readiness for self-sacrifice for achieving larger societal goals. We should devise effective governmental and non-governmental mechanisms to make this happen so that our youth can develop as responsible and capable citizens of tomorrow. Our young men and women are the greatest asset of our country. I will commit myself to encourage every action that can make this dream to become a reality very soon.

India as a Knowledge Superpower

Friends, science, technology and their applications have been my main calling in life so far. Accordingly, my vision for the future of India is strongly rooted in my faith in the power of scientific and technological knowledge and their beneficial applications. Our greatest and most precious national resource is our one billion people, who have inherited a priceless intellectual, cultural, artistic and artisanal heritage. But how can their minds be ignited? How can their talents, skills and knowledge be rendered more productive, and more rewarding to them so that they become active agents of a society-wide transformation in education, healthcare, agriculture, industry, and services; so that we will witness large-scale employment generation, high productivity, rural prosperity and urban renewal; so that our national security becomes impregnable; so that we achieve greater societal harmony and peace; so that we vastly expand the scope of e-governance, which is crucial even from the point of view of making our democracy perform and deliver better?

I share the conviction of our political leaders and others as enshrined in the Scientific Policy Resolution, and reiterated many times by our own academic and R&D establishment, that the answer lies, chiefly, in making India a science- and technology-driven nation. We have already demonstrated our core competence in agriculture, Information Technology, space research, atomic energy, defence, some aspects of healthcare and select areas of manufacturing and services, and have started to reap its benefits. We should now develop similar core competence in some critical technologies to address our national priorities. We should aim to become a Knowledge Superpower within this decade, so that India can face the challenges of growing competition in the era of globalisation and our hard-earned freedom is reliably nurtured.

If I get an opportunity, we will work together, within the Parliamentary system, to generate a road map for transforming India from a 'Developing Nation' into a 'Developed Nation'. In my book *India 2020: A Vision for the New Millennium,* I have said,

> "A developed India by 2020, or even earlier, is not a dream. It need not even be a mere vision in the minds of many Indians. It is a mission we can all take up—and succeed."

Youth and Children, the Source of Our Hope

You might ask me: "What is the source of your optimism?" My answer will be: "India's youth and India's children."

In the past twelve months, I have interacted with over 55,000 school children from most of the States of our country. They are all dreaming to live in a prosperous India, with peace and harmony, and looking for role models for exemplary leadership in every field and also looking for opportunities for themselves to contribute. When I look into their eyes, when I listen to them speak, I am awestruck by the heavy responsibility that rests on the shoulders of elders like us. Together with you, I want to work to fulfill their dreams—to fulfill our dreams. O'Almighty! Empower my mind to always think and act that my nation is bigger than me.

May I, therefore, appeal to you to cast your valuable vote to elect me to serve this great Nation as its next President and work towards the fulfillment of our commonly cherished vision of India as a Developed Nation.

Jai Hind!

Yours sincerely,

(A.P.J. Abdul Kalam)

Appendix V

When Can I Sing a Song of India ?

I am indeed delighted to participate in the lecture series organised by the Department of Administrative Reforms "The Ideas that have worked". I was thinking how I could interact with such a powerful team in front of me. It occurs to me that I will put forth some of my experiences, which I have, came through during my professional career and it will be mostly on personalities and events. Of course, in the beginning itself, I must mention to you that I had a rare privilege of working with three great scientific thinkers and fantastic human beings... Prof. Vikram Sarabhai, founder of space technology in India and a visionary; Prof. Satish Dhawan, former Chairman, ISRO, who gave to the country multiple missions like satellite communication and remote sensing and is a great thinker and teacher; and Prof. Brahm Prakash, Former Director of VSSC and the father of nuclear material in India, who in the later years shaped launch vehicle technology. They were responsible for unifying multiple technologies with management and lead successfully satellite and launch vehicle programmes. Above all they provided many scientific and technological leaders to the country. We all also learnt from these great three, management with nobility. They created together a reliable and efficient leaderhsip in multiple field of science, technology and management. With this background let me sequence my thoughts and find a topic. Throughout my talk, you will see the umbilical chord of my career connected to this great Trinity.

Youth Meet

Recently, I was addressing a Youth meet of India at Ahmedabad. About 3000 youth from all over the country were participating. Of course my aim was to communicate to them the importance of science and technology to the young people and to attract them towards further education in science and also a career in science and technology. At the end of the address one girl who is in the 10+2 came to me with certain hesitation and said " Uncle, Can I ask a question to you?, I said go ahead Lady. She said, I have an elder brother studying in USA, he came home last summer and almost sang a song of USA. I asked the young girl what is the song, She said, my brother says, "America is beautiful, America is rich, America is clean and they are hard working. Even Indians who go to USA become hard working and rich". Please tell me uncle, 'when can I sing a song of India'. Friends, hence, the topic I have selected to discuss with you is "When I can sing a song of India" . Let us jointly work to make atleast our growing children sing the song of India.

Dream to Action: India Launches its Satellite Launch Vehicle

I was appointed as the Project Director of SLV-3 after nearly 10 years of work in space centre in 1973. This was the first important assignment at the VSSC. As it called for, India building satellite launch vehicles to put satellites in the lower earth orbit. The choice of the Project Director was a big event in the ISRO, it is a prestigious appointment with full of challenges accompanied by hard work, pains and finally success. There was tremendous competition for this position. Prof. Brahm Prakash the then Director, VSSC selected me from among experienced highly foreign qualified and holding very senior scientific and managerial posts. Yet I was selected because I completed an important project, and showing performance in the meteorological rocket development. This winning of competition in the midst of eminent personalities led me to feel the weight and responsibility to work for it vigorously. With this environment we were also able to attract excellent scientists, technologists, managers because the mission was challenging. Prof. Brahm Prakash helped me in the flow of multiple technologies from not only from VSSC also from ISRO Satellite centre and SHAR Space Centre.

The First Challenge

I would like to quickly come to the event, which will be important for the subject of discussion today. On 10th August 1979, the first SLV-3 experiemental launch planned to take-off at 1500 hrs . I was the Mission Director and along with a 50 member strong team within the SHAR Control Centre with 6 specialists to assist me in critical decision making before take off. The automated computer count stopped indicating a possible anomaly in the propulsion system. My specialist team saw at the display that in the second stage of flight the pressure dropped in the reaction control system oxidiser tank that provides the 3 axis altitude control after the first stage rocket is separated. The specialist team advised me to go ahead with the count down ignoring the pressure drop as they felt that propellant stored was sufficient enough to last for twice the flight duration, I was advised to go ahead with the launch. I concurred and pushed the computer button to the launch sequence.

At T-0 the SLV-3 took off beautifully. The first stage had given predicted thrust and altitude and velocity needed at given altitude. The second stage initiated as per the tele data, but within a few seconds we witnessed the second stage and third stage and the satellite got caught into a tumbling motion and we lost the flight to the Bay of Bengal. It was 7 am in the morning. The whole team inspite of all its day and night hard work and sweat they were busy in collecting the data and was trying to establish the reason for the flight failure Meanwhile, I was called by Prof Satish Dhavan to attend a press conference. Before the press conference, Prof. Satish Dhawan told me he is going to handle the situation and I should be present with many of the senior scientists and technologists. The press conference room was full with media. There was gloom , many questions were posed, some very powerful, thoughtful and also criticisms. Prof Satish Dhawan, announced " Friends, today we had our first Satellite launch vehicle to put satellite in the orbit, we could not succeed. It is our first mission of proving multiple technologies in satellite and satellite launch vehicles. In many technologies we have succeeded and a few more we have to succeed, above all I realise my team members has to be given all the technological support. I am going to do that and the next mission will succeed. Subsequently, a failure analysis board was formed to establish the cause.

Now I will move to the second mission of SLV-3 that took place on 18th July 1980, it was 6.30 in the morning. The whole nation's attention was towards the SHAR launch complex and the control centre. The mission team were busy and computer took over the flight sequence from T-4 minutes. At T-0 the flight took off text book trajectory we were witnessing. After nearly 600 secs of the flight I realised every stage has given the required velocity including the 4 th stage. I made an announcement, "Mission Director calling all stations. The SLV-3 has given the required velocity and right altitude to put Rohini satellite in the orbit. Our down range stations and global stations will get the orbit satellite beam the required data within an hour". There was a thunderous applause from all the stations and visitors gallery. The most important thing happened then. Prof Satish Dhawan asked me to handle the press conference with our team members. The message I would like to convey is, " When success comes in after hard work the leader should give the credit of the success to the team members. When failure comes the leaders should absorb the failures and protect the team members". I could not get this beautiful, technological education of failure management in any of the text books written by any of the Harvard or any of the management institutes at that time. I would like to say particularly to this audience, since we will be managing hundreds of persons, dealing with a challenging task : There will be failure in a system, failure in a project, failure in the procurement action or failure in the administrative action even failure in the political system. It is vital to protect the team immediately after a failure from the onslaught effect of failures. Equally we should celebrate success of individuals and team. About us, Mahatma Gandhi has said in his autobiography; " it is always been a mystery to me how men can feel themselves honoured by the humiliation of their fellow men". A prophetic saying, it is.

Three Technological Events

I would like to share with you certain experiences from the events I have participated recently. This happened in a year's period. On 11th May 98 the Chairman, Atomic Energy Commission Dr R Chidambaram and myself and some of our team members were working for the results of the underground nuclear three tests followed by another two. We were at very close to the test site and the countdown was progressing. At T-5 seconds and hundreds of parameters from instrumentation were displayed. The mission was to take place in a few seconds. At T-0, we witnessed the whole earth shrugged and thundered in front of us and all around. We saw part of the earth raising. What a powerful energy India generated through nuclear weapons?. This successful mission was the great partnership of DAE and DRDO. Self-reliant technology made the nation to become a nuclear weapon state. The idea to the event, it was indeed weaponisation mission completion. India can do it.

The second event is about a missile system. On 11th April 1999, the AGNI-II took off with computer command from the beautiful island range. 600 parameters from the missile were monitored in real time through a series of radars, telemetry stations and ship borne instrumentations networked with our own communication satellites. The AGNI with its payload reached with close accuracy on the target 2000 kms away. Also an Island Mission Range was born. The partnership of DRDO labs with academic institutions and industries brought this important success and it is another triumph for self reliance, inspite of the technology denials.

Another event is about India's rocket technology. It reached its prime when the ISRO launched successfully the operational Polar Satellite Launch Vehicle on 26 May 99. The PSLV that has the third largest booster in the world, has become a cost-effective launch vehicle, and above all the ISRO reached a stage of integrating its own satellite IRS, a German and a South Korean satellites in that launch. India can compete in the launch vehicle services for satellite launching for other countries. This is the result of a great vision of self-reliance and sustained hardwork of ISRO and multiple institutions and industries.

These three events demonstrate that India has the capability to achieve a higher level of technological goals in spite of technology denials and control regimes. It means, if we have mission oriented programmes with leadership and political commitment, we will achieve these goals, however difficult they are. Can India bring technology to make impossible, possible.

If you scan the time from green revolution onwards, there have been successes in other commercial sector also. We are aware the green revolution made India self sufficient. The pharma sector, not only meeting domestic demands, but also play a major competitive role in the international market. Some of the industries have competitive strengths in automobile products and also some areas of textiles. Ofcourse, in software products we have substantive presence in the world. Many foreign companies are also happy to source Indian industries and intellectual capabilities. I am also aware of a number of small industries who show technological innovations. If we network right inputs in correct time, we can multiply such industrial "tribes" manifold.

Birth of a Vision

It was indeed a great experience working with Prof Vikram Sarabhai from 1963-1971. At that time, I was an young engineer progressing multiple task of composite technology and explosive systems, rocket engineering systems at Thiruvananthapuram Space centre. Prof Sarabhai unfurled the vision for space programme in 1970, India primarily should build its own satellite launch vehicles and launch from Indian soil with remote sensing at sun synchronous orbit and communication satellite in the geo synchronous orbit.Today, almost his vision has been realised in all and India has operationalised Polar Satellite Launch Vehicles and this year will achieve GSLV capability. ISRO has also operationalised IRS and INSAT satellite system.

One personal experience I would like to share with you in conjunction with Prof Sarabhai's vision for space programmes. Design project of India's first satellite launch vehicle was approved. Design of each stage of rocket, heat shield , guidance system was given to selected project leaders. I was given the 4th stage SLV-3, that is upper stage rocket to give final velocity to put Rohini into orbit. The 4th stage SLV, uses an apogee motor, it should give the maximum thrust with minimum weight condition. It has critical technology. Hence, it was made out of composite structures which gives light weight. It is in early 1969 I remember, I received a call from Prof Sarabhai from Ahmedabad stating that he will be visiting Trivandrum along with Prof. Curien, President of a French Space organisation. I was asked to give a presentation about the 4 th stage to Prof Curien's team. When the presentation by my team was over, we realised that SLV-3 4th stage is also being considered for a French 4th stage launch vehicle 'Diamont' P-4 and French Organisation was looking for an apogee rocket motor nearly double the propellant weight and also size of the stage what we had designed.

A decision was taken in the same meeting that SLV's fourth stage should be reconfigured to match and suit both French satellite launch vehicles and Indian launch vehicles. I would like to give the picture of the status at that time of our rocket technology. It was in the drawing board and of design status. Here is a visionary whose dream that Indian scientist's will build an upper stage rocket system compatible both for Indian and French satellite launch vehicle system. What a confidence he put on the Indian scientific community? A decision was taken that this upper stage has to be designed and developed. This event was remarkable and motivating for us. We went on full swing. A series of reviews took place between the two teams. The 4th stage graduated from drawing board to developing stage. Then in 1971 Prof Sarabhai passed away at the same time the Diamont P-4 programme was called off and to be reconfigured in future. When the 4 th stage was developed and series of tests were going on a new requirement appeared in the horizon that is India building small communication satellites to be integrated as one of the piggy back satellite in the Ariane programmes (European Space Launch Programme). For our Indian Apple programme that is communication satellite - the SLV-3 4 th stage exactly fitted and we flew in 1980s integrated in the European space launch from French Guiana Kourou. The vision seeded in 1969 by Prof Vikhram Sarabhai was indeed realised when the apple satellite started transmitting a communication to Indian earth stations. This gives some insight of a visionary with committed scientific and support, we can realise the vision. Even we can built our rockets can be flown in foreign soil. This achievement triggered rocket technologists in the country .

Second Green Revolution from Ninety Plus

Recently, there was a function in Chennai organised by the Manipal Academy of Higher Education to felicitate 3 personalities. They were Sri C Subramaniam for his vision for agriculture and Shri N A Palkiwala for his work on social justice and myself for Specific science and technology area. What I witnessed in this meeting was, Mr C Subramaniam who is 90 + and who spearheaded the green revolution in 1960s, was putforth planning a second green revolution and said he will establish a National Agro Foundation based on the experience of success of first green revolution. Developing hybrid seed backed by scientific and agriculture packages.He unfurled second green revolution with a strategy for adoption of small and marginal famers must be introduced entrusted with high value products to labs for soil testing and provide access to information on weather and markets. The Foundation aims at bringing a million farmers under the scheme. For this he has enlisted a top agrilcuture consultancies and managers and technologists for promoting this foundation. I was really inspired to be with him and his unfurling concept of soil testing and marketing fertilizers of seed and water management and finally the crop to marketing. This meeting with him, I found I must share with you here as a person of young and old have to get inspired to build the developed India.

Second Vision for the Nation

After 50 years of progress, the aspirations are mounting that India should become a developed country. This is the second vision for the nation. How we can prepare ourselves to this challenge? To become a developed India, the essential needs are:

(a) India has to be economically and commercially powerful, at least to be one of the six top nations in terms of size of the economy. Our target should be a GDP growth of 9 -11% annually and that the people below poverty line to be reduced to 10%.
(b) near self-reliance in defence needs of weapon, equipment with no umbilical attached to any outside world.
(c) India should have a right place in world forums.

Technology Vision 2020 is a pathway to realise this cherished mission. The Technology Vision 2020 consisted of 17 technology packages in the core sectors such as agriculture and food, healthcare, infrastructure and strategic industries. The Task Teams with nearly 500 experts of our country worked for two years, deliberated national status of various branches of national development and generated 35 documents detailing the steps to be taken for creating wealth for the nation and the well being of our people. "Technology" is the most vital key for achieving the goals. The vision deals with agro food processing, food and agriculture, health -care, electric power, civil aviation, waterways, engineering industries, life sciences and bio-technology, strategic industries and materials and processing. There is a tremendous link between each technology package.

Five Mega Projects to Transform the Nation to Developed Country

We have identified five areas where India has a core competence for an integrated action.

(1) Agriculture and food processing - we have to put a target of 360 million tons of food and agricultural production. Other areas of agriculture and agro food processing would bring prosperity to rural people and speed up the economic growth.
(2) Reliable and quality electric power for all parts of the country.
(3) Education and Healthcare - we have seen, based on the

experience, education and healthcare are interrelated. For example, Kerala with education and better healthcare can bring down the population growth and provide improvements in quality of life of the people. Similarly, in Tamil Nadu also we have seen the downward growth of population resulting from a unique system of "mid-day meal" coupled with education. Studies about Andhra Pradesh also have different facets. These experiences, we feel, should be taken and spread in big states like Bihar and Uttar Pradesh. Beginning of agricultural prosperity through better yields in these States will help this process.

(4) Information Technology - This is one of our core competence. We believe, this area can be used to promote education in remote areas and also to create national wealth. (5) Strategic sectors - This area, fortunately, witnessed the growth in nuclear technology, space technology and defence technology.

These five areas are closely inter-related and lead to national, food, economic and security. A strong partnership among the R&D, academy, Industry and the community as a whole with the Government departments will be essential to accomplish the vision.

In the Budget of 2000-2001, I am delighted to say that the Finance Minister announced certain budget provision for Vision 2020. I am sure, ignited minds will generate action. India will be transformed into a developed India before the year 2020.

Conclusion: Results from Experiences

Having shared some ideas that have worked, I was wondering about how to conclude with this enlightened gathering of decision makers and sensors of the society. Can we derive a message from our successes and shortcomings?

Yesterday, I received a phone call from a girl hailing from Maharashtra. An IAS aspirant from a very poor family, this girl was supported by her teacher to travel to Delhi. She borrowed two decent dresses for the visit and made a gruelling search to locate a distant relative where she could get shelter. What made her to call me? She said she read the Marathi translation of my book 'Wings of Fire' that dared her to dream and solace and strength to endure her struggle. I felt satisfied in the sense that a few souls could identify themselves with book. They find my life resonating with their own. Poverty is a curse. Forty percent of our people live below poverty line and unless our GDP gallops to double digits, we will remain a land of isolated islands of prosperity and affluence in an ocean of misery and hardships.

What can change the present cast where we appeared to have been trapped as a society. Technology is the only tool that can free us from our shackles - both physical and psychological. The advent of information technology can be seen across the entire cross-section of our lives. Similar spread of technological transformation is needed in the area of healthcare and value-added production. This is the only way to become a developed nation. Fortunately we have all components of technology to succeed - people, material, skills, infrastructure. The time has come when we come out from our mindset of a suffering civilization and strive for our destiny to be a developed nation. There is no need for the Peacock to turn in to an ostrich. The rhythm and harmony that signifies a song and the grace of a peacock that goes with that is something that is so innate and natural of India. It has to be preserved in to our social fabric and the benefits of the technology must percolate down to the lowest strata of the Society to change. This is the idea that seems to be knocking on our door. Why don't we open it?

Empower the Leader

I still remember after selecting me as the Project Director, Chairman ISRO stated, "I will now on work for the Project Director." Hence the whole organization works for the Project Director. It remained true for the Missile Project too. During the Missile Development Programme a new generation of team leaders emerged - Project Directors, Technology Directors, System Managers, Group Heads. These young scientists were made explicitly responsible and empowered to develop missile systems in a multi-organizational environment where traditional boss-subordinate hierarchy will not work. These leaders had to deal with officials much older and experienced in their respective fields. We instill in them full financial and administrative authority to take and implement decisions. They would chair the Project Management and Design Review meetings and I would join them as a member, as and when required. While this arrangement led to very fast progress, it also made these young leaders butt of envy and target of uncharitable criticism of not only their peers and subordinates but also superiors. After nearly two decades, I can very confidently tell you that unless you identify a person, declare him a leader, empower him, and shield him until he delivers, things will not move much differently. The fear psychosis of big brother is watching, peers-leg-pulling, and adverse publicity would only lead to more intrigue and shell locking. It would create a generation of play-safe, puritans rather than mission driven zealots for who end drives means. Hence empower the leader and protect him while he is facing adversity. Stand by him in the difficult times.

Friends, I shared with you a few thoughts that have worked. Transformation of thoughts into action and subsequently as results demanded team work and courage to combat pain of failures.

Billion people of our nation is a big resource. Vision for the nation ignites the minds. In ignited India, our children will sing the song of India

Index

Song by Dr. A P J Abdul Kalam

Song of Youth

ME AND MY NATION—INDIA

As a young citizen of India,

armed with technology, knowledge and
love for my nation,

I realize, small aim is a crime.

I will work and sweat for a great vision,
the vision to transforming India into a
developed nation, powered by economic
strength with value system.

I am one of the citizens of the billion,
only the vision will ignite the billion souls.

It has entered into me,

the ignited soul compared to any resource .

Is the most powerful resource
on the earth, above the earth and under the earth.

I will keep the lamp of knowledge burning.